Android™ *Tablets*

FOR DUMMIES®

A Wiley Brand

Android™ Tablets

FOR DUMMIES®

A Wiley Brand

By Dan Gookin

FOR DUMMIES®

A Wiley Brand

Android Tablets™ For Dummies®

Published by
John Wiley & Sons, Inc.
111 River Street
Hoboken, NJ 07030-5774

www.wiley.com

For general information on our other products and services, please contact our Customer Care Department within the U.S. at 877-762-2974, outside the U.S. at 317-572-3993, or fax 317-572-4002.

For technical support, please visit www.wiley.com/techsupport.

Wiley publishes in a variety of print and electronic formats and by print-on-demand. Some material included with standard print versions of this book may not be included in e-books or in print-on-demand. If this book refers to media such as a CD or DVD that is not included in the version you purchased, you may download this material at http://booksupport.wiley.com. For more information about Wiley products, visit www.wiley.com.

Library of Congress Control Number: 2013933954

ISBN 978-1-118-54319-1 (pbk); ISBN 978-1-118-54325-2 (ebk);
ISBN 978-1-118-67132-0 (ebk); ISBN 978-1-118-67133-7 (ebk)

Manufactured in the United States of America

10 9 8 7 6 5 4 3 2 1

About the Author

Dan Gookin has been writing about technology for over 25 years. He combines his love of writing with his gizmo fascination to create books that are informative, entertaining, and not boring. Having written more than 130 titles with millions of copies in print translated into over 30 languages, Dan can attest that his method of crafting computer tomes seems to work.

Perhaps his most famous title is the original *DOS For Dummies,* published in 1991. It became the world's fastest-selling computer book, at one time moving more copies per week than the New York Times #1 bestseller (though as a reference book, it could not be listed on the NYT bestseller list). From that book spawned the entire line of *For Dummies* books, which remains a publishing phenomenon to this day.

Dan's most popular titles include *Android Phones For Dummies, Word For Dummies,* and *Laptops For Dummies*. He also maintains the vast and helpful website, www.wambooli.com.

Dan holds a degree in Communications/Visual Arts from the University of California, San Diego. Presently, he lives in the Pacific Northwest, where he serves as Councilman for the City of Coeur d'Alene. Dan enjoys spending time with his sons playing video games inside while they watch the gentle woods of Idaho.

Publisher's Acknowledgments

We're proud of this book; please send us your comments at `http://dummies.custhelp.com`. For other comments, please contact our Customer Care Department within the U.S. at 877-762-2974, outside the U.S. at 317-572-3993, or fax 317-572-4002.

Some of the people who helped bring this book to market include the following:

Acquisitions and Editorial

Project Editor: Susan Pink

Acquisitions Editor: Katie Mohr

Copy Editor: Susan Pink

Technical Editor: Andrew Moore

Editorial Manager: Jodi Jensen

Editorial Assistant: Anne Sullivan

Sr. Editorial Assistant: Cherie Case

Cover Photo: © iStockphoto.com / Cary Westfall

Composition Services

Project Coordinator: Kristie Rees

Layout and Graphics: Joyce Haughey

Proofreaders: Lindsay Amones, Shannon Ramsey

Indexer: Christine Karpeles

Publishing and Editorial for Technology Dummies

> **Richard Swadley,** Vice President and Executive Group Publisher

> **Andy Cummings,** Vice President and Publisher

> **Mary Bednarek,** Executive Acquisitions Director

> **Mary C. Corder,** Editorial Director

Publishing for Consumer Dummies

> **Kathleen Nebenhaus,** Vice President and Executive Publisher

Composition Services

> **Debbie Stailey,** Director of Composition Services

Contents at a Glance

Table of Contents

Introduction

Somewhere filling the void between the smartphone and the computer lies the premiere device of the 21st century. It's probably something you've never used before but will soon be unable to live without. It's the tablet, specifically an Android tablet.

The Android tablet is a gizmo that could fully replace your computer, as well as several other pieces of electronics you may tote around. It's an all-in-one, lightweight, battery-powered, long-lasting, fully mobile, telecommunications, information, and entertainment gizmo.

Oh, but I do go on.

As an Android tablet owner, or someone who's interested in purchasing such a device, you obviously want to get the most from your technology. Perhaps you've attempted to educate yourself using that flimsy *Getting Started* booklet that came with the thing. Now you're turning to this book, a wise choice.

New technology can be intimidating. Frustrating. No matter what, your experience can be made better by leisurely reading this delightful, informative, and occasionally entertaining book.

About This Book

Please don't read this book from cover to cover. This book is a reference. It's designed to be used as you need it. Look up a topic in the table of contents or the index. Find something about your tablet that vexes you or something you're curious about. Look up the answer, and get on with your life.

The overall idea for this book is to show how things are done on the Android tablet and to help you get the most from the device without overwhelming you with information or intimidating you into despair.

Sample sections in this book include

- Locking the tablet
- Activating voice input
- Importing contacts from your computer
- Setting up an e-mail account
- Running Facebook on your tablet
- Talking and video chat

    ✔ Placing a Skype phone call

    ✔ Helping others find your location

    ✔ Flying with an Android tablet

You have nothing to memorize, no sacred utterances or animal sacrifices, and definitely no PowerPoint presentations. Instead, every section explains a topic as though it's the first thing you read in this book. Nothing is assumed, and everything is cross-referenced. Technical terms and topics, when they come up, are neatly shoved to the side, where they're easily avoided. The idea here isn't to learn anything. My philosophy when writing this book was to help you look it up, figure it out, and get on with your life.

How to Use This Book

This book follows a few conventions for using an Android tablet. First of all, no matter what name your tablet has, whether it's a manufacturer's name or some cute name you've devised on your own, this book refers to your tablet as an *Android tablet* or often just *tablet*.

The way you interact with the Android tablet is by using its *touchscreen,* the glassy part of the device as it's facing you. The device also has some physical buttons, as well as some holes and connectors. All these items are described in Chapter 1.

The various ways to touch the screen are explained and named in Chapter 3.

Chapter 4 discusses text input on an Android tablet, which involves using an onscreen keyboard. You can also input text by speaking to the Android tablet, which is also covered in Chapter 4.

This book directs you to do things by following numbered steps. Each step involves a specific activity, such as touching something on the screen; for example:

    3. Touch the Apps icon.

This step directs you to touch the graphical Apps icon on the screen. When a button is shown as text, the command reads:

    3. Touch the Download button.

You might also be directed to *choose* an item, which means to touch it on the screen.

Some settings can be turned off or on, as indicated by a box with a check mark in it, similar to what's shown in the margin. By touching the box on the screen, you add or remove the check mark. When the check mark appears, the option is on; otherwise, it's off.

Foolish Assumptions

Even though this book is written with the gentle hand-holding required by anyone who is just starting out, or who is easily intimidated, I've made a few assumptions. For example, I assume that you're a human being and not a colony creature from the planet Zontar.

My biggest assumption: You have an Android tablet, one that uses the Android operating system distributed by Google. Your tablet could be a cellular tablet (one that uses the mobile data network) or a Wi-Fi only model. This book covers both.

This book addresses two releases of the Android operating system, Ice Cream Sandwich (ICS) and Jelly Bean. To determine which operating system your tablet uses, follow these steps:

1. **At the Home screen, touch the Apps icon.**

   Refer to Chapter 3 for a description of the Apps icon.

2. **Open the Settings app.**

3. **Choose About Tablet.**

   This item might be named About Device.

4. **Look at the item titled Android Version.**

   The number that's shown indicates the Android operating system version.

Android ICS is version 4.0.x, where the x could be any number.

Android Jelly Bean is versions 4.1.x and 4.2.x.

This book does not cover tablets running Android Honeycomb, which was version 3.x.

Although you don't need a computer to use an Android tablet, I do reference having a computer at various points in the text. The computer can be a PC or Windows computer or a Macintosh. Oh, I suppose it could also be a Linux computer. In any event, I refer to the computer as a "computer" throughout this book. When directions are specific to a PC or Mac, the book says so.

Programs that run on an Android tablet are *apps,* which is short for *applications.* A single program is an app.

Finally, this book doesn't assume that you have a Google account, but already having one helps. Information is provided in Chapter 2 about setting up a Google account — an extremely important part of using the Android tablet. Having a Google account opens up a slew of useful features, information, and programs that make using the tablet more productive.

How This Book Is Organized

This book is divided into five parts, each of which covers a certain aspect of the Android tablet or how it's used.

Part 1: Getting Started with Android Tablets

Part I covers setup and orientation to familiarize you with how the device works. It's a good place to start if you're new to the concept of tablet computing, mobile devices, or the Android operating system.

Part II: Stay in Touch

In Part II, you read about various ways that an Android tablet can electronically communicate with your online friends. There's texting, e-mail, the web, social networking, and even the much-wanted trick of using the non-phone Android tablet to make phone calls and do video chat.

Part III: Omni Tablet

The Android tablet is pretty much a limitless gizmo. To prove it, the chapters in Part III cover all the various and wonderful things the tablet does: It's an e-book reader, a map, a navigator, a photo album, a portable music player, a calendar, a calculator, and potentially much more.

Part IV: Nuts and Bolts

Part IV covers a lot of different topics. Up first is how to connect the Android tablet wirelessly to the Internet as well as to other gizmos, such as a Bluetooth printer. There's a chapter on sharing and exchanging files with a computer. You'll find information on using the tablet elsewhere, even overseas. Then come the customization, maintenance, and troubleshooting chapters.

Part V: The Part of Tens

I wrap things up with the traditional *For Dummies* Part of Tens. Each chapter in this part lists ten items or topics. The chapters include tips, tricks, shortcuts, things to remember, and things not to forget — plus, a smattering of useful apps that no Android tablet should be without.

Icons Used in This Book

This icon flags useful, helpful tips or shortcuts.

This icon marks a friendly reminder to do something.

This icon marks a friendly reminder not to do something.

This icon alerts you to overly nerdy information and technical discussions of the topic at hand. Reading the information is optional, though it may win you the Daily Double on *Jeopardy!*

Where to Go from Here

Start reading! Observe the table of contents and find something that interests you. Or look up your puzzle in the index. When these suggestions don't cut it, just start reading Chapter 1.

My e-mail address is dgookin@wambooli.com. Yes, that's my real address. I reply to all e-mail I get, and you'll get a quick reply if you keep your question short and specific to this book. Although I do enjoy saying Hi, I cannot answer technical support questions, resolve billing issues, or help you troubleshoot your Android tablet. Thanks for understanding.

You can also visit my web page at www.wambooli.com for more information or as a diversion. Go to www.wambooli.com/help/tablets/ for specific support for the Android tablet on my website.

Enjoy this book and your Android tablet!

Part I
Getting Started with Android Tablets

Visit www.dummies.com for great Dummies content online.

In this part . . .

- ✔ Get things set up on your new Android tablet.

- ✔ Work through activation and initial tablet configuration.

- ✔ Learn how to turn a tablet on and off and to lock and unlock the screen.

- ✔ Discover the many sensual ways you can manipulate the touchscreen.

- ✔ Use the onscreen keyboard and dictation to create text.

- ✔ Visit www.dummies.com for great Dummies content online.

That Out-of-the-Box Experience

*Y*our Android tablet adventure begins by opening the device's box. Sure, you've probably already done that. I don't blame you; I already opened the box that my Android tablet came in before I read this chapter. No problem. So to help you remember the experience, or get yourself oriented if you found the experience daunting, or just prepare you for that out-of-the-box experience yet to come, this chapter provides you with a gentle introduction to your new Android tablet.

Initial Procedures

Setting up an Android tablet isn't that complex. Then again, people with an IQ of 240 don't find brain surgery that complex. As Einstein said, "It's all relative."

The most important thing about setting up an Android tablet is that there's no time limit. Further, there's no secret ingredient. And you don't need to don an apron or wear a funny hat. That's all good news.

For your tablet, setup is merely an initial process through which you must labor. The process, which you need to do only once, involves liberating the tablet from its box, perhaps some assembly, charging the battery, and then setting up a Google account. This section gets you started by pointing you in the right direction.

✔ Software setup is required to get your Android tablet up and running. That setup involves linking your tablet with your Google account on the Internet. I avoid writing about those details until Chapter 2.

✔ Android tablets that use the digital cellular network require extra setup: You need to identify the tablet with the cellular provider's network, assigning the device a network ID so that you can get all those nifty monthly bills. This process is also avoided until Chapter 2.

✔ Noncellular tablets — those that use only a Wi-Fi network to connect to the Internet, and thereby avoid the monthly bills — don't require a cell phone subscription.

Liberating the tablet from the box

Thanks to an excess of funds, your federal government has conducted numerous studies on how people use electronic devices. Men and women wearing white lab coats and safety goggles, and wielding clipboards, drew solid conclusions by thoroughly examining hundreds of Android tablets. The results were unanimous: An Android tablet works better when you first remove it from its box. Thank you, federal grant!

I assume that you're pretty good at the box-opening thing, so I probably don't need to detail that procedure. I can affirm, however, that it's perfectly okay to remove and throw away those plastic sheets stuck to the front, back, and sides of the tablet.

Along with the tablet, you'll find the following items in the box:

✔ **A USB cable:** You can use it to connect the tablet to a computer or a wall charger.

✔ **A wall charger:** Use this thing (and the USB cable) to charge the tablet.

✔ **Useless pamphlets:** Cheerfully avoid reading the booklets, sheets, and guides rattling around inside the box. Don't throw them away, but don't bother studying them, either.

Go ahead and free the USB cable and wall charger from their clear plastic cocoons.

I recommend keeping the box for as long as you own your Android tablet. If you ever need to return the thing, or ship it anywhere, the original box is the ideal container. You can shove all those useless pamphlets and papers back into the box as well.

Charging the battery

The very first thing that I recommend you do with your Android tablet is give it a full charge. Obey these steps:

1. **Connect the wall charger and USB cable.**

   They snap together only one way.

2. **Attach the USB cable to the Android tablet.**

   Look for the tiny connector on one of the tablet's sides. It may or may not be labeled. There may also be an HDMI video connector, which is about the same size, but it's considered vulgar to plug the USB cable into that hole.

3. **Plug the plug-thing into the wall.**

Upon success, a large "battery charging" type of icon might appear on the Android tablet's touchscreen. That icon lets you know that the tablet is functioning properly, but don't be alarmed if the battery icon fails to appear.

   ✔ If the tablet turns on, don't panic! Chapter 2 discusses how to proceed next, or how to turn off the tablet if you're not yet ready to play with it.

   ✔ Even if your Android tablet came fully-charged from the factory, I still recommend giving it an initial charge, to at least familiarize yourself with the process.

   ✔ The USB cable is used for both charging the Android tablet and connecting it to a computer for sharing information, exchanging files, or using the tablet as a computer modem. The latter process is called *tethering* and is covered in Chapter 16.

   ✔ You can also charge the tablet by connecting it to a computer's USB port. As long as the computer is on, the tablet charges.

   ✔ The battery charges more efficiently if you plug it into a wall, as opposed to charging it from a computer's USB port.

   ✔ Most Android tablets I've seen don't feature a removable battery, so the battery cannot be replaced should it be defective. If the battery doesn't charge or keep a charge, you need to return the tablet for a refund or replacement.

Tablet Exploration

Second star to the right and straight on 'till morning may get Peter Pan to Neverland, but for navigating your way around the Android tablet you're going to need more specific directions.

Finding things on the tablet

Take heed of Figure 1-1, which is my attempt at illustrating a generic Android tablet's hardware features. Use that figure as a guide as you follow along on your own tablet to locate some key features, described in this section.

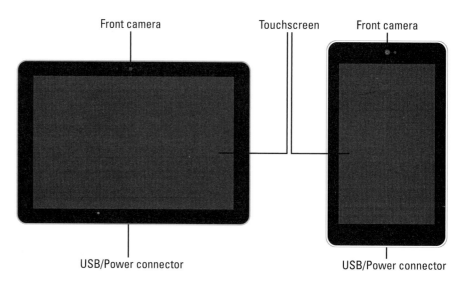

Figure 1-1: Things to find on your Android tablet.

On the front of the Android tablet, find the following goodies:

Touchscreen display: The biggest part of the tablet is the touchscreen display, which occupies almost all the territory on the front of the device. The touchscreen display is a look-touch gizmo. You look at it, but also touch it with your fingers to control the tablet.

Front camera: The Android tablet's front-facing camera is found above the touchscreen on the device's center line. For larger tablets, the camera is on top when the tablet is oriented horizontally (Figure 1-1, left). For small format tablets, the camera is on top when the tablet is oriented vertically (Figure 1-1, right).

Light sensor: It's difficult to see, but a teensy light sensor is just to the left of the front camera. It is used to help adjust the brightness level for the touchscreen and probably serves other functions as well, none of which has to do with mind-reading.

Dock/USB power connector: A slot on the bottom of the tablet is where you connect the USB cable, which is used to both charge the battery and connect your Android tablet to a computer. The slot is also where the tablet connects to the dock, should you have one of those. See the section, "Getting optional accessories."

Around the Android tablet you'll find a variety of buttons, holes, connectors, and other doodads. Try to find all these items on your tablet, making a note of their location:

Power/Lock: The Power/Lock button is labeled with the universal power icon, shown in the margin. Press this button to turn on the tablet, to lock it (put it to sleep), to wake it up, and to turn off the tablet. Directions for performing those activities are found in Chapter 2.

Volume up/volume down: The tablet's volume control adjusts the noise the thing makes. One of the buttons turns the volume up, the other one turns the volume down. (Well, actually, it's a rocker switch, so volume up and volume down are the same button.)

Memory slot: The memory slot is where you'll find the Android tablet's microSD card, a media card on which information is stored. Details about the microSD card are covered in the next section, but be aware that not every tablet sports a microSD card slot.

Headphone jack: This hole is where you can connect standard headphones.

Speaker(s): Stereo speakers are found left and right on the tablet, sometimes on the front, mostly on the sides, occasionally on the back.

Microphone: A miniscule circular opening found on the tablet's edge is used as the device's microphone. Some tablets may feature two microphone holes. Don't worry if you can't find them; they're there.

The typical Android also has a back side. It's not shown in Figure 1-1 because the censors won't let me do an illustration and also because the back is boring: On it you may find the tablet's main camera and LED flash. That's it.

✔ Some tablets lack a rear-facing camera. I can recommend to those tablet owners getting a painting program for your tablet and using it to paint the images you would otherwise photograph.

✔ Not every rear-facing camera features a flash.

✔ Some tablets use NFC, or Near Field Communications, so that you can send and receive information by touching your tablet with another NFC device. The NFC technology is internal, which means you don't really see it on your tablet, although it's typically found on the back of the device.

✔ Don't stick anything into the microphone hole. Yes, it's tempting, but don't. Only stick things into your tablet that you're supposed to, such as the USB cable, headphones, and microSD memory card.

Inserting and removing the microSD card

Some Android tablets use a removable media card on which they can store your stuff — photos, videos, music, evil plans. The card uses the microSD format, so it's referred to as a microSD card or often (incorrectly) as an SD card.

The microSD card is teensy, which is a scientific description. The card fits into a slot on the edge of your tablet but can also be inserted into your computer and read like any removable media card.

To insert a microSD card into your Android tablet, follow these steps:

1. **Ensure that the Android tablet is turned off.**

   Specific directions are offered in Chapter 2, but for now, press and hold the Power/Lock button (see the margin), and choose the Power Off command from the menu.

2. **If the microSD card slot is covered by a tiny tab or hatch, open the tiny tab or hatch.**

   Use your thumbnail to pry open the cover. Some covers come off completely; others just flop over to the side, like an annoying leaf caught under your car's windshield wiper.

3. **Orient the microSD card so that the printed side is facing you and the teensy triangle on the card is pointing in toward the Android tablet.**

4. **Use your fingernail or a paperclip to gently shove the card all the way into the slot.**

   The card makes a faint clicking sound when it's fully inserted.

5. **Close the hatch covering the microSD card slot.**

After the microSD card is installed, turn on your Android tablet. See Chapter 2 for details, though basically you just press and hold the Power/Lock button until the touchscreen comes to life.

Most of the time, you'll leave the microSD card inside your Android tablet. When the urge hits to remove it, heed these steps:

1. **Turn off your Android tablet.**

   You can damage the media card if you just yank it out of the tablet, which is why I recommend first turning off the tablet.

2. **Open the itty-bitty hatch covering the microSD card slot.**

3. **Use your fingernail to press the microSD card inward a tad.**

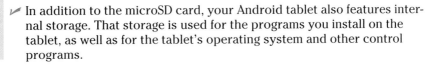

The microSD card is spring-loaded, so pressing it in eventually pops it outward.

4. **Pinch the microSD card between your fingers and remove it completely.**

The microSD card is too tiny to leave laying around. Put it into a microSD card adapter for use in your PC or another electronic device. Or store it inside a miniature box that you can label with a miniature pen in miniature letters, "MicroSD Card Inside." Don't lose it!

- ✔ Some Android tablets come with a microSD card, but most often you have to purchase one.

- ✔ MicroSD cards come in a smattering of capacities, measured in gigabytes (billions of bytes), abbreviated GB or just G. Common capacities include 8GB, 16GB, and 32GB. The higher the capacity, the more stuff you can store but also the more expensive the card.

- ✔ To use a microSD card with your computer, you'll need an SD card adapter. Insert the microSD card into the adapter, and then plug the SD card adapter into your computer. The adapters are an extra purchase, though some microSD cards come with an adapter.

- ✔ SD stands for *Secure Digital*. It is but one of about a zillion media card standards.

- ✔ In addition to the microSD card, your Android tablet also features internal storage. That storage is used for the programs you install on the tablet, as well as for the tablet's operating system and other control programs.

Getting optional accessories

Your credit card company will be thrilled when you discover that an assortment of handy Android tablet accessories are available for purchase. You can find them at the place where you purchased your tablet, online or in the real world. Here are just a few of the items that you can consider getting to complete your tablet experience:

Earphones: You can use any standard cell phone or portable media player earphones with an Android tablet. Simply plug the earphones into the headphone jack at the top of the tablet, and you're ready to go.

HDMI cable: For tablets with an HDMI (video output) port, you can get an HDMI cable. The cable connects the tablet to an HD monitor, where you can view videos or pictures on the Big Screen. Not every Android tablet features an HDMI port.

Pouches and sleeves: Answering the question "Where do I put this thing?" is the handy Android tablet pouch or sleeve accessory. Try to get one designed for your tablet. If not, check the size before you buy. Not every 10-inch tablet fits into the same 10-inch pouch.

Screen protectors: These plastic, clingy things are affixed to the front of the tablet, right over the touchscreen. They help protect the touchscreen glass from finger smudges and sneeze globs, while still allowing you to use the touchscreen.

Vehicle charger: You can charge the Android tablet in your car if you buy a vehicle charger. It's an adapter that plugs into your car's 12-volt power supply, in the receptacle that was once known as a cigarette lighter. The vehicle charger is a must if you plan on using the Android tablet's navigation features in your auto or when you need a charge on-the-road.

Docks, various and sundry: Most people manhandle their tablets. Tsk, tsk. You can be more refined and get your Android tablet a dock. There are several kinds, from the simple prop-dock that holds up the tablet at a pleasant viewing angle to docks that contain keyboards to multimedia docks that feature HDMI and USB ports.

Other exciting and nifty accessories might be available for your tablet. Check the location where you bought your tablet frequently for new garnishes and frills.

- ✔ None of this extra stuff is essential to using the tablet.

- ✔ The only way to get HDMI output with some tablets is to obtain a multimedia docking station.

- ✔ You can use Bluetooth earphones or a cell phone Bluetooth headset with any Android tablet.

- ✔ If the earphones feature a microphone, you can use that microphone for dictation, recording, and even chatting with friends.

- ✔ If the earphones feature a button, you can use the button to pause and play music. Press the button once to pause, again to play.

- ✔ Android tablets generally don't recognize more than one earphone button. So, for example, if you use earphones that feature a volume or mute button, pressing that extra button does nothing.

- ✔ A useful accessory to get is a microfiber cloth to help clean the tablet's screen, plus a special cleaning solution wipe. See Chapter 20 for more information about cleaning an Android tablet's screen.

Where to Keep Your Tablet

Like your car keys, glasses, wallet, and light saber, your Android tablet should be kept in a safe, easy to find, always handy place, whether you're at home, at work, on the road, or in a galaxy far, far away.

Making a home for the tablet

I recommend keeping your Android tablet in the same spot when you've finished using it. If you have a computer, my first suggestion is to make a spot right by the computer. Keep the charging cord handy, or just plug the cord into the computer's USB port so that you can synchronize information with your computer on a regular basis, not to mention keep the tablet charged.

If you have a docking stand, plug your tablet into that when you're not toting it about.

Above all, avoid keeping the tablet in a place where someone could sit on it, step on it, or otherwise damage it. For example, don't leave the tablet on a table or counter under a stack of newspapers, where it might get accidentally tossed out or put in the recycle bin.

Never leave the tablet on a chair!

As long as you remember to return the tablet to the same spot when you're done with it, you'll always know where it is. I don't know why I have to write this suggestion, although it may have something to do with the presence of teenagers in the house.

Taking the Android tablet with you

If you're like me, you probably carry the Android tablet around with you when you leave the office, at the airport, in the air, or in your car. I hope you're not using the tablet while you're driving. Regardless, it's best to have a portable place to store your tablet while you're on the road.

The ideal place for the tab is a specially designed pouch or sleeve. That pouch keeps the tablet from being dinged, scratched, or even unexpectedly turned on while it's in your backpack, purse, carry-on luggage, or wherever you put the tablet when you're not using it.

Also see Chapter 18 for information on using an Android tablet on the road.

Android Tablet On and Off

The bestselling *Pencils For Dummies* (Wiley) has no chapter describing how to turn on a pencil. *Pens For Dummies* (also Wiley) does have a chapter "Enabling the Pen to Write," but that's not really an on-off thing, and the author of that book does describe in great detail how awkward an on-off switch or power button would be on a pen. Aren't you and I lucky to live in an age when such things are carefully described?

Your Android tablet is far more complex than a pen or a pencil, and often it's more useful. As such an advanced piece of technology, your tablet features not an on-off button but a Power/Lock button. That button does more than just turn the Android tablet on or off, which is why this book has an entire chapter devoted to the subject.

Initial Tablet Nonsense

The first time you turn on your Android tablet — the very first time — it prompts you to complete a setup process. This step is necessary, although it may have already been completed for you by the cheerful people who sold you the tablet. Better read through this section just to be sure.

The tablet will not start unless the battery is charged. Or unless you plug it in. See Chapter 1.

Activating your Android tablet

Tablets that use the digital cellular network require activation before they can use that network. The process works like activating a cell phone, and it's basically the same technology. The purpose is to associate your tablet with an account number so that you can receive a monthly bill.

Activation of your cellular tablet was most likely done at the Phone Store or elsewhere if you purchased the device online. If not, you'll be prompted to run through activation steps when you first turn on the tablet.

Follow through with these instructions to activate your Android tablet. Even if you have a Wi-Fi–only tablet, peruse these initial steps:

1. **Press the Power/Lock button.**

   You may have to press it longer than you think. You can release the button when you see the manufacturer's logo or animation appear on the tablet's touchscreen.

2. **If necessary, unlock your tablet.**

   To unlock the tablet, slide your finger across the touchscreen or touch and move the Lock icon outward toward a circle that appears. Figure 2-1 illustrates these two popular methods. Your tablet may have a different unlocking screen, in which case directions on the screen generally explain what to do.

3. **Select your mother tongue.**

   If you're reading this in English, choose English as the language for your Android tablet. Если ты говоришь русский, выбрать Русский язык.

4. **Touch the Activate button.**

   The tablet contacts your cellular provider to confirm that you have an active account.

   The Activate prompt doesn't appear for Wi-Fi tabs. Instead, you may be asked to scope out a Wi-Fi network. See Chapter 16.

5. **Obey the directions of your cellular provider.**

   The specifics of what happens next depend on your cellular provider.

6. **Touch the Next button when you see the text *Device Is Activated*.**

   The Android tablet restarts.

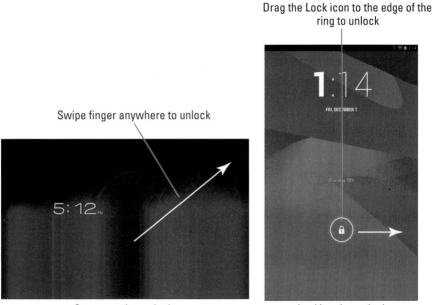

Drag the Lock icon to the edge of the ring to unlock

Swipe finger anywhere to unlock

Screen-swipe unlock   Locking ring unlock

Figure 2-1: Unlocking an Android tablet.

If you have trouble activating your tablet, contact your cellular provider. You'll need to read information from the Android tablet's box, which has activation information printed on a label.

The next step in the initial setup process is to connect the tablet with your Google account. Continue reading in the next section.

Setting up a Google account

To get the most from your Android tablet, you must have a Google account. If you don't already have a Google account, drop everything (except this book) and follow these steps to obtain one:

1. **Open a web browser program.**

   I believe these steps work best when you use a computer, not your tablet. If you don't have access to a computer, skip to the next section, "Linking your Google account," for an alternative approach.

2. **Visit the main Google page at** www.google.com.

   Type **www.google.com** in the web browser's Address box.

3. **Click the Sign In link.**

   Another page opens where you can log into your Google account, but you don't have a Google account, so:

4. **Click the link to create a new account.**

   The link is typically found below the text boxes where you would log into your Google account. As I write this chapter, the link is titled Sign Up. It was once titled Create an Account Now.

5. **Continue heeding the directions until you've created your own Google account.**

Eventually your account will be set up and configured.

To try things out, log off from Google and then log back in. That way, you'll ensure that you've done everything properly and remembered your password. (The web browser program may even prompt to remember the password for you.)

I also recommend creating a bookmark for your account's Google page: The Ctrl+D or Command+D keyboard shortcuts are used to create a bookmark in just about any web browser.

Continue reading in the next section for information on synchronizing your new Google account with the Android tablet.

Linking your Google account

Information on your Android tablet is synchronized with the information from your Google account on the Internet. Information including your contact list, Gmail messages, calendar appointments, and other Googly things are updated between your tablet and the Internet nearly instantaneously. But none of that happens until you tell the tablet about your Google account. Obey:

1. **Start the Android tablet, if you haven't already, and unlock the screen.**

   If you're prompted to activate the tablet, see the section, "Activating your Android tablet."

2. **Keep working through the screens until you see the one prompting you to sign in with your Google account.**

3. **Touch the Sign In button to sign into your Google account.**

   Or, if you haven't yet set up your Google account, choose the option that lets you create a new Google account.

4. **Touch the Username text box and type your Google account name.**

   Use the onscreen keyboard to type. If you need help, see Chapter 4 for information on typing text on your Android tablet.

5. **Touch the Password field and type your Google account's password.**

6. **Touch the Sign In button.**

   If you can't see the Sign In button, press the Hide icon (shown in the margin) to hide the onscreen keyboard.

7. **Continue working through the Google account setup, touching Next at each screen, until you get to the Finish Setup button.**

8. **Touch the Finish Setup button.**

   Sorry, but you're not really done yet. Instead, you'll see the Account Setup screen. You can choose to add more accounts, though that topic is covered in the section, "Adding more accounts."

9. **Touch the Next button.**

10. **If prompted for location information, ensure that there are check marks by each item.**

    You may see up to three items, though the name of each item may change depending on which cellular provider you're using. Generically speaking, the items are:

      Location Services: Enable your cellular data provider to access location information, which aids in maps and other location apps.

      Standalone GPS Services: Allow location information to be accessed by your tablet's apps as well as by the Internet.

      Google Location Services: Allow Google to collect your location data anonymously.

    You may be prompted to touch the Agree button after activating each service. Do so.

11. **Touch the Next button.**

12. **If you see a Backup Assistant Screen, touch the Skip button.**

    Only a few tablets offer Backup Assistant, which I don't use. If you want more information on backing up data on your tablet, see Chapter 20.

13. **Touch the Begin button to start using your Android tablet.**

The good news is that you're done with most of the initial setup. The better news is that you need to do this setup only once on your Android tablet. From this point on, you can start using your Android tablet without being pestered about initial configuration.

✔ Another task worth doing at this point is connecting your tablet with a Wi-Fi network. See Chapter 16 for details.

✔ One of the first things you may notice synchronized between your tablet and Google is your Gmail inbox. See Chapter 6 for more information on Gmail.

✔ See the sidebar "Who is this Android person?" for more information about the Android operating system.

Adding more accounts

You're not stuck using only Google and Gmail on your Android tablet. You can add just about any online, e-mail, or Internet account you have for use on the tablet. Heed these steps:

1. **At the Home screen, touch the Apps icon.**

   If you're completely confused, refer to Chapter 3 for information on the Home screen and Apps icon.

2. **On the Apps screen, touch the Settings icon to run the Settings app.**

3. **Under the Account heading, choose Add Account. On some tablets, you need to first choose the Accounts and Sync item, and then touch Add Account.**

   You'll see a list of accounts you can add on the tablet. The variety depends on what the manufacturer has provided, but don't despair if you don't see the type of account you want; there are many ways to add accounts on your tablet, as described elsewhere in this book.

4. **Choose the account to add.**

5. **Fill in the information on the screen, such as your user name and password, to add the account to your tablet.**

Repeat these steps to add more accounts to your tablet.

✔ To access information for individual accounts, choose the account from the list on the Settings app screen. If the account is associated with a specific app, you might also be able to change account information from that app.

✔ It's best to set up new accounts using the Internet. You can do so on the tablet, or you can use a computer with its nice big monitor and comfy keyboard.

✔ Specific information on adding e-mail accounts is found in Chapter 6. To add social networking accounts, such as Facebook and Twitter, see Chapter 8.

Regular, Everyday Tablet Nonsense

With initial setup and configuration out of the way, you follow a regular routine when it comes to turning on your Android tablet. Your tablet day starts by turning the thing on, unlocking it, waking it up, or angrily shaking it. Almost all these methods are covered in this section.

Turning on your Android tablet

To turn on your Android tablet, press and hold the Power/Lock button. After a few seconds, you'll see the manufacturer's logo or animation. The tablet is starting.

Eventually you behold the main unlock screen (refer to Figure 2-1). Use your finger to swipe the screen or otherwise manipulate the locking mechanism. Once your Android tablet is unlocked, start using it. The various fun and interesting things you can do are described throughout this book.

- Some unlocking screens not only unlock the tablet but start specific apps, such as the camera. In those cases, you must swipe the screen or drag the Lock icon to a specific icon that appears. Lift your finger from the touchscreen to start the indicated app or tablet feature.

- It's rare that you'll be turning the tablet off. Most of the time you just unlock the tablet, waking it up after a snooze. See the next section.

Unlocking the tablet

I recommend that you leave your Android tablet on all the time. It was designed to be used that way. The battery lasts quite a while, so when the tablet is bored, or when you've ignored it for a while, it falls asleep and the screen locks.

You unlock a snoozing tablet by pressing the Power/Lock button. Unlike turning your tablet on, a quick button press is all that's needed.

Once awake, the tablet displays a locking screen. It could be the standard unlocking screen (refer to Figure 2-1) or a more secure locking screen, such as the Face Unlock, Pattern, PIN, or Password locks. (See the next section.)

After your Android tablet is unlocked, you can begin using it.

- The Android tablet continues to run while it's sleeping. Mail is received, social networking updates are made, and so on. The tablet also continues to play music while it's locked.

- Touching the touchscreen doesn't unlock the tablet unless you've configured the tablet not to use a screen lock. See Chapter 19.

✔ Loud noises will not wake up your tablet.

✔ Android tablets don't snore while sleeping.

✔ See the section "Locking the tablet," later in this chapter, for more information.

Working the secure lock screens

If you've added more security to your Android tablet, you could see any one of several lock screens. The variety depends on what's available on your tablet, as well as how you've configured security.

The most unique screen lock is face unlock. To work that lock, press the Power/Lock button, and then hold up your tablet and stare at it. Don't press your face against the glass. That's wrong. Instead, use the tablet like a mirror to position your face in the middle of the box, as shown in Figure 2-2. The tablet should unlock.

If the tablet doesn't unlock when you attempt to use face unlock, you'll be prompted with a pattern or PIN lock.

The pattern lock, shown in Figure 2-3, requires that you trace your finger along a pattern that includes up to nine dots on the screen.

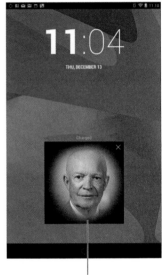

Position your face here

Figure 2-2: The face unlock screen.

Trace your fingers over the dots

Keep tracing the pattern

Figure 2-3: The pattern lock screen.

The PIN and password locks are shown in Figure 2-4. In both cases, you need to type the PIN or password using the onscreen keyboard. Touch the Enter, OK, or Done key to accept input; use the Delete key to back up and erase.

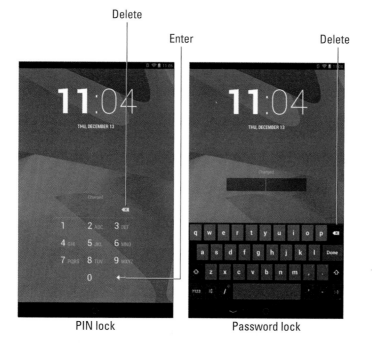

Figure 2-4: The PIN and password lock screens.

After you match the pattern, PIN, or password, your tablet is unlocked and you can start using it.

- See Chapter 19 for details on how to configure the various Android tablet screen locks.

- The pattern lock can start at any dot, not necessarily the upper-left dot as shown in Figure 2-3.

- The password lock must contain at least one letter and number, though it can also include a smattering of symbols and other characters.

- For additional information on working the onscreen keyboard, see Chapter 4.

Who is this Android person?

Just like a computer, your Android tablet has an operating system. It's the main program in charge of all the software (apps) inside the tablet. Unlike a computer, however, Android is a mobile device operating system, designed primarily for use in cell phones but also tablets. For that reason, you may see your tablet referred to as a "phone" in various apps.

The Android operating system is used on many of today's most popular smartphones, including the Droid, Nexus, and Galaxy. By using Android, your tablet has access to all the apps available to Android phones and other mobile devices. You'll read how to add those apps in Chapter 15.

Android is based on the Linux operating system, which is a computer operating system, though it's much more stable and bug-free than Windows so it's not as popular. Google owns, maintains, and develops Android, which is why

your online Google information is synced with the Android tablet.

The Android mascot, shown nearby, often appears on Android apps or hardware. He has no official name, though he's called Andy.

The End of Your Android Tablet Day

I know of three ways to say goodbye to your Android tablet; only one of them involves renting a steamroller. The other two methods are documented in this section.

Locking the tablet

Locking the tablet is cinchy: Simply press the Power/Lock button. The display goes dark; your tablet is locked.

- ✔ Your Android tablet still works while locked; it receives e-mail and can play music, but it's not using as much power as it would with the display on.

- ✔ The tablet will probably spend most of its time locked.

✔ Locking the tablet isn't the same as turning off the tablet. It's more like a computer's sleep mode. Indeed, a locked tablet is often described as a sleeping or snoozing tablet.

✔ Any timers or alarms you set still activate when your tablet is locked. See Chapter 14 for information on setting timers and alarms.

✔ To unlock your tablet, press and release the Power/Lock button. See the section "Unlocking the tablet," earlier in this chapter.

Setting the lock timeout

You can manually lock your tablet at any time by pressing the Power/Lock button. That's probably why it's called the Power/*Lock* button, although I have my doubts. Anyway, when you don't manually lock the tablet, it automatically locks after a given period of inactivity.

You can control the tablet's self-lock timeout value, which can be set anywhere from 15 seconds to 1 hour. Obey these steps:

1. **At the Home screen, touch the Apps icon.**

2. **Open the Settings app.**

3. **Choose Display.**

4. **Choose Screen Timeout.**

5. **Choose a timeout value from the list provided.**

    I prefer a value of 1 minute.

6. **Touch the Home icon to return to the Home screen.**

The lock timer begins after a period of inactivity. Specifically, when you don't touch the screen, the timer starts ticking. About 5 seconds before the timeout, the touchscreen dims. Then it turns off and your tablet locks. If you touch the screen before then, the timer is reset.

Turning off your Android tablet

To turn off your tablet, heed these steps:

1. **Press and hold the Power/Lock button.**

    You'll see the Device Options menu, shown in Figure 2-5.

    If you chicken out and don't want to turn off your tablet, touch the Back icon.

2. **Touch the Power Off item.**

    The Android tablet turns itself off.

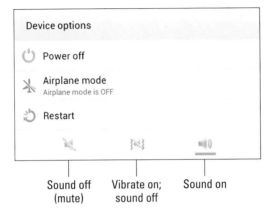

Figure 2-5: The Device Options menu.

The tablet doesn't run when it's off, so it won't remind you of appointments and won't collect e-mail, nor will you hear any alarms you've set. The tablet won't be angry with you for turning it off, though you may sense some resentment when you turn it on again.

- The Restart option (refer to Figure 2-5) may not be available on all Android tablets.

- Some tablets may have a Silent Mode option instead of the sound icons shown in Figure 2-5.

- The Device Options menu is titled Tablet Options on some Android tablets. Other tablets may not title the menu at all.

- Ensure that your tablet is kept in a safe place while it's turned off. See the section "Where to Keep Your Tablet" in Chapter 1.

How the Tablet Works

In This Chapter

▶ Working the touchscreen
▶ Changing the volume
▶ Getting around the Home screen
▶ Using icons
▶ Running apps (programs)
▶ Accessing recently used apps
▶ Checking notifications
▶ Finding all the apps

It used to be that you could judge how advanced something was by how many buttons it had. Starting with the dress shirt and progressing to the first computer, more buttons meant fancier technology. Your Android tablet tosses that rule right out the window. Beyond the Power/Lock button and Volume Up/Down button, the device is bereft of buttons. In fact, to add insult to injury, some manufacturers refer to the Power/Lock button as a *key*.

My point is that to use your tablet, you're going to have to understand how a touchscreen works. That touchscreen is the tablet's main input device, the gizmo you'll use to do all sorts of wondrous and useful things. Using a touchscreen may be a new experience for you, so this chapter provides a general orientation to the touchscreen and how an Android tablet works.

Basic Operations

To control a unique and benevolent gizmo like an Android tablet, you have to familiarize yourself with some basic operations, as covered in this section.

Touching the touchscreen

Minus any buttons and knobs, the way you control an Android tablet is to manipulate things on the touchscreen with one or two fingers. It doesn't matter which fingers you use, and feel free to experiment with other body parts as well, though I find fingers to be handy.

Here are the many ways the touchscreen can be touched:

Touch: The simplest way to manipulate the touchscreen is to touch it. You touch an object, an icon, a control, a menu item, a doodad, and so on. The touch operation is similar to a mouse click on a computer. A touch may also be referred to as a *tap* or *press.*

Double-tap: Touch the screen twice in the same location. Double-tapping can be used to zoom in on an image or a map, but it can also zoom out. Because of the double-tap's dual nature, I recommend using the pinch or spread operation instead when you want to zoom.

Long-press: A long-press occurs when you touch part of the screen and keep your finger down. Depending on what you're doing, a pop-up menu may appear or the item you're long-pressing may get "picked up" so that you can drag (move) it around. *Long-press* might also be referred to as *touch and hold* in some documentation.

Swipe: To swipe, you touch your finger on one spot and then drag it to another spot. Swipes can go up, down, left, or right, which moves the touchscreen content in the direction you swipe. A swipe can be fast or slow. It's also called a *flick* or *slide.*

Pinch: A pinch involves two fingers, which start out separated and then are brought together. The effect is used to *zoom out,* to reduce the size of an image or see more of a map.

Spread: The opposite of pinch is spread. You start out with your fingers together and then spread them. The spread is used to *zoom in,* to enlarge an image or see more detail on a map.

Rotate: A few apps let you rotate an image on the screen by touching with two fingers and twisting them around a center point. Think of turning a combination lock on a safe, and you get the rotate operation.

You can't manipulate the touchscreen while wearing gloves unless they're gloves specially designed for using electronic touchscreens, such as the gloves that Batman wears.

Inevitably, you must clean the touchscreen, so see Chapter 20 for recommendations on doing so properly.

Changing the orientation

Because your Android tablet can be used in either vertical or horizontal orientation, it features an *accelerometer*. This gizmo determines in which direction the tablet is pointed or whether you've reoriented the device from an upright to a horizontal position (or vice versa) or even upside down. That way, the information on the tablet always appears upright, no matter how you hold it.

To demonstrate how the tablet orients itself, rotate the tablet to the left or right. Most apps change their orientation to match however you've oriented the tablet, such as the Home screen shown in Figure 3-1.

Vertical orientation   Horizontal orientation

Figure 3-1: Android tablet orientation.

The rotation feature may not work for all apps, and it may not even work for the Home screen. In that case, open the web browser app to experiment with rotation; see Chapter 7.

  ✔ Most games present themselves in one orientation only.

  ✔ You can lock the orientation if the rotating screen bothers you. See the section "Making Quick Settings," later in this chapter.

  ✔ A great application for demonstrating the Android tablet accelerometer is the game *Labyrinth*. You can purchase it at the Google Play Store, or download the free version, *Labyrinth Lite*. See Chapter 15 for more information about the Google Play Store.

Setting the volume

There are times when the sound level is too loud. There are times when it's too soft. And, there are those rare times when it's just right. Finding that just-right level is the job of the Volume button that clings to the side of your Android tablet.

Pressing the top part of the Volume button makes the volume louder; pressing the bottom part makes the volume softer. As you press the button, a graphic appears on the touchscreen to illustrate the relative volume level, similar to what's shown in Figure 3-2.

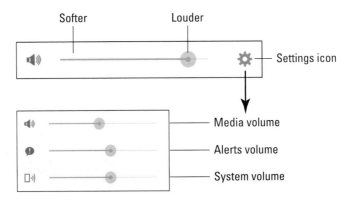

Figure 3-2: Setting the volume.

Touch the Settings icon, shown in Figure 3-2, to see more detailed volume controls. You can individually set the volume for media, alerts, and the system, as shown in the expanded onscreen volume control: Drag the dot left or right to set the volume.

✔ The Settings icon may appear as shown in the margin instead of as the Gear icon (refer to Figure 3-2).

✔ When the volume is set all the way down, the tablet is silenced.

✔ Silencing the tablet by sliding down the volume level may place it into vibration mode.

✔ The Volume button works even when the tablet is locked (when the touchscreen display is off). That means you don't need to unlock the tablet if you're playing music and need to adjust the volume.

✔ Refer to Chapter 19 for information on placing the tablet into vibration mode.

There's No Place Like Home Screen

The main base from which you begin domination of your Android tablet is the *Home screen.* It's the first thing you see after unlocking the tablet, and the place you go to whenever you quit an app.

Touring the Home screen

Examples of typical Android tablet Home screens are illustrated in Figure 3-3. The primary difference between the two is the location of the notification icons, the status icons, and the Apps icon.

Figure 3-3: Android Home screens.

Several fun and interesting things appear on the Home screen. Find these items on your own tablet's Home screen:

App icons: The meat of the meal on the Home screen plate is where the action takes place: app (application) icons. Touching an icon runs its program.

Widgets: A widget is a teensy program that can display information, let you control the tablet, access features, or do something purely amusing. You can read more about widgets in Chapter 19.

Apps icon: Touch this icon to view the collection of apps and widgets available on your tablet. It may be called the Apps Menu icon, the All Apps icon, or even the Launcher. See the later section "The Apps Screen."

Notification icons: These icons come and go, depending on what happens in your digital life. For example, new icons appear whenever you receive a new e-mail message or have a pending appointment. The section "Checking notifications," later in this chapter, describes how to deal with notifications.

Status icons: These icons represent the tablet's current condition, such as the type of network to which it's connected, signal strength, and battery status, as well as whether the tablet is connected to a Wi-Fi network or using Bluetooth, for example.

Google Search: Use this gizmo to invoke a powerful search of the items stored on the Android tablet or the entire Internet.

Ensure that you recognize the names of the various parts of the Home screen because these terms are used throughout this book and in whatever other scant Android tablet documentation exists. Directions for using the Home screen gizmos are found throughout this chapter.

✔ The Home screen is entirely customizable. You can add and remove icons from the Home screen, add widgets and shortcuts, and even change wallpaper (background) images. See Chapter 19 for more information.

✔ Touching a part of the Home screen that doesn't feature an icon or a control does nothing. That is, unless you're using the *live wallpaper* feature. In that case, touching the screen changes the wallpaper in some way, depending on the wallpaper that's selected. You can read more about live wallpaper in Chapter 19.

Accessing multiple Home screens

The Home screen is more than what you see. It's actually an entire street of Home screens, with only one Home screen *page* displayed at a time.

To switch from one page to another, swipe the Home screen left or right. There are pages to the left of the main Home screen page, and pages to the right. The number of pages depends on the tablet, with five pages being the average.

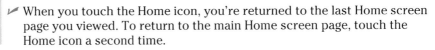

✔ Home screen pages might also be referred to as Home screen *panels*.

✔ When you touch the Home icon, you're returned to the last Home screen page you viewed. To return to the main Home screen page, touch the Home icon a second time.

✔ The main Home screen is often the center Home screen page, though some Android tablets let you choose any page as the main one.

✔ See Chapter 19 for information on adding, removing, and organizing Home screen pages.

Icons, Icons, Icons

Your Android tablet's touchscreen has no physical buttons but does have a host of icons. They ring the Home screen and appear in various apps, providing a consistent way to control various activities.

Table 3-1 lists the most common icons, which appear at the bottom of the screen in just about every app in the Android kingdom. If you don't see them, touch the bottom of the screen and they'll appear.

Table 3-1		Common Icons
Icon	*Name*	*Function*
⬅	Back	Go back, close, or dismiss the onscreen keyboard
⌂	Home	Go to the Home screen
⧉	Recent Apps	Display recently opened apps
⌄	Hide	Dismiss the onscreen keyboard or recent apps list

In addition to the common icons shown in Table 3-1, you'll find other icons used on the Home screen as well as in various apps. Table 3-2 lists these icons and their functions.

Table 3-2		Other Icons
Icon	*Name*	*Description*
⁝	Menu	Displays the menu for an app. It's often found in the upper-right corner of the screen.
≡	Menu	Displays the menu for an app.

(continued)

Table 3-2 *(continued)*

Icon	Name	Description
☰	Old Menu	Displays the menu for older Android apps. It often appears at the bottom of the screen, next to the Recent Apps icon.
+	Add	Adds or creates a new item. The plus symbol may be used in combination with other symbols, depending on the app.
☆	Favorite	Flags a favorite item, such as a contact or a web page.
⚙	Gear	Displays a settings menu or options for an app or a feature.
≡	Settings	Displays a settings menu or options for an app or a feature. The Settings icon is another version of the Gear icon.
✕	Close	Closes a window or clears text from an input field.
⤳	Share	Shares information stored on the tablet via e-mail, social networking, or other Internet services.

Various sections throughout this book give examples of using the icons. Their images appear in the book's margins where relevant.

- ✔ The little triangle in the lower-right corner of the Menu icon is used in many apps to denote a pop-up or shortcut menu attached to something on the screen. Touch that triangle to see the shortcut menu.

- ✔ Other common symbols are used on icons in various apps. For example, the standard Play and Pause icons are used as well as variations on the symbols shown in Tables 3-1 and 3-2.

- ✔ Samsung tablets, as well as other Android tablets, feature a Screen Capture icon, on the bottom of the screen. Touch that icon to convert the image on the screen into a picture file. To access the screen capture feature, use the Gallery app. See Chapter 12 for more information on the Gallery app.

Home Screen Chores

To become a zombie, you must know how to perform several duties: moan, limp, and eat brains. A zombie's life isn't difficult, and neither is your Android tablet life, as long as you know how to do a few basic duties on the Home screen.

Starting an app

It's blissfully simple to run an app on the Home screen: Touch its icon. The app starts.

- ✓ App is short for *application*.
- ✓ Not all apps appear on the Home screen, but all of them appear when you display the Apps screen. See the section "The Apps Screen," later in this chapter.
- ✓ Samsung tablets feature *mini-apps*, which are summoned by touching the bottom center of the Home screen. A mini-app is a combination app and widget, which appears in the middle of the screen while it runs.
- ✓ When an app closes or you quit the application, you're returned to the Home screen.

Accessing a widget

Like app icons, widgets can appear on the Home screen. To use a widget, touch it. What happens next depends on the widget and what it does.

For example, touch the YouTube widget to view a video right on the Home screen. Swipe your finger across that widget to peruse videos like you're flipping the pages in a book.

Other widgets do interesting things, display useful information, or give you access to the Android tablet's features.

See Chapter 19 for details on working with widgets; Chapter 15 discusses getting more widgets at the Google Play Store.

Reviewing recent apps

If you're like me, you probably use the same apps over and over on your Android tablet. You can easily access that list of recent apps by touching the Recent Apps icon on the Home screen. When you do, you see a pop-up list of apps most recently accessed, similar to the list shown in Figure 3-4.

Recent app thumbnails

Scroll up and down

Choose a thumbnail to
switch to that app

Recent icon

Figure 3-4: Recently used apps.

To reopen an app, choose it from the list. You can hide the recently used
apps list by touching the Hide icon.

For the programs you use all the time, consider creating shortcuts on the
Home screen. Chapter 19 describes how to create shortcuts for apps, as well
as shortcuts to popular contacts, shortcuts for e-mail, and all sorts of fun stuff.

Checking notifications

Notifications appear as icons, either at the top or bottom of the Home screen,
as illustrated earlier, in Figure 3-3. To check out notifications, swipe down
from the top or up from the bottom of the Home screen. You see a scrolling
list of all notifications in something called the Notification shade, as shown in
Figure 3-5.

Scroll through the list of notifications by swiping the shade up and down. To
peruse a specific notification, touch it. Choosing a notification displays more
information, and it may also dismiss the notification.

Swipe down   Clear all

Notification shade

Swipe up

Notification shade

Figure 3-5: The Notification shade.

You can dismiss a notification by sliding it to the right. If a Close icon appears to the right of the notification, touching that icon dismisses the notification. To dismiss all the notifications, touch the Dismiss All or Clear button.

To hide the notification list, touch the Back icon, the X (Close) icon on the Notification shade, or anywhere else on the Home screen.

✔ Some tablets require you to swipe the screen from the top-left edge to see the Notification shade. When you swipe from the top-right edge, you see the Quick Settings shade. See the next section.

✔ Dismissing some notifications doesn't prevent them from appearing again in the future. For example, notifications to update your programs continue to appear, as do calendar reminders.

✔ Ongoing notifications cannot be dismissed. They include items such as USB (shown in Figure 3-5), Bluetooth, and Wi-Fi connections.

✔ Some programs, such as Facebook and the various Twitter apps, don't display notifications unless you're logged in. See Chapter 8.

✔ The Android tablet plays a sound, or *ringtone,* when a new notification floats in. You can choose which sound plays; see Chapter 19 for more information.

✔ See Chapter 14 for information on dismissing calendar reminders.

Making Quick Settings

Quick Settings are a clutch of popular tablet features, such as Bluetooth, Wi-Fi, Airplane Mode, and Auto Rotate. Shortcuts to popular places, such as the Settings app, might also be in with Quick Settings. The point is to keep these items handy in one specific location. What drives you nuts, of course, is finding where Quick Settings lurk.

Some Android tablets feature Quick Settings as its own shade, accessed by swiping down from the top-right of the screen, as shown in Figure 3-6. Other tablets may crowd up the Notifications shade with Quick Settings, found on the right in Figure 3-5.

Swipe down

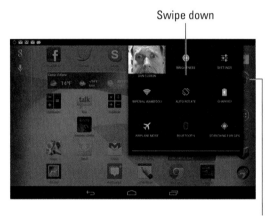

Quick Settings shade

Figure 3-6: The Quick Settings shade.

To access the Quick Settings shade (refer to Figure 3-6), swipe down from the top where the status icons are found. That's the upper-right edge of the screen for most tablets. If your tablet shows settings at the lower-right edge, swipe *up* from there instead.

Here are common items you may find lurking in the Quick Settings shade on your Android tablet:

Airplane Mode: Disables the wireless radios not allowed while using the tablet on an airplane. See Chapter 18 for additional information.

Battery Info: Provides quick access to the tablet's Battery Settings screen, where you can monitor battery consumption and change battery options.

Bluetooth: Turns the tablet's Bluetooth wireless radio on or off. See Chapter 16 for information on Bluetooth.

Brightness: Sets the screen's brightness or provides access to the Settings screen, where brightness options are set. In some cases, you may even see a Brightness slider (refer to Figure 3-4) right on the Quick Settings shade. Touch the Auto check box to enable automatic brightness based on ambient light.

Driving Mode: Sets options that make it easier to use the tablet while driving. This setting may sound terrifying, but the driving mode options include voice commands (dictation) and text-to-speech control for reading e-mail.

GPS: Controls the tablet's global positioning system radio, which helps various apps pinpoint your location.

Power Saving: Activates the tablet's capability to save power when the battery is getting woefully low.

Screen Rotation Lock: Enables or disables the tablet's capability to rotate and reorient the touchscreen based on which way you're holding the thing. See the section "Changing the orientation," earlier in this chapter.

Settings: Opens the Settings app, where all of the tablet's configuration settings and options are located.

Sound: Controls the tablet's noise-making capabilities, either by muting all sound or placing the tablet into vibration mode — or both!

Sync: Turns on background data synchronization with your Google (and other) Internet accounts.

Users: Lets you log out of the tablet and allow another user access. Each user can customize how the tablet looks and control various settings. They can also log in by choosing their account when the tablet is first unlocked. See Chapter 21.

In Figure 3-5, you see the Quick Settings item near the top of the Notification shade. That item can be swiped left and right to access more Quick Settings options and features. So don't think that you're getting gypped out of any options because the shade is too narrow.

The Apps Screen

The app icons you see on the Home screen don't represent all the apps in your Android tablet. Those icons aren't even apps; they're shortcuts. To see all apps installed on your Android tablet, you must visit the Apps screen, shown in Figure 3-7.

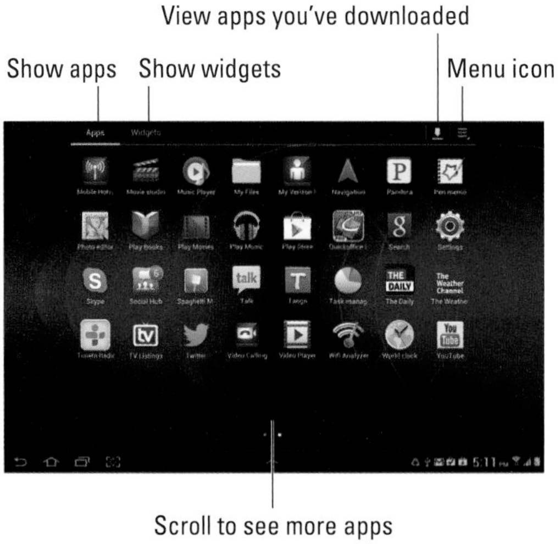

View apps you've downloaded

Show apps   Show widgets   Menu icon

Scroll to see more apps

Figure 3-7: The Apps screen.

To summon the Apps screen, touch the Apps icon on the Home screen. The Apps icon looks like one of these two icons, though it may also have another appearance, depending on the tablet:

You can find any additional apps by swiping the Apps screen to the left. If you scroll too far, you'll start looking at widgets; choose the Apps category from the top of the screen to peruse only apps.

- ✔ All Apps installed, built-in, or downloaded to your tablet appear on the Apps screen.

- ✔ See Chapter 15 for information on getting more apps for your Android tablet.

- ✔ Apps appear on the Apps screen in alphabetical order. Some Android tablets let you sift and sort the apps on the Apps screen. To do so, touch the Menu icon and use the commands there to help you arrange or sort the icons. If there is no Menu icon, you cannot rearrange the app icons.

Creating and Editing Text

In This Chapter

▶ Using the onscreen keyboard

▶ Choosing another keyboard

▶ Creating text by typing or swiping

▶ Accessing special characters

▶ Editing text

▶ Selecting, cutting, copying, and pasting text

▶ Dictating text with voice input

*H*uman beings create text in a variety of ways. From stone tablets to paper, text was mostly crafted by hand. With the advent of the typewriter, humans typed their text. Then came the computer and word processing. Since 1840 or so, people have assumed that text was created by using some form of keyboard.

Your Android tablet lacks a keyboard, a real one at least. To sate the tablet's text-input desires, you use something called an *onscreen keyboard*. It works like a real keyboard, but with the added frustration of lacking moveable keys. Don't fret! You can add a real keyboard to your tablet, and you can even forgo typing and just dictate your text. It's all covered here.

Everybody Was Touchscreen Typing

The old mechanical typewriters required a lot of effort to press their keys: clackity-clack-clack. Electronic typewriters made typing easier. And, of course, the computer is the easiest thing to type on. A tablet? That device takes some getting used to because its keys are merely flat rectangles on a touchscreen. Whether your fingers love it or hate it, you must tolerate it.

Using the onscreen keyboard

When you touch a text field or are given the opportunity to type something, an onscreen keyboard pops up conveniently. The standard Android onscreen keyboard layout is shown in Figure 4-1. You'll be relieved to know that it's similar to the standard computer keyboard, though some of the keys change their function depending on what you're typing. Computer keyboards are incapable of that feat, unless you provide them with an ample supply of hallucinogens.

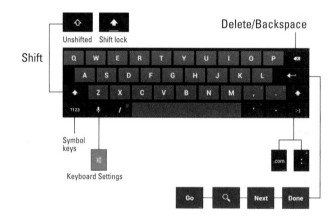

Figure 4-1: The Google Voice Typing onscreen keyboard.

The typical onscreen keyboard's alphabetic mode is illustrated in Figure 4-1. You see keys from A through Z, albeit not in that order. You also see a Shift key for changing the letter case, and a Delete key, which backspaces and erases. Your tablet may show more keys — such as Tab and Caps Lock — or it may show fewer keys.

The Enter key, shown in the margin, changes its look depending on what you're typing. Five variations are shown in Figure 4-1. Here's what each one does:

Enter (or Return): Just like the Enter or Return key on your computer keyboard, this key ends a paragraph of text. It's used mostly when filling in long stretches of text or when multiline input is available.

Go: This action key directs the app to proceed with a search, accept input, or perform another action.

Search: You see this key appear when you're searching for something on the tablet. Touching the key starts the search.

Next: This key appears when you're typing information in multiple fields. Touching this key switches from one field to the next, such as when typing a user name and password.

Done: This key appears whenever you've finished typing text in the final field of a screen that has several fields. Sometimes it dismisses the onscreen keyboard; sometimes it doesn't.

Some of the keys in the bottom row change depending on what you're typing. For example, you may see .com and www. keys when typing a web page address. Use those keys to insert all those characters with one touch.

Other keys on the onscreen keyboard may change as you type, such as the apostrophe key changing to an underline. When does that happen? I don't know, but watch out for it.

- If you pine for a real keyboard, one that exists in the fourth dimension, you're not stuck. See the nearby sidebar, "A real keyboard?"

- To dismiss the onscreen keyboard, touch the Hide icon, which replaces the standard Back icon on the touchscreen.

- Some onscreen keyboards label the Space key with a large, ugly U symbol.

- You may find a Keyboard Settings key, labeled with a Gear or Settings icon, which you use to make adjustments to the onscreen keyboard. In Figure 4-1, that key is shared with the Microphone key; long-press the Microphone key to see the Keyboard Settings key.

- The keyboard changes its widget when you reorient the tablet. The vertical position is narrow; the horizontal position is wider and easier for typing.

- The Microphone key is used for dictation. If you don't see a Microphone key on the keyboard, dictation must be activated. See the section "Activating voice input," later in this chapter, for the secret instructions.

A real keyboard?

If typing is your thing and the onscreen keyboard doesn't do it for you, consider getting your Android tablet a real keyboard. You can do so in two ways. First, you can see whether your tablet features an optional *keyboard dock.* This docking stand props up the tablet at a good viewing angle and also provides a laptop-size keyboard.

When no docking station is available, you can obtain a Bluetooth keyboard for your tablet. The Bluetooth keyboard connects wirelessly, giving you not only a larger, full-action keyboard but also all the divine goodness that wireless brings. You can read more about Bluetooth in Chapter 16.

Selecting another onscreen keyboard

The onscreen keyboard that your tablet presents is preset by the tablet's manufacturer. It could be the generic Android or Google Voice keyboard, or it could be a custom keyboard or even the fancy Swype keyboard. To determine which onscreen keyboard you're using, or to switch to another keyboard, heed these steps:

1. **At the Home screen, touch the Apps icon.**

   The Apps screen appears, listing all the apps on your tablet.

2. **Open the Settings app.**

3. **Choose Language and Input.**

   The Language and Input screen appears. In the Keyboard and Input Methods area, you'll see a list of keyboard configurations available for your tablet.

4. **Touch a keyboard to choose it.**

   A check mark appears by the keyboard you've chosen, such as the Google Voice Typing keyboard, Samsung Keypad (for Samsung tablets), or the Swype keyboard.

5. **If you want to further customize the keyboard's options, touch the Settings icon and make your changes.**

6. **Touch the Home button when you're done.**

Most people don't change their tablet's onscreen keyboards, probably because they don't know it's possible! I recommend that you choose the Google Voice Typing keyboard, which is what I use for this book.

Keyboard varieties are also available at the Google Play Store. Search for alternative keyboards there; see Chapter 15 for information on the Play Store.

Hunt and Peck and Swipe

Typing should be a basic activity. It *should* be. Typing on a touchscreen keyboard can be, well, touchy. Use my advice in this section to get some basics and perhaps discover a few tricks.

Typing duties

It's cinchy to type on the onscreen keyboard: Just touch a letter button to produce the character. It works just like a computer keyboard in that respect, though the onscreen keyboard is flat and there's no key action.

As you type, the key you touch is highlighted. The tablet may give a wee bit of tactile feedback. Typing on a touchscreen is easy to get used to; after a few months of practice, you may even forget how much you dislike it.

- ✔ Above all, it helps to type *slowly* until you get used to the keyboard.

- ✔ When you make a mistake, press the Delete key to back up and erase.

- ✔ A blinking cursor on the touchscreen shows where new text appears, which is similar to how text input works on your computer.

- ✔ Need more room for your stubby fingers? Turn the tablet horizontally and the keyboard grows in size.

- ✔ When you type a password, each character you type appears briefly but is then replaced by a black dot for security reasons.

- ✔ See the later section, "Text Editing," for more details on editing your text so that you can fix those myriad typos and boo-boos.

Swiping duties

Both the Google Voice Typing keyboard and the Swype keyboard allow you to rapidly input text by follow a special typing procedure: Don't lift your finger from the onscreen keyboard. That's correct, you just drag your finger from key to key and the keyboard is smart enough to interpret your scribbling as text.

If you opt for this type of typing (or swiping), I recommend that you start with simple, short words: Keep your finger on the touchscreen and drag it over the letters in the word, such as the word *howdy,* shown in Figure 4-2. Lift your finger when you've completed the word, and the word appears in whichever app you're using.

Figure 4-2: Swipe the word *howdy.*

The keyboard's predictive text capabilities show you potential matches, with the best match shown in the center. That's the word inserted into the text automatically when you lift your finger. If it's not the correct word, you can long-press the center word to choose an alternative.

- ✔ On the Swype keyboard, capital letters are typed by dragging your finger above the keyboard after touching the letter. So, for example, to swipe the word *Utah*, you'd start on the *u*, swipe your finger above the keyboard, and then swipe the *t*, *a*, and *h*.

- ✔ To create a double letter, such as the *oo* in *book*, you do a little loop on that key. For example, to type the word *spoon*, drag your finger over *s* and *p*, dawdle a bit on *o*, and then drag to the *n*. Lift your finger to type *spoon*.

- ✔ The swiping software interprets your intent as much as it interprets your accuracy. Even being *close to* the target letter is good enough; as long as you create the correct pattern over the keyboard, the tablet usually displays the right word.

- ✔ Slow down and you'll get the hang of it. If not, you can still hunt-and-peck using a swiping keyboard.

Accessing special symbols

You're not limited to typing only the symbols you see on the alphabetic keyboard. Touch the 123 key to get access to additional keyboard layouts, samples of which are shown in Figure 4-3.

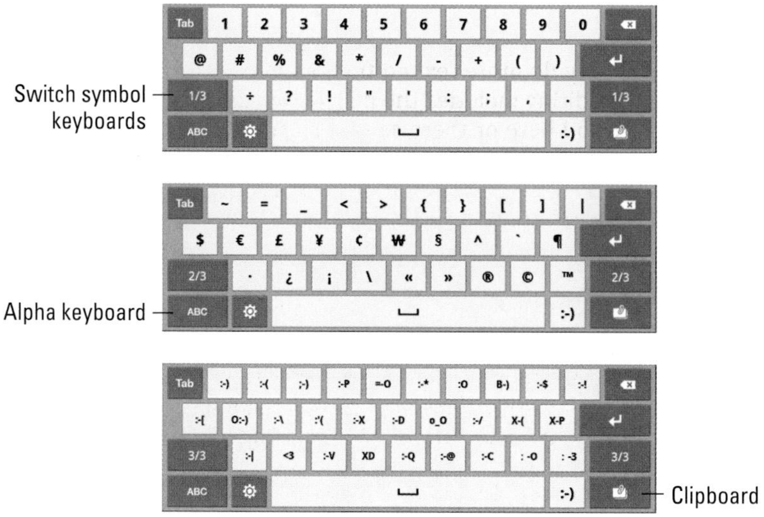

Figure 4-3: Number and symbol keyboards.

Touch the 1/3, 2/3, or 3/3 key to switch between various symbol keyboards, as illustrated in Figure 4-3.

With some onscreen keyboards, the symbol keys are accessed by touching the key labeled ~\{. The 123 key may merely access the numeric keys.

To return to the standard alphabetic keyboard (refer to Figure 4-1), touch the ABC key.

You can access special character keys from the main alphabetic keyboard, providing you know a secret: Long-press (touch and hold) a key. When you do, you see a pop-up palette of additional characters, similar to the ones shown for the A key in Figure 4-4.

Figure 4-4: Special symbol pop-up palette thing.

Choose a character from the pop-up palette or touch the X button to close the palette.

Not every character has a special pop-up palette.

Text Editing

You'll probably do more text editing on your Android tablet than you antici-pated. That editing includes the basic stuff, such as spiffing up typos and adding a period here or there as well as complex editing involving cut, copy, and paste. The concepts are the same as you find on a computer, but the pro-cess can be daunting without a physical keyboard and a mouse. This section irons out the text-editing wrinkles.

Moving the cursor

The first part of editing text is to move the cursor to the right spot. The *cursor* is that blinking, vertical line where text appears. On most computing devices, you move the cursor by using a pointing device. The Android tablet has no pointing device, but you do: your finger.

To move the cursor, simply touch the spot on the text where you want to move the cursor. To help your precision, a cursor tab appears below the text, similar to what's shown in the margin. You can move that tab with your finger to move the cursor around in the text.

After you move the cursor, you can continue to type, use the Delete key to back up and erase, or paste text copied from elsewhere.

You may see by the cursor tab a pop-up containing a Paste button. That button is used to paste text, as described in the later section, "Cutting, copying, and pasting."

Selecting text

Selecting text on an Android tablet works just like selecting text in a word processor: You mark the start and end of a block. That chunk of text appears highlighted on the screen.

Text selection starts by long-pressing a chunk of text. Sometimes you have to press for a while, and you might try double-tapping the text, but eventually you see the Text Selection toolbar appear on the top of the screen. You also see a chunk of selected text, as shown in Figure 4-5.

Figure 4-5: Android tablet text selection.

Drag the start and end markers around the touchscreen to define the block of selected text. Or you can touch the Select All command at the top of the screen to mark all the text as a single block.

After you select the text, you can delete it by touching the Delete key on the keyboard. You can replace the text by typing something new. Or you can cut or copy the text. See the section "Cutting, copying, and pasting," later in this chapter.

To cancel the text selection, touch the Done button, or just touch anywhere on the touchscreen outside the selected block.

✔ Seeing the onscreen keyboard is a good indication that you can edit and select text.

✔ You may see a pop-up menu when you long-press text. If so, choose the Select Text command. You'll then see the Text Selection toolbar and be able to select text on the screen.

Selecting text on a web page

It's possible to select text on a web page even if the text isn't "editable" text. Because the text isn't editable, or even edible, you need to follow these steps:

1. **Long-press the web page near the text you want to copy.**

   The start and end block markers appear, as does the Text Selection toolbar. The toolbar may not look exactly like the one in Figure 4-5: In addition to the Copy and Select All commands, you may find Share, Find, and Web Search commands.

2. **Move the tabs to mark the beginning and end of the block.**

   If your tablet displays a resizable rectangle instead of tabs, drag the rectangle's edges to select the block of text.

3. **Choose Copy from the Text Selection toolbar.**

The text is copied to the tablet's clipboard. From there, it can be pasted into any app that accepts text input. See the next section.

✔ You can only copy text from a web page. Obviously, you cannot cut text, even when the web page is just horribly wrong.

✔ Choose the Share command to copy the chunk o' text to another app, send it in an e-mail message, or post it to a social networking site.

✔ Choose the Web Search command to perform a Google search on the selected text.

✔ Refer to Chapter 7 for more information on surfing the web with your Android tablet.

Cutting, copying, and pasting

Selected text is primed for cutting or copying, which works just like it does in your favorite word processor. After you select the text, choose the proper command from the Text Selection toolbar. To copy the text, choose the Copy command. To cut the text, choose Cut.

Just like on a computer, cut or copied text on an Android tablet is stored on a clipboard. To paste any previously cut or copied text, move the cursor to the spot where you want the text pasted.

If you're lucky, you'll see a Paste button above the blinking cursor, as shown in Figure 4-6. If not, touch the cursor tab to see the Paste button. Touch that command to paste the text.

The Paste command can be accessed also from the Text Selection toolbar, although in that case the pasted text replaces any highlighted text on the screen.

The Paste command can appear anywhere text is input on the tablet, such as in an e-mail message, in a Twitter Tweet, or in any text field.

Figure 4-6: The Paste button.

- The Paste button shows up only when there's text to paste.

- You can paste text only into locations where text is allowed. Odds are good that if you can type, or whenever you see the onscreen keyboard, you can paste text.

- Some Android tablets let you view items stored on the clipboard. You may find a Clipboard app on the Apps screen, or you may see a Clipboard command when you cut, copy, or paste text. Some keyboards feature a Clipboard button (refer to Figure 4-3), which you can use to summon the clipboard.

Android Tablet Dictation

The Android tablet has the amazing capability to interpret your dictation as text. It works almost as well as computer dictation in science fiction movies, though I can't seem to find the command to locate intelligent life.

Activating voice input

To ensure that voice input is listening to you and available with the onscreen keyboard, obey these steps:

1. **At the Home screen, touch the Apps icon.**

2. **Touch the Settings icon to run the Settings app.**

3. **Choose Language and Input.**

4. **Ensure that a check mark appears next to Google Voice Typing.**

   If not, touch the box to place a check mark there.

5. **Touch the Home icon to return to the Home screen.**

The Microphone key now appears on the onscreen keyboard. See the next section for instructions on how to use it.

Speaking instead of typing

Talking to your tablet really works, and works quite well, providing that you touch the Microphone key on the keyboard and properly dictate your text.

After touching the Microphone key, you see a special window at the bottom of the screen. When the text *Speak Now* appears, dictate your text, speaking directly at the tablet. Try not to spit.

As you speak, a Microphone graphic on the screen flashes. The flashing doesn't mean that the Android tablet is embarrassed by what you're saying. No, the flashing merely indicates that the tablet is listening, detecting the volume of your voice.

As you blab, the tablet digests what you say and the text you speak — or a close approximation — appears on the screen. It's magical and sometimes comical.

 ✔ The first time you try voice input, you might see a description displayed. Touch the OK button to continue.

 ✔ You can edit your voice input just as you edit any text. See the section "Text Editing," earlier in this chapter.

 ✔ If you don't like a word chosen by the dictation feature, touch the word on the screen. You'll see a pop-up list of alternatives from which to choose.

 ✔ Speak the punctuation in your text. For example, you would say, "I'm sorry comma and it won't happen again" to have the tablet produce the text *I'm sorry, and it won't happen again* or something close to that.

 ✔ Common punctuation you can dictate includes the comma, period, exclamation point, question mark, and colon.

 ✔ Pause your speech before and after speaking punctuation.

 ✔ There is no way presently to capitalize words you dictate.

 ✔ Dictation may not work where no Internet connection exists.

Uttering s**** words

The Android tablet features a voice censor. It replaces those naughty words you might utter, placing the word's first letter on the screen, followed by the appropriate number of asterisks.

For example, if *spatula* were a blue word and you uttered *spatula* when dictating text, the dictation feature would place *s******* on the screen rather than the word *spatula*.

Yeah, I know: silly. Or should I say "s****."

The tablet knows a lot of blue terms, including the infamous "Seven Words You Can Never Say on Television," but apparently the terms *crap* and *damn* are fine. Don't ask me how much time I spent researching this topic.

See Chapter 21 if you'd like to disable the dictation censor.

Commanding the tablet with your voice

Dictation shouldn't just be for writing text. No, you desire more from your Android tablet! You want to bark orders! Unlike the cat, your tablet actually understands your commands and — most of the time — dutifully obeys. The secret is to use the Voice Search app.

You'll find the Voice Search app nestled among the many apps on the Apps screen. If not, you can utter your dictates by using the Google Search item found at the top of the Home screen.

To get things started, touch the Microphone icon. You see the Google *Speak now* prompt, along with a glowing microphone icon. Dictate what you want, such as "Restaurants near me." In a few moments, the tablet runs the proper app (or it prompts you to select an app) and finds what you're looking for.

Examples of what you can utter in the Voice Search app include

> *Find a good Chinese restaurant*
>
> *Send e-mail to Obama*
>
> *Listen to The Monkees*

I admit that this feature is a tad unreliable, especially compared with how well voice input works overall. Still, it's worth a try if you truly want to play Mr. Spock and say aloud your commands to a cold, impersonal piece of electronics.

Part II
Stay in Touch

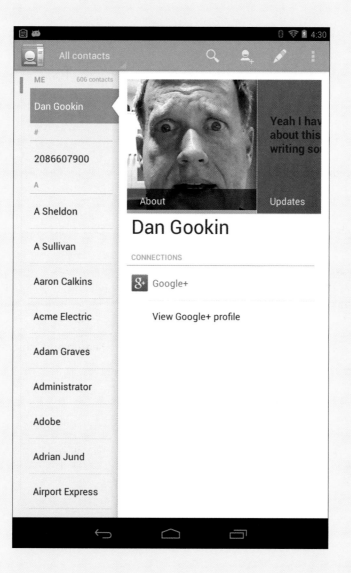

Get more from the tablet's address book by organizing your contacts into groups in the article "Working with Contact Groups" online at www.dummies.com/extras/androidtablets.

In this part . . .

✔ Organize your contacts in the tablet's address book, keeping them handy for e-mail, social networking, voice chat, and video chat.

✔ Send and receive e-mail using your tablet.

✔ Explore the web using the tablet's web browser or the innovative Google Chrome app.

✔ Share your life using your Android tablet and various social networking apps.

✔ Secretly turn your tablet into a phone using the Talk and Skype apps.

All Your Friends

In This Chapter

▶ Exploring the tablet's address book

▶ Searching and sorting your contacts

▶ Adding new contacts

▶ Using the Maps app to add contacts

▶ Editing contacts

▶ Putting a picture on a contact

▶ Deleting contacts

*I*t may seem puzzling that your Android tablet features an address book, chock full of contact information. Such a thing makes sense for a phone. After all, how good are you at keeping phone numbers in your head? But why bother for a tablet, a device that isn't a phone? The answer is communications.

To best use your tablet for communications, you need to keep track of people. That means having their e-mail information, website addresses, social networking info, plus phone numbers because — and this isn't really a secret — it's possible to make phone calls with your tablet. That communication all starts with keeping all your friends in a single app.

The Tablet's Address Book

You most likely already have contacts in your Android tablet's address book because your Google account was synchronized with the tablet when you first set things up. All your Gmail contacts as well as other types of contacts on the Internet were duplicated on the tablet, so you already have a host of friends available. The place where you can access these folks is the Contacts (or People) app.

✔ Whether the app is called Contacts or People — or even something else — it does basically the same thing. For the sake of consistency, this chapter refers to the app as the Contacts app.

✔ If you haven't yet set up a Google account, refer to Chapter 2.

✔ Adding more contacts is covered later in this chapter, in the section "Even More Friends."

✔ Contact information from the Contacts app is used by most apps on the Android tablet, including Email, Gmail, Talk, as well as any app that lets you share information, such as photographs or videos.

Using the address book

To peruse your Android tablet's address book, start the Contacts app. You may be blessed to find that app's icon on the Home screen. If not, touch the Apps icon on the Home screen, and then touch the Contacts app icon on the Apps screen.

The Contacts app may have a different name on your tablet. It may be called the People app, for example.

The Contacts app shows a list of all contacts in your Android tablet, organized alphabetically by first name, similar to the one shown in Figure 5-1.

Scroll the list by swiping with your finger. Or you can drag your finger along the left side of the screen to quickly scan the list.

To do anything with a contact, you first have to choose it: Touch a contact name, and you see detailed information on the right side of the screen, as shown in Figure 5-1. The list of activities you can do with the contact depends on the information shown and the apps installed on your tablet. Here are some options:

Send e-mail: Touch the contact's e-mail address to compose an e-mail message using either the Gmail or Email app. When the contact has more than one e-mail address, you can choose to which one you want to send the message. Chapter 6 covers using e-mail on your tablet.

View social networking status: Contacts who are also your social networking buddies can display their current status. The status may appear at the bottom of the info list in the Contacts app. You might see a View Profile item or a Social Network Feeds button, which lets you see all social networking status updates for that contact. See Chapter 8 for more information on social networking.

Place a phone call: Yes, an Android tablet is not a phone, but when you install Skype, touching a contact's phone number activates that app, and you can use the tablet to make a call. See Chapter 9 for details.

View address on a map: When the contact has a home or business address, you can choose that item to view the address using the Maps app. When you choose the Maps app, you can then get directions, look at the place using the Street View tool, or do any of a number of interesting things, covered in Chapter 10.

Some tidbits of information that show up for a contact don't have an associated action. For example, the tablet doesn't sing *Happy Birthday* when you touch a contact's birthday information.

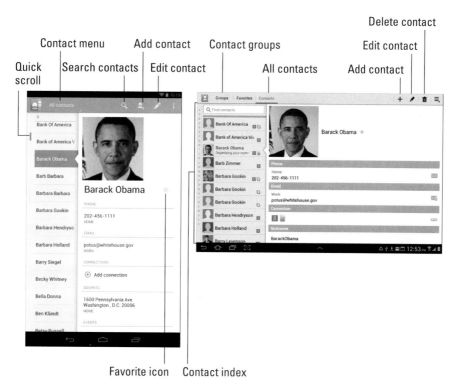

Figure 5-1: Samples of the Android tablet address book.

Sorting your contacts

Your contacts are displayed in the Contacts app in a certain order. Most often, that order is alphabetically by first name. You can change that order if the existing arrangement drives you nuts. Here's how:

1. **Start the Contacts app.**

2. **Touch the Menu icon.**

3. **Choose Settings.**

   The screen that appears contains options for viewing your contacts.

4. **Choose the Sort List By or List By command.**

   This command sorts contacts by first name or by last name. Some tablets may use *given name* for *first name* and *family name* for *last name.* It's European.

5. **Choose View Contact Names By or Display Contacts By.**

   This command specifies how the contacts appear in the list: first name first or last name first.

There's no right or wrong way to display your contacts — only the method that you prefer.

Searching contacts

You might have a massive number of contacts. Although the Contacts app doesn't provide a running total, I'm certain that I have more than 250,000 contacts on my tablet. That's either because I know a lot of people or they just owe me money.

Rather than endlessly scroll the Contacts list and run the risk of rubbing your fingers down to nubs, you can employ the tablet's powerful Search command. Touch the Search icon or use the Find Contacts text field if it's visible, as shown in Figure 5-1. Type the name you want to locate. The list of contacts quickly narrows to show only the contacts matching the text you type.

   ✔ To clear a search, touch the X, at the right side of the Find Contacts text box.

   ✔ No, there's no correlation between the number of contacts you have and how popular you are in real life.

Even More Friends

Having friends is great. Having more friends is better. Keeping all those friends is best. You and all your new friends will be thrilled to know the myriad ways to add friends or create contacts for your tablet's address book app. This section lists a few of the more popular and useful methods.

Building a contact from scratch

Sometimes it's necessary to create a contact when you actually meet another human being in the real world. Or maybe you finally got around to transferring information to the tablet from a traditional address book. In either instance, you have information to input, and it starts like this:

1. **Open the tablet's address book app.**

   The app may be named Contacts or People or Unwashed Masses or something similar.

2. **Touch the Add Contact icon.**

   Refer to Figure 5-1 for this button's potential location and design. If you don't see an Add Contact icon, ensure that you're viewing all the contacts and not a specific contact group: Choose All Contacts from the Contact menu or touch the All Contacts item at the top of the screen.

3. **If prompted, choose your Google account from the menu.**

   I recommend creating new contacts using Google because it synchronizes the information with the Internet and any other Android gizmos you may own.

4. **On the New Contact screen, fill in the information as best you can.**

   Fill in the text fields with the information you know. Figure 5-2 illustrates a typical new contact screen. Touch a field to display the onscreen keyboard.

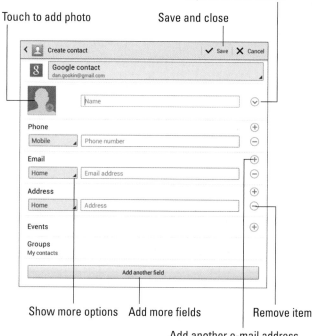

Figure 5-2: Creating a contact.

Scroll the New Contact screen up or down to view all the fields. To add more fields, use the Add Another Field button (shown in Figure 5-2) or, if you don't readily see that field, touch the Menu icon to choose which fields to add.

5. Touch the Done button to complete editing and add the new contact.

New contacts are automatically synced with your Google account. That's one beauty of your tablet's Android operating system: You don't have to duplicate your efforts; contacts you create on the tablet are instantly updated with your Google account on the Internet.

Creating a contact from an e-mail message

Perhaps one of the easiest ways to build up the Contacts list is to create a contact from an e-mail message. Follow these general steps when you receive a message from someone not already in your Android tablet address list:

1. Touch either the contact's name in the From field or the picture by the contact's name at the top of the message.

The contact's name or picture is really a menu, as shown by the little lower-right corner triangle. That's your clue that a menu exists.

2. Choose whether to create a contact or add the e-mail address to an existing contact.

- **For an existing contact:** Scroll through the list to choose the contact. The e-mail address is added to that contact.

- **For a new contact:** Fill in the rest of the contact's information on the New Contact screen. Building the contact works just like creating a contact from scratch, though the e-mail address and potentially the person's name is already available.

3. Touch the OK, Done, or Save button to create the contact.

If you accidentally create a contact when you already have that contact, you can join the two. See the later section "Joining identical contacts" for information on combining two address book entries.

Importing contacts from your computer

Your computer's e-mail program is doubtless a useful repository of contacts you've built up over the years. You can export these contacts from your computer's e-mail program and then import them into your tablet. It's not simple, but it's possible.

The key is to save or export your computer e-mail program's records in the vCard (.vcf) file format. These records can then be imported by the Android tablet into the Contacts app. The method for exporting contacts varies depending on the e-mail program:

- **In the Windows Live Mail program,** choose Go⇨Contacts and then choose File⇨Export⇨Business Card (.VCF) to export the contacts.

- **In Windows Mail,** choose File⇨Export⇨Windows Contacts, and then choose vCards (Folder of .VCF Files) from the Export Windows Contacts dialog box. Click the Export button.

- **On the Mac,** open the Address Book program and choose File⇨Export⇨ Export vCard.

After the vCard files are created on your computer, connect the Android tablet to the computer and transfer them. Transferring files from your computer to the Android tablet is covered in Chapter 17.

With the vCard files stored on your tablet, follow these steps in the Contacts app to complete the process:

1. **Touch the Menu icon.**
2. **Choose the Import/Export command.**
3. **Choose Import from Storage.**

   The command might instead read Import from USB Storage.

4. **Choose your Google account.**
5. **Choose the Import All vCard Files option.**
6. **Touch the OK button.**

   The contacts are saved on your tablet and also synchronized to your Gmail account, which instantly creates a backup copy.

The importing process may create some duplicates. That's okay: You can join two entries for the same person in your tablet's address book. See the section "Joining identical contacts," later in this chapter.

Beaming contacts

If your Android tablet features Near Field Communications (NFC), you can receive contact information from another Android gizmo simply by touching the two devices. As long as both devices feature NFC, you use the Android Beam feature to make the transfer: Open the Contacts app and display the contact's information. Touch your tablet's back (or wherever the NFC field is located) to the other Android device. When the Touch to Beam prompt appears, tap the screen. The contact information is sent to the other device.

Finding a new contact on the map

When you use the Maps app to locate a coffee house, milliner, or parole office, you can quickly create a contact for that location. Here's how:

1. **After searching for your location, touch the cartoon bubble that appears on the map.**

   You'll see a pop-up window that describes more details about the location. Refer to Chapter 10 for more information on finding locations and touching cartoon bubbles that appear.

2. **Touch the Menu icon.**

   The Menu icon doesn't appear in the pop-up window; look for it elsewhere on the screen.

3. **Choose Add as a Contact.**

4. **If prompted, choose your Google account as the location under which to create the contact.**

   You see the New Contact screen with much of the information already filled in because the Maps app shared that info with the Contacts app. It's good when apps play together nicely.

5. **(Optional.) Add more information if you know it.**

6. **Touch the Done or Save button.**

   The new contact is created.

See Chapter 10 for detailed information on how to search for a location using the Maps app.

Manage Your Friends

Don't let your friends just sit there, occupying valuable storage space inside your tablet! Put them to work. Actually, the tablet does the work; you just give the orders. This section lists some routine and common address book chores and activities.

Editing contact information

To make minor touch-ups on any contact, start by locating and displaying the contact's information. Touch the Edit icon (at the top of the screen) to start making changes.

Change or add information by touching a field and then typing using the onscreen keyboard. You can edit information as well: Touch the field to edit and change whatever you want.

If the contact has been joined (so it's a single entry in the address book but contains information combined from more than one source), you'll see additional contact information by scrolling down.

Some contact information cannot be edited. For example, fields pulled in from social networking sites can be edited only by that account holder on the social networking site.

When you're finished editing, touch the Save or Done button.

Taking a picture of a contact

Nothing can be more delicious than snapping an inappropriate picture of someone you know and using the picture as his or her contact picture on your Android tablet. Then, every time the person e-mails you, that embarrassing, potentially career-ending photo comes up.

Oh, and I suppose you could use nice pictures as well, but what's the fun in that?

The simplest way to add a picture to one of your contacts is to have the image already stored in the tablet. You can snap a picture and save it (covered in Chapter 11), grab a picture from the Internet (covered in Chapter 7), or use any image stored in the Gallery app (covered in Chapter 12). The image doesn't even have to be a picture of the contact — any image will do.

After you store the contact's photo or any other suitable image on your tablet, follow these steps to update the contact's information:

1. **Locate and display the contact's information.**

2. **Touch the Edit icon.**

3. **Touch the Contact Picture icon.**

   The picture shows a generic icon instead of a photograph. (If a photograph is already there, you can change it.)

4. **Choose Picture or Album to fetch the image from the tablet's storage.**

   If you have other image management apps on your tablet, you can instead choose the app's command from the list. Otherwise:

5. **Choose Gallery.**

   The photo gallery is displayed. It lists all photos and videos stored on your tablet.

6. **Browse the photo gallery to look for a suitable image.**

   See Chapter 12 for more information on using the Gallery app.

7. **Touch the image you want to use for the contact.**

8. Crop the image.

Use Figure 5-3 as a guide for how to crop the image.

Figure 5-3: Cropping a contact's image.

9. Touch the OK or Done button.

The image is cropped but not yet assigned.

10. Touch the OK, Save, or Done button to finish editing the contact.

The image is now assigned, and it appears whenever the contact is referenced.

You can add pictures to contacts in your Google account by using any computer. Just visit your Gmail Contacts list to edit a contact. You can then add to that contact any picture stored on your computer. The picture is eventually synced with the same contact on your tablet.

✔ If the contact is in your presence, you can always take his or her picture using your Android tablet. In Step 4 in the preceding list, choose the command Take Photo or Take New Photo, and then snap that picture. See Chapter 11 for details on using the tablet's camera.

✔ Your Gmail contacts can add contact images when they add their own images to their Google accounts.

✔ Some images in the Gallery app may not work for contact icons. For example, images synchronized with your online photo albums may be unavailable.

✔ To remove or change a contact's picture, choose the Remove or Remove Photo command in Step 4.

Making a favorite

A *favorite* contact is someone you stay in touch with most often. The person doesn't have to be someone you like — just someone you (perhaps unfortunately) contact often, such as your bookie.

The favorite contacts are kept in the Starred or Favorite group. To view that group, choose the Groups view from the Contact button menu or choose the Groups item from the top of the Contact app's screen. (Refer to Figure 5-1.)

To make a contact a favorite, display the contact's information and touch the Favorite (star) icon by the contact's image, as shown in Figure 5-1. When the star is filled, the contact is one of your favorites and is stored in the Starred group.

To remove a favorite, touch the contact's star again, and it loses its highlight. Removing a favorite doesn't delete the contact but instead removes it from the Favorite or Starred group.

By the way, contacts have no idea whether they're among your favorites, so don't believe that you're hurting their feelings by not making them favorites.

Joining identical contacts

Your tablet pulls contacts from multiple sources, such as Gmail, Facebook, Yahoo!, and even other apps such as Skype. Because of that, you may discover duplicate contact entries in the Contacts app. Rather than fuss over which entry to use, you can join the contacts. Here's how:

1. **Wildly scroll the Contacts list until you locate a duplicate.**

   Well, maybe not *wildly* scroll, but locate a duplicated entry. Because the Contacts list is sorted, the duplicates usually appear close together.

2. **Select one of the contacts to view it on the right side of the screen.**

3. **Touch the Edit icon as if you were editing the duplicate contact.**

4. **Touch the Menu icon, and then choose the Join command.**

   If you don't see the Join command, you may not have to edit the contact before joining: Touch the Cancel icon to stop editing, and then, while viewing the contact, touch the Menu icon and choose Join Contact.

   The Join Contact(s) window appears. If you're fortunate, it may list some suggested similar contacts.

   If you don't see matching contacts, scroll through the list of all contacts to find a match.

5. **Touch a matching contact in the list to join the two contacts.**

The accounts are merged. Well, they appear together on your Android tablet.

Some tablets may let you select multiple contacts from a list. In that case, place a check mark by each duplicate contact you want to join, and then touch a Join button to paste them all together.

6. **Touch the Save or Done button to finish editing the contact.**

   Some tablets may join the contacts immediately, in which case you won't see the Save or Done button.

Joined contacts contain multiple sets of information. You can see the different sets when you edit the contact; each set features its own header that lists the contact's source, such as Google Contact or Google+ Contact.

To split up a contact, edit that entry, touch the Menu icon, and choose the Separate command. Touch the OK button to burst the single entry into multiple contact entries. This procedure is often necessary when the tablet guesses about joining contacts but doesn't do a good job of it.

Removing a contact

Every so often, consider reviewing your contacts. Purge those folks whom you no longer recognize, have forgotten, or just flat-out dislike. It's simple:

1. **Display the contact you want to get rid of.**

2. **Touch the Trash icon while viewing the contact.**

3. **Touch OK to confirm.**

If you don't see a Trash icon, touch the Menu icon and choose the Delete command. Touch OK to remove the contact from your tablet.

Because the Contacts list is synchronized with your Gmail contacts for your Google account, the contact is also removed there.

Removing a contact doesn't kill the person in real life.

6

You've Got E-Mail

In This Chapter

▶ Configuring e-mail on your tablet

▶ Receiving e-mail

▶ Reading, replying to, and forwarding e-mail

▶ Composing a new message

▶ Dealing with e-mail attachments

▶ Changing your e-mail signature

The first e-mail message was sent back in the early 1970s. Programmer Ray Tomlinson doesn't remember the exact text but guesses that it was probably something like QWERTYUIOP. Although that's not as memorable as the first telegraph sent ("What hath God wrought?") or the first telephone message ("Mr. Watson, come here. I want you."), it's one for the history books.

Today, e-mail has become far more functional and necessary, well beyond Mr. Tomlinson's early tests. Although you could impress your e-mail buddies by sending them QWERTYUIOP, you're more likely to send and reply to more meaningful communications. Your Android tablet is more than up to the task.

Android Tablet E-Mail

Electronic mail is handled on the Android tablet by two apps: Gmail and Email.

The Gmail app hooks directly into your Google Gmail account. In fact, they're exact echoes of each other: The Gmail you receive on your computer is received also on your tablet.

You can also use the Email app to connect with non-Gmail electronic mail, such as the standard mail service provided by your ISP or a web-based e-mail system such as Yahoo! Mail or Windows Live Mail.

Regardless of the app, electronic mail on the Android tablet works just like it does on a computer: You can receive mail, create messages, forward e-mail, send messages to a group of contacts, and work with attachments, for example. As long as the tablet can find an Internet connection, e-mail works just peachy.

✔ Both the Gmail and Email apps are located on the Apps screen. You may also find shortcuts to the apps on the Home screen.

✔ Although you can use your tablet's web browser to visit the Gmail website, you should use the Gmail app to pick up your Gmail.

✔ If you forget your Gmail password, visit this web address:

```
www.google.com/accounts/ForgotPasswd
```

Setting up an Email account

The Email app is used to access web-based e-mail, or *webmail,* from Yahoo! Mail, Windows Live, and what-have-you. It also lets you read e-mail provided by an Internet service provider (ISP), office, or other large, intimidating organization. To get things set up regardless of the service, follow these steps:

1. **Start the Email app.**

   Look for it on the Apps screen.

   If you've run the Email app before, you'll see the Email inbox and you're done. See the next section for information on adding additional e-mail accounts.

   If you haven't yet run the Email app, the first screen you see is Account Setup.

2. **Type the e-mail address you use for the account.**

3. **Type the password for that account.**

4. **Touch the Next button.**

   If you're lucky, everything is connected and you can move on to Step 5. Otherwise, you'll have to specify the details as provided by your ISP, including the incoming and outgoing server information, often known by the bewildering acronyms POP3 and SMTP. Plod through the steps on the screen.

   Your ISP most likely has a support web page for setting up e-mail accounts. That page may list specific account setup information for an Android device. Use it.

5. **Set the account options on the aptly named Account Options screen.**

   You might want to reset the Inbox Checking Frequency to something other than 15 minutes.

   If the account will be your main e-mail account, place a check mark next to the Send Email from this Account by Default option.

6. **Touch the Next button.**

7. **Give the account a name and check your own name.**

   The account is given the name of the mail server, which may not ring a bell when you receive your e-mail. I name my ISP's e-mail account Main because it's my main account.

   The Your Name field lists your name as it's applied to outgoing messages. So if your name is really, say, Cornelius the Magnificent and not bill76, you can make that change now.

8. **Touch the Next button.**

   You're done.

The next thing you'll see is your e-mail account inbox. Your tablet synchronizes any pending e-mail you have in your account, updating the inbox immediately. See the section "Message for You!" for what to do next.

Adding even more e-mail accounts

The Email app can be configured to pick up mail from multiple sources. If you have a Yahoo! Mail or Windows Live account and maybe an evil corporate account in addition to your ISP's account, you can add them. Follow through with these steps:

1. **Visit the Apps screen and start the Settings app.**

2. **Choose Add Account.**

   It's found in the Accounts area, by the big plus sign. If not, choose the Accounts & Sync item, and then touch the Add Account item.

3. **If the account type you need is shown in the list, such as Yahoo! Mail, choose it. Otherwise, choose the Email icon.**

   For accessing your evil organization's Microsoft Outlook Exchange server, choose the Corporate option.

4. **Type the account's e-mail address.**

5. **Type the password for the account.**

6. **Touch the Next button.**

   In a few magical moments, the e-mail account is configured and added to the account list.

If you goofed up the account name or password, you're warned: Try again. Or if the account requires additional setup, use the information provided by the ISP or other source to help you fill in the appropriate fields.

7. Set any options that thrill you.

Most of the preset choices are fine for a web-based, or IMAP, e-mail account. For a corporate account, you'll need to confirm the settings with your corporate IT Benevolent Dictator (although they'll probably just set up the account for you).

8. Touch the Next button.

9. Name the account.

On my tablet, the account was named with my e-mail address. Wrong! So I typed in the web-based e-mail service name.

You may see a prompt to set your own name. That name is attached to all outgoing e-mail, so if you want to change it, do so now.

10. Touch the Next button.

The e-mail account is set up. You'll now see it listed on the account screen.

You can repeat the steps in this section to add more e-mail accounts. All the accounts you configure will be made available through the Email app.

 ✔ Be on the lookout for e-mail–specific apps, although not every tablet has them. For example, I've seen a Yahoo! Mail app. If you find such an app specific to your e-mail service, be sure to use it.

 ✔ For some corporate accounts, you may be prompted to activate the Device Administrator, which is a fancy term for allowing your corporate IT overlords remote access to your Android tablet to control e-mail. If you're shackled to corporate e-mail, you've probably already agreed to such a thing when you signed up to be an employee. Otherwise, keep in mind that you can always get your corporate e-mail at work and may not really need to use your Android tablet for that purpose.

Message for You!

All Android tablets work flawlessly with Gmail. In fact, if Gmail is already set up to be your main e-mail address, you'll enjoy having access to your messages all the time by using your tablet.

Non-Gmail e-mail, handled by the Email app, must be set up before it can be used, as covered earlier in this chapter. After completing the quick and occasionally painless setup, you can receive e-mail on your tablet just as you can on a computer.

Getting a new message

You're alerted to the arrival of a new e-mail message in your tablet by a notification icon. The icon differs depending on the e-mail's source.

For a new Gmail message, the New Gmail notification, similar to what's shown in the margin, appears at the top of the touchscreen.

For a new e-mail message, you see the New Email notification.

Conjure the Notification shade to review your e-mail notifications. You'll see either a single notification representing the most recent message or the total number of pending messages listing the various senders and subjects.

Choosing an e-mail notification takes you to the appropriate e-mail inbox.

Checking the inbox

To peruse your Gmail, start the Gmail app. The Gmail inbox is shown in Figure 6-1.

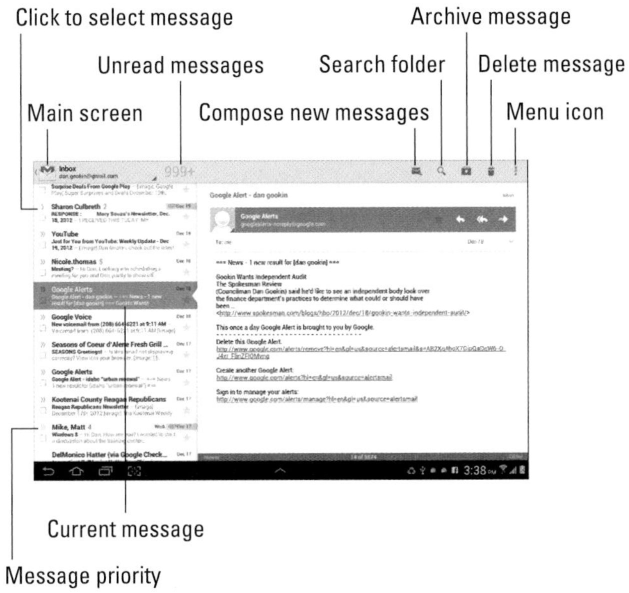

Click to select message   Archive message

Unread messages   Search folder   Delete message

Main screen   Compose new messages   Menu icon

Current message

Message priority

Figure 6-1: The Gmail inbox.

To check your Email inbox, open the Email app. You're taken to the inbox for your primary e-mail account.

When you have multiple e-mail accounts accessed through the Email app, you can view your universal inbox by choosing the Combined View command from the Account menu, as shown in Figure 6-2.

New message

Click to select message   Reply

Mailbox overview   Refresh   Forward

Account menu   Search   Delete message

Figure 6-2: Messages in the Email app.

Don't bother looking for your Gmail inbox in the Email app. Gmail is its own app; your Gmail messages don't show up in the Email app, even when you choose Combined View from the Account menu.

- ✔ See the section "Setting the primary e-mail account" for information on setting the primary e-mail account.

- ✔ Search your Gmail messages by pressing the Search button, as shown in Figure 6-1.

- ✔ Gmail is organized using labels, not folders. To see your Gmail labels from the inbox, touch the Folder Overview button. It's found in the upper-left corner of the screen.

- ✔ Multiple e-mail accounts gathered in the Email app are color coded. When you view the combined inbox, you see the color codes to the left of each message — providing that messages from multiple accounts are available.

- ✔ Scroll the message list in the Email app to view older messages. The Newer and Older buttons move you through the messages one at a time.

Reading an e-mail message

As mail comes in, you can read it by choosing a new e-mail notification, as described earlier in this chapter. Reading and working with the message operate much the same whether you're using the Gmail or Email app.

Choose a message to read by touching the message on the left side of the screen, as illustrated in Figures 6-1 and 6-2. The message text appears on the right side of the window, which you can scroll up or down by using your finger.

To access additional e-mail commands, touch the Menu icon. The commands available depend on what you're doing in the Gmail or Email app when you touch the button.

- ✔ Before reading a message, you may have to choose the inbox from the labels or folders on the left side of the screen.

- ✔ Touch the star by a message to help you more quickly find that message in the future. Starred messages can be viewed or searched separately.

- ✔ If you properly configure the Email program, there's no need to delete messages you read. See the section "Configuring the manual delete option," later in this chapter.

- ✔ I find it easier to delete (and manage) Gmail messages when using a computer.

Replying to or forwarding a message

After you read an incoming message, you may choose to reply. That chore, as well as the task of forwarding a message, is handled by choosing the proper icon that appears when you read a Gmail or Email message (refer to Figures 6-1 and 6-2). You can choose between three icons:

Touch the Reply icon to reply to a message. A new message window appears with the To field already filled out. The same subject is also referenced, and the original message text is quoted.

Touch the Reply All icon to respond to *everyone* who received the original message, including folks on the CC line.

Touch the Forward icon to copy the message contents to someone else.

After choosing any option — Reply, Reply All, or Forward — the next step is to create the message, which works as described in the next section.

Use Reply All only when everyone else must get a copy of your reply. Because most people find endless Reply All e-mail threads annoying, use the Reply All option judiciously.

Write a New E-Mail Message

The Gmail and Email apps not only receive electronic mail but can also be used to spawn new mail. This section describes the various ways to create a message using your tablet.

Starting a message from scratch

Crafting an e-mail epistle on your tablet works exactly like creating one on a computer. Figure 6-3 shows the basic setup, though the screen you see on your tablet might look subtly different.

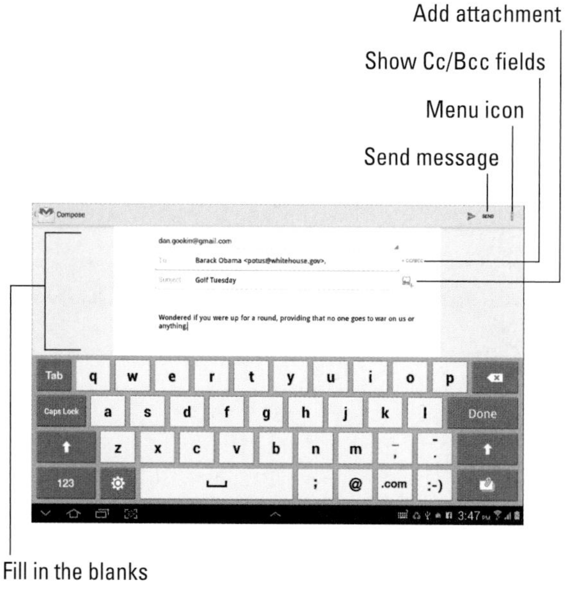

Add attachment

Show Cc/Bcc fields

Menu icon

Send message

Fill in the blanks

Figure 6-3: Writing a new e-mail message.

Here's how to get started with a new message:

1. **Start an e-mail app, either Gmail or Email.**

2. **Touch the Compose or New Message icon.**

3. **Touch the To field and type the e-mail address.**

   You can type the first few letters of a contact's name and then choose a matching contact from the list that's displayed.

4. **Type a subject.**

5. **Type the message.**

6. **Touch the Send icon to whisk your missive to the Internet for immediate delivery.**

Copies of the messages you send in the Email program are stored in the Sent mailbox. If you're using Gmail, copies are saved in your Gmail account, which you can access from your Android tablet or from any computer or mobile device connected to the Internet.

✔ See the later section "Saving a draft" for information on saving a message for later sending or rescuing a previously saved message.

✔ To cancel a message in Gmail, touch the Trash icon and choose the Discard command. Touch the OK button to confirm. In the Email app, cancel a new message by touching the X button in the upper-right corner of the New Mail window.

✔ To summon the Cc field in Gmail, press the +CC/BCC button, as shown in Figure 6-3. The CC (carbon copy) and BCC (blind carbon copy) fields appear, eager for you to fill them in.

Sending e-mail to a contact

A quick and easy way to compose a new message is to find a contact and then create a message using that contact's information. Heed these steps:

1. **Open the tablet's address book app.**

   The app may be called Contacts or People, depending on your tablet. See Chapter 5 for details.

2. **Locate the contact to whom you want to send an electronic message.**

3. **Touch the contact's e-mail address.**

4. **Choose the Compose command to send an e-mail message using the Email app; Choose Gmail to send the message using Gmail.**

   The options you see may appear differently on the screen, but you'll be given choices for Email and Gmail, as well as any other e-mail app that you've installed on the tablet.

At this point, creating the message works as described in the preceding section.

Saving a draft

When you're not quite ready to send a message, you can save it as a draft. The message stays in the Drafts folder until you're ready to edit or send it.

To save a draft in Gmail, touch the Menu icon and choose Save Draft.

In the Email app, touch the Save icon (which looks like an old floppy disk).

To edit the message, choose the Drafts folder and then touch the message. The message is sent by touching the Send button.

Message Attachments

E-mail attachments on an Android tablet work pretty much the same in both the Gmail and Email apps. The key is the paper clip icon, not only for receiving attachments but for sending them as well.

Dealing with attachments

Your Android tablet lets you view or save most e-mail attachments, depending on what's attached. You can also send attachments, though it's more of a computer activity, not something that's completely useful on a mobile device. (Tablets aren't really designed for creating or manipulating information.)

E-mail messages with attachments are flagged in the inbox with the paper clip icon, which seems to be the standard I-have-an-attachment icon for most e-mail programs. When you open one of these messages, you may see the attachment right away, specifically if it's a picture.

When you don't see the attachment right away, you see buttons in the message, which you can touch to preview or save the attachment.

   ✔ Touch the Preview button to witness the attachment on your tablet.

   ✔ Touch the View button to download and see the attachment.

   ✔ Touch the Save button to save the attachment without viewing it.

What happens after you touch the Preview or View button depends on the type of attachment. Sometimes you see a list of apps from which you can choose one to open the attachment. PDF and Microsoft Office documents are opened using an app such as Document Viewer or Quickoffice.

Some attachments cannot be opened. In these cases, use a computer to fetch the message and attempt to open the attachment. Or you can reply to the message and inform the sender that you cannot open the attachment on your tablet.

- ✔ Sometimes, pictures included in an e-mail message aren't displayed. You can touch the Show Pictures button in the message to display the pictures.

- ✔ See Chapter 12 for more information on the Gallery app and how image sharing and video sharing work on your Android tablet.

Sending an attachment

The most common e-mail attachment to send from a tablet is a picture or video. Some tablets may limit you to that choice, but other tablets may allow you to attach documents, music, and even random files if you're so bold.

The key to adding an attachment to an outgoing message is to touch the paper clip (Add Attachment) icon in the Compose window. This technique works in both the Gmail and Email apps. After touching the Add Attachment icon, you see the Choose Attachment menu. The number of items on that menu depends on what's installed on your Android tablet. There are a few basic items:

Gallery: Pluck a picture or video from the Gallery app.

Quickoffice: Choose a document that you've saved on your tablet.

Select music track: Choose music stored in the music library.

Other items: If you've installed another photo manager or a file manager, it also appears on the list.

The number of items you see depends on which apps are installed on your Android tablet. Also, the variety is different between the Gmail and Email apps.

You'll use the program you've chosen to locate the specific file or media tidbit you plan to send. That item is attached to the outgoing message.

To select more than one attachment, touch the paper clip icon again.

 It's also possible to send an attachment by using the various Share commands and icons located in various apps. After choosing the Share command, select Gmail or Email as the app to use for sharing whatever it is you want to share.

E-Mail Configuration

You can have oodles of fun and waste oceans of time confirming and customizing the e-mail experience on your Android tablet. The most interesting things you can do are to modify or create an e-mail signature, specify how mail you retrieve on the tablet is deleted from the server, and assign a default e-mail account for the Email app.

Creating a signature

I highly recommend that you create a custom e-mail signature for sending messages from your Android tablet. Here's my signature:

```
DAN

This was sent from my Android tablet.
Typos, no matter how hilarious, are unintentional.
```

To create a signature for Gmail, or to change the existing signature, obey these directions:

1. **In the Gmail app, touch the Menu icon.**

2. **Choose Settings.**

3. **Choose your Gmail account (your address).**

4. **Choose Signature.**

   Any existing signature appears on the screen, ready for you to edit or replace it.

5. **Type or dictate your signature.**

6. **Touch OK.**

To set a signature for the Email app, heed these steps:

1. **In the Email app, touch the Menu icon.**

2. **Choose Settings.**

3. **Choose an account.**

   The accounts are named after your e-mail address, unless you gave them another name when you first set up the account.

4. **Choose the Signature or Add Signature command.**

   If you don't see either command, choose an account from the left side of the screen.

5. **Type or dictate your new outgoing e-mail signature, or edit any exist-ing signature.**

6. **Touch the OK button.**

When you have multiple e-mail accounts, repeat these steps to configure a signature for each one.

Configuring the manual delete option

Non-Gmail e-mail you fetch on your Android tablet is typically left on the e-mail server. That's because, unlike a computer's e-mail program, the Email app doesn't delete messages after it picks them up. The advantage is that you can retrieve the same messages later using a computer. The disadvantage is that you end up retrieving mail you've already read and possibly replied to.

You can control whether the Email app removes messages after they're picked up. Follow these steps:

1. **In the Email app, touch the Menu icon.**

2. **Choose Settings.**

3. **Choose a specific account from the left side of the window.**

4. **Choose the command Incoming Settings.**

   If there is no Incoming Settings, you're dealing with a web-based e-mail account, in which case there is no need to worry about the manual delete option.

5. **Touch the Delete Email from Server item.**

   The item is a menu, shown by the triangle in the lower-right corner.

6. **Choose the When I Delete from Inbox option.**

7. **Return to the Email app by touching the Back icon a few times.**

When you delete a message in the Email app on your Android tablet, the mes-sage is deleted also from the mail server. It isn't picked up again, not by the tablet, another mobile device, or any computer that fetches e-mail from that same account.

  ✔ Mail you retrieve using a computer's mail program is deleted from the mail server after it's picked up. That's normal behavior. Your Android tablet cannot pick up mail from the server if your computer has already deleted it.

  ✔ Deleting mail on the server isn't a problem for Gmail. No matter how you access your Gmail, from your tablet or from a computer, the inbox lists the same messages.

Setting the primary e-mail account

When you have more than one e-mail account, the main account — the default — is the one used by the Email app to send messages. To change that primary mail account, follow these steps:

1. **Start the Email app.**

2. **From the Account menu, choose Combined View.**

   The Account menu is labeled in Figure 6-2. If you have only one e-mail account, you won't see the Combined View item; proceed with Step 3.

3. **Touch the Menu icon and choose Settings.**

4. **Choose the e-mail account you want to mark as your favorite from the left side of the screen.**

5. **On the right side of the screen, place a check mark next to the Default Account item.**

The messages you compose and send using the Email app are sent from the account you specified in Step 4.

7

Tablet Web Browsing

In This Chapter

- Browsing the web on your tablet
- Adding a bookmark
- Working with tabs
- Searching for text on a web page
- Sharing and saving web pages
- Downloading images and files
- Configuring the web browser app

'm certain that the World Wide Web was designed to be viewed on a computer. The monitor is big and roomy. Web pages are displayed amply, like Uncle Carl on the sofa watching a ballgame. The smaller the screen, however, the more difficult it is to view web pages designed for those roomy monitors. The web on a cell phone? Tragic. But on an Android tablet?

Your tablet doesn't have the diminutive screen of a cell phone, nor does it have a widescreen computer monitor. Instead, the tablet's screen is a good size in between, like a younger, thinner version of Uncle Carl. That size is enjoyable for viewing the web, especially when you've read the tips and suggestions in this chapter.

AK Notepad   Bluetooth   Em

Evernote - Create Note   Facebook   Gm

Skype

> If possible, activate the tablet's Wi-Fi connection before you venture out on the web. Although you can use the cellular data connection, a Wi-Fi connection incurs no data usage charges.

> Many places you visit on the web can instead be accessed directly and more effectively by using specific apps. Facebook, Gmail, Twitter, YouTube, and other popular web destinations have apps that you may find already installed on your tablet or are otherwise available free from the Google Play Store.

The Web on Your Tablet

It's difficult these days to find someone who has no experience with the World Wide Web. More common is someone who has used the web on a computer but has yet to sample the Internet waters on a mobile device. If that's you, consider this section your quick mobile web orientation.

Getting a better web browser

All Android tablets come with a basic web browser app. The app may be called Browser or Internet. Regardless of the name, the app offers the traditional web browser features and works similarly to typical computer web browser programs.

If you're fortunate, your tablet came with the Chrome app, which is Google's own web browser. If you weren't so fortunate, you can obtain a free copy of Chrome from the Google Play Store; see Chapter 15 for details.

I highly recommend installing and using the Chrome app, not only for its speed and features but also for its integration with the desktop Chrome browser and your Google account.

This chapter refers to the Chrome web browser as the tablet's main web browser, though many of the steps listed here apply also to the Browser or Internet app.

Viewing the web

Begin your mobile web browsing experience by opening the tablet's web browser app, such as the Chrome app illustrated in Figure 7-1. That app may be found on the Home screen or, like all apps, on the Apps screen.

Here are some handy Android tablet web browsing and viewing tips:

- ✔ Pan the web page by dragging your finger across the touchscreen. You can pan up, down, left, or right when the page is larger than the tablet's screen.

- ✔ Pinch the screen to zoom out or spread two fingers to zoom in.

- ✔ You can orient the tablet vertically to read a web page in portrait mode. Doing so may reformat some web pages, which can make long lines of text easier to read.

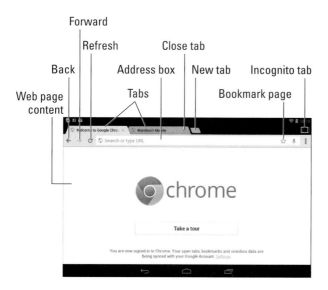

Figure 7-1: The Chrome web browser.

Visiting a web page

To visit a web page, type its address in the Address box (refer to Figure 7-1). You can also type a search word or phrase if you don't know the exact address of a web page. Touch the Go button on the onscreen keyboard to search the web or visit a specific web page.

If you don't see the Address box, touch the web page's tab atop the screen. The Address box, along with the various icons left and right, appears on the screen.

You "click" links on a page by touching them with your finger. If you have trouble stabbing the right link, zoom in on the page and try again.

✔ To reload a web page, touch the Refresh icon to the left of the Address box.

✔ When a web page is loading, the Refresh icon is replaced by an X icon. To stop a web page from loading, touch the X.

✔ Many websites feature special mobile editions, which automatically appear when you visit those sites using a device like the Android tablet. If you'd prefer not to automatically visit the mobile version of a website, touch the Menu icon and choose the command Request Desktop Site. After that item is selected, the Chrome app no longer shows the mobile version of a website.

Browsing back and forth

To return to a web page, you can touch the Back icon at the top of the screen (refer to Figure 7-1) or the Back icon at the bottom of the screen (see the margin).

Touch the Forward icon (refer to Figure 7-1) to go forward or to return to a page you were visiting before you touched Back.

Although Chrome lacks it, many web browser apps feature a browser history screen. Use that screen to review the long-term history of your web adventures. For most common web browsing apps, you access the history screen by touching the Bookmarks icon and then choosing the History tab from the top of the screen.

Working with bookmarks

Need to remember a favorite website? For heaven's sake, don't turn down the corner of your tablet! Instead, just create a bookmark for that site. It's cinchy: Touch the Favorite icon to the right of the Address box. Tap that icon, and you see the Add Bookmark window, shown in Figure 7-2.

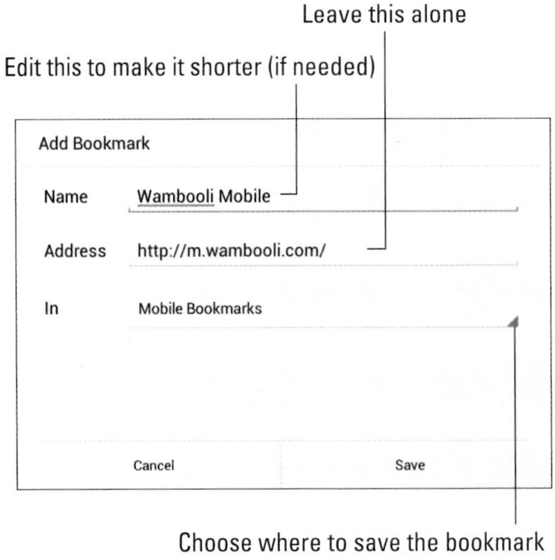

Leave this alone

Edit this to make it shorter (if needed)

Add Bookmark

Name   Wambooli Mobile

Address   http://m.wambooli.com/

In   Mobile Bookmarks

Cancel   Save

Choose where to save the bookmark

Figure 7-2: Creating a bookmark.

I typically edit the name to something shorter, especially if the web page's title is long. Shorter names look better in the Bookmarks window. Touch the Save or OK button to create the bookmark.

After the bookmark is set, it appears in the list of bookmarks. To see the bookmark list in the Chrome app, touch the Menu icon and choose the Bookmarks command. Chrome has three categories for bookmarks: Desktop Bookmarks, Other Bookmarks, and Mobile Bookmarks. (You choose the category from the Add Bookmark window; refer to Figure 7-2.)

The Desktop Bookmarks folder contains any bookmarks you've used on the desktop version of Chrome, which is a handy way to import your computer's bookmarks. That information is coordinated with your Android tablet courtesy of your Google account.

To browse bookmarks, open a bookmark folder. If necessary, touch a subfolder to open it. Then touch a bookmark to visit that page.

✔ Remove a bookmark by long-pressing its entry in the Bookmarks list. Choose the command Delete Bookmark.

✔ Bookmarked websites in the Chrome app can also be placed on the Home screen: Long-press the bookmark thumbnail and choose the command Add to Home Screen.

✔ If your desktop Chrome bookmarks are not coordinated with your Android tablet, start Chrome on your desktop. Click the Settings (wrench) icon and ensure that you're signed in using your Google account.

✔ A handy way to create new bookmarks is to review the Most Visited sites in the Chrome app: When perusing your Bookmarks, touch the Most Visited tab at the bottom of the screen. Touch a web page thumbnail to view that page, and then touch the Favorite icon to bookmark that page.

Managing web pages in multiple tabs

The Chrome app uses a tabbed interface to help you access more than one web page at a time. Refer to Figure 7-1 to see various tabs marching across the Chrome app's screen, just above the Address box.

Here's how you work the tabbed interface:

✔ *To open a blank tab,* touch the teeny tab stub to the right of the last tab, as shown in Figure 7-1.

✔ *To open a link in a new tab,* long-press that link. Choose the Open in New Tab command from the menu that appears.

✔ *To open a bookmark in a new tab,* long-press the bookmark and choose the Open in New Tab command.

You switch between tabs by choosing one from the top of the screen.

Close a tab by touching its Close (X) icon; you can close only the tab you're viewing.

- ✔ The tabs keep marching across the screen, left to right. You can scroll the tabs to view the ones that have scrolled off the screen.

- ✔ If you close all the tabs, you'll see a blank screen in the Chrome app. A New Tab command appears atop the screen.

- ✔ New tabs open to the last web page you viewed. Or if you were viewing the bookmarks, the tab opens with the bookmarks.

- ✔ Shhh! For secure browsing, you can open an *incognito tab:* Touch the Menu icon and choose the New Incognito Tab command. When you go incognito, the web browser won't track your history, leave cookies, or provide other evidence of which web pages you've visited in the incognito tab. A short description appears on the incognito tab page describing how it works.

- ✔ To switch between your incognito tabs and regular tabs, touch the rectangle that appears in the upper-right corner of the Chrome app's screen (refer to Figure 7-1).

Searching the web

Ha! You probably thought I was going to write something about visiting the Google website using your tablet's web browser.

Wrong!

At the top of each Home screen on your Android tablet is the Google Search box, shown in Figure 7-3. The Search box is the best way to search the web, your tablet, or just about anything in your digital life.

Figure 7-3: The Google Search box.

Touch the Google Search box, and then type what you're looking for. Or, if you want to join the twenty-first century, touch the Microphone icon and dictate your search info. In mere moments, you'll see the search results in the web browser or — if you're lucky — your tablet has the Google Now app installed and a robot voice dictates the answer.

Searching for something on a web page

To search for something when you're viewing a web page in the Chrome app, follow these steps:

1. **Visit the web page where you want to find a specific tidbit o' text.**

2. **Touch the Menu icon.**

3. **Choose Find in Page.**

4. **Type the text you're searching for.**

5. **Use the up- or down-arrow to locate that text on the page — up or down, respectively.**

   The found text appears highlighted on the web page.

Touch the Cancel (X) icon when you're done searching.

Sharing a page

There it is! That web page that you just *have* to talk about to everyone you know. The gauche way to share the page is to copy and paste it. Because you're reading this book, though, you know there's a better way to share a web page. Heed these steps:

1. **Go to the web page you want to share.**

2. **Touch the Menu icon and choose the Share command.**

   The Share Via menu appears, listing apps and methods by which you can share the page, similar to what's shown in Figure 7-4.

   The variety and number of items on the Share Via menu depend on the apps installed on your tablet. For example, you might see Twitter and Facebook, if you've set up those social networking sites as covered in Chapter 8.

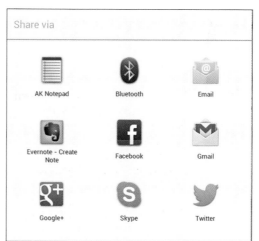

Figure 7-4: Options for sharing a web page.

3. **Choose a method for sharing the link.**

   For example, choose Email to send the link by mail, or Twitter to share the link with your legions of followers.

4. **Do whatever happens next.**

   Whatever happens next depends on how you're sharing the link: Compose the e-mail, create a comment in Facebook, or whatever. Refer to various chapters in this book for specific directions.

If your Android tablet sports the NFC feature, you can share a web page by using the feature commonly known as Android Beam (not to be confused with Jim Beam). Simply visit the web page you want to share, and then touch your Android tablet's back to the other device's rear (or wherever NFC is enabled on that device). To send the page you're viewing, touch the screen when you see the prompt Touch to Beam.

Saving a web page

I like to save web pages of long diatribes or interesting text so that I can read them later, such as when I'm cooped up in an airplane for a cross-country trip or sitting around bored at an AA meeting.

The Chrome app lacks a method for saving a website. A future update may add that feature, but other web browsing apps are fully capable of saving a web page. To do so, visit the page you want to save, touch the Menu icon, and choose the Save for Offline Reading command.

The web page may be available through the Downloads app (found on the Apps screen), or the web browser app may feature a Saved Pages folder, which you can access from the Bookmarks button.

If you use Chrome and want to save web pages for offline viewing, get the Pocket app. Even if you don't use Chrome, the Pocket app is brilliant to have for viewing web pages and other media when you're far away from an Internet connection.

The Art of Downloading

There's nothing to downloading, other than understanding that most people use the term without knowing exactly what it means. Officially, a *download* is a transfer of information over a network from another source to your gizmo. For your Android tablet, that network is the Internet and the other source is a web page.

- The Downloading Complete notification appears after your tablet has downloaded something. You can choose that notification to view the downloaded item.

- There's no need to download program files to an Android tablet. If you want new software, you obtain it from the Google Play Store, covered in Chapter 15.

- Most people use the term *download* to refer to copying or transferring a file or other information. That's technically inaccurate, but the description passes for social discussion.

- The opposite of downloading is *uploading.* That's the process of sending information from your gizmo to another location on a network.

Grabbing an image from a web page

The simplest thing to download is an image from a web page. It's cinchy: Long-press the image. You see a pop-up menu appear, from which you choose the Save Image command.

To view images you download from the web, you use the Gallery app. Downloaded images are saved in the Download album.

- Refer to Chapter 12 for information on the Gallery app.

- The image is stored on the tablet's internal storage. The location of the download folder where the files are stored depends on the tablet. You can read about Android tablet file storage in Chapter 17.

Downloading a file

The web is full of links that don't open in a web browser window. For example, some links automatically download, such as links to PDF files or Microsoft Word documents or other types of files that a web browser is too afeared to display.

To save other types of links that aren't automatically downloaded, long-press the link and choose the Save Link command from the menu that appears. If that command doesn't appear, your tablet is unable to save the file, either because the file is of an unrecognized type or because there could be a security issue.

You view the saved file by using the Downloads app. See the next section.

Reviewing your downloads

To review a history of your downloaded stuff, both from the web as well as e-mail attachments saved, open the Downloads app on the Apps screen. You'll see the list of downloads sorted by date, similar to what's shown in Figure 7-5.

Delete selected item(s)

Toolbar appears only when something is selected

Share selected item(s)

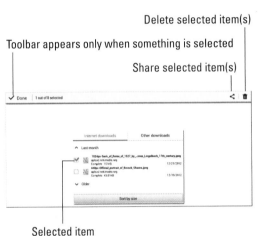

Selected item

Figure 7-5: The Download Manager.

To view a download, choose it from the list. The Android tablet opens the appropriate app to view the download.

✔ The Download Manager may also list any web pages you've downloaded.

✔ To remove an item from the Downloads list, place a check mark in its box, as shown in Figure 7-5. Touch the Trash icon at the top of the screen to remove that download.

✔ Sharing a downloaded item is done by placing a check mark by the downloaded file and choosing the Share icon at the top of the screen (refer to Figure 7-5).

✔ You can quickly review any download by choosing the Download notification.

Web Browser Controls and Settings

More options and settings and controls exist for web browser apps than just about any other Android app I've used. Rather than bore you with every dang-doodle detail, I thought I'd present just a few of the options worthy of your attention.

Setting a home page

The *home page* is the first page you see when you start a web browser app. That rule holds true for just about every web browser app but Chrome; no option exists for setting a home page in that browser. But for other browsers, set a home page by heeding these directions:

1. **Browse to the page you want to set as the home page.**

2. **Touch the Menu icon.**

3. **Choose Settings.**

   The Settings screen appears.

4. **Choose the General category.**

5. **Choose Set Home Page.**

   The Set Home Page menu appears.

6. **Touch the Current Page button.**

   The home page is set.

If you want your home page to be blank (not set to any particular web page), choose the Blank Page item from the Set Home Page menu. I prefer a blank home page because it's the fastest web page to load. It's also the web page with the most accurate information.

Rather than have a home page, the Chrome app either opens to the last web page you've viewed or displays a list of web pages you frequent.

Changing the way the web looks

You can do a few things to improve the way the web looks on your Android tablet. First and foremost, don't forget that you can orient the device horizontally or vertically, which rearranges the way a web page is displayed.

From the Settings screen, you can also adjust the zoom setting used to display a web page. Heed these steps:

1. **Touch the Menu icon.**

2. **Choose Settings.**

3. **Choose Accessibility or Advanced**

4. **Choose Default Zoom or, if that option isn't available, use the Text Scaling bar to enlarge or reduce the text size.**

You can enlarge or reduce text on any web page by pinching or spreading your fingers on the touchscreen.

Setting privacy and security options

With regard to security, my advice is always to be smart and think before doing anything questionable on the web. Use common sense. One of the most effective ways that the Bad Guys win is by using *human engineering* to try to trick you into doing something you normally wouldn't do, such as click a link to see a cute animation or a racy picture of a celebrity or politician. As long as you use your noggin, you should be safe.

As far as your tablet's web browser settings go, most of the security options are already enabled for you, including the blocking of pop-up windows (which normally spew ads).

If web page cookies concern you, you can clear them from the Settings window. Follow Steps 1 and 2 in the preceding section and choose Privacy. Touch the option Clear Browsing Data, which is found near the upper-right part of the screen.

You can also choose the Clear Form Data command and remove the check mark from Remember Form Data. These two settings prevent any text you've typed in a text field from being summoned automatically by someone who may steal your tablet.

On the main Settings screen, you can choose the time Autofill Forms and adjust the slider to the Off position. Ditto for the Save Passwords setting: Adjust the slider to the Off position. You add security by not saving sensitive information about the websites you visit.

As you use the Android tablet, you may see various warnings regarding location data. What they mean is that the tablet can take advantage of your location on planet Earth (using the GPS or satellite position system) to help locate businesses and people near you. I see no security problem in leaving that feature on, though you can disable location services from the Content Settings page of the Chrome app's Settings screen: Remove the check mark by Enable Location.

8

Digital Social Life

In This Chapter

▶ Getting Facebook on your tablet

▶ Sharing your life on Facebook

▶ Setting up Twitter

▶ Tweeting

▶ Exploring other social networking opportunities

The original reason everyone wanted on the Internet was to send and receive e-mail. Having an official Internet e-mail address — with a dot-com at the end — was considered far more prestigious than having a lowly CompuServe or silly AOL address. It was *the* thing to put on a business card.

Today, social networking has eclipsed e-mail as the number one reason for using the Internet. It has nearly replaced e-mail, has definitely replaced having a personalized website, and has become an obsession for millions across the globe. Your Android tablet is ready to meet your social networking desires. This chapter covers the options.

Your Life on Facebook

Of all the social networking sites, Facebook is the king. It's the online place to go to catch up with friends, send messages, express your thoughts, share pictures and video, play games, and waste more time than you ever thought you had.

✔ Although you can access Facebook on the web by using your tablet's web browser app, I highly recommend that you use the Facebook app described in this section.

✔ If your tablet didn't ship with the Facebook app, you can easily obtain it from the Google Play Store. See the section "Getting the Facebook app."

✔ Future software updates to the Android tablet may include a Facebook or other social networking app. If so, you can read about updates on my website at

```
www.wambooli.com/help/tablets
```

Setting up your Facebook account

The best way to use Facebook is to have a Facebook account, and the best way to do that is to sign up at www.facebook.com by using a computer. Register for a new account by setting up your user name and password.

Don't forget your Facebook user name and password!

Eventually, the Facebook robots send you a confirmation e-mail. You reply to that message, and the online social networking community braces itself for your long-awaited arrival.

After you're all set up, you're ready to access Facebook on your Android tablet. To get the most from Facebook, you need a Facebook app. Keep reading in the next section.

Getting the Facebook app

If your Android tablet doesn't come with a Facebook app, you can get the Facebook app free from the Google Play Store. That app is your red carpet to the Facebook social networking kingdom.

The official name of the app is *Facebook for Android*. It's produced by the Facebook organization itself. You can search for and install this app from the Google Play Store. See Chapter 15.

Running Facebook on your tablet

The first time you behold the Facebook app, you'll probably be asked to sign in. Do so: Type the e-mail address you used to sign up for Facebook and then type your Facebook password. Touch the Log In button or the onscreen keyboard's Done key.

Eventually, you see the Facebook news feed, similar to what's shown in Figure 8-1.

Choose what to view (show sidebar)
Upload picture   Show friends

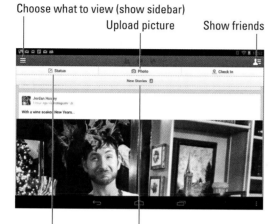

Status update   New items to read

Figure 8-1: Facebook on an Android tablet.

To set Facebook aside, touch the Home icon to return to the Home screen. The Facebook app continues to run until you either sign out of the app or turn off your Android tablet. To sign out of the Facebook app, touch the Menu icon (at the bottom-right of the screen) and choose the Logout command.

- Refer to Chapter 19 for information on placing a Facebook app shortcut on the Home screen.

- Also see Chapter 19 for information on adding a Facebook widget to the Home screen. The Facebook widget displays recent status updates and allows you to share your thoughts directly from the Home screen.

- The news feed can be updated by swiping down the screen.

- The Facebook app generates notifications for new news items, mentions, chat, and so on. Look for them on the status bar along with the tablet's other notifications.

Setting your status

The primary thing you live for on Facebook, besides having more friends than anyone else, is to update your status. It's the best way to share your thoughts with the universe, far cheaper than skywriting and far less offensive than a robocall.

To set your status, follow these steps in the Facebook app:

1. **Touch the Status button at the top of the screen.**

   You see the Update Status screen, where you can type your musings, similar to what's shown in Figure 8-2.

Status update text   Share status

Upload photo   Choose sharing audience
Share your location
Choose friends to join you

Figure 8-2: Updating your Facebook status.

2. **Type something pithy, newsworthy, or typical of the stuff you read on Facebook.**

3. **Touch the Post button.**

You can set your status also by using the Facebook widget on the home page, if it's been installed: Touch the text box, type your important news tidbit, and touch the Share button.

Uploading a picture to Facebook

One of the many things your Android tablet can do is take pictures. Combine that feature with the Facebook app, and you have an all-in-one gizmo designed for sharing the various intimate and private moments of your life with the ogling throngs of the Internet.

The key to sharing a picture on Facebook is to locate the wee Camera icon, which is found on the Update Status screen (refer to Figure 8-2). There's also a Photo button on other Facebook screens, similar to what's shown in Figure 8-1. Sharing a picture works similarly no matter where you start.

Here's how to work that button and upload an image or a video to Facebook:

1. **Touch the Photo button.**

   You see a thumbnail overview of all the pictures in your phone, including those you've taken as well as images from other sources.

2. **Touch to select a photo.**

   You can select multiple photos if you like; any photo tagged for uploading features a green check mark.

3. **Touch the Compose button, found in the lower-right corner of the screen.**

   The button features a little green circle with a number that indicates how many images are selected.

   After selecting or taking a picture, the image appears as a thumbnail on the Write Post screen, which looks nearly identical to the Update Status screen (refer to Figure 8-2).

4. **(Optional) Type some text to accompany the image.**

5. **Touch the Post button.**

   The image is posted as soon as it's transferred over the Internet and digested by Facebook.

The image can be found as part of your status update or news feed, but it's also saved to the Mobile Uploads album.

If you'd rather snap a picture instead of choosing one from the Gallery, touch the Camera icon in Step 2. The tablet switches over to camera mode, allowing you to take a new picture. See Chapter 11 for more information on using the tablet's camera.

- ✔ You can use the Facebook app to view the image on Facebook, or you can use Facebook on any computer connected to the Internet.

- ✔ To view your Facebook photo albums, touch the Menu icon in the upper-left corner of the main Facebook screen. Touch the first item in the side-bar, which is your Profile. Choose the Photos button when viewing your Facebook Profile.

- ✔ A few Android tablets lack a rear camera. For those devices, you can still upload images to Facebook, but you can't use the tablet's camera to snap a photo and upload.

- ✔ Facebook appears also on the Share menus you find in various tablet apps. Choose Facebook from the Share menu to send to Facebook what-ever it is you're looking at. (Other chapters in this book give you more information about the various Share menus and where they appear.)

Configuring the Facebook app

The commands that control Facebook are stored on the Settings screen, which you access while viewing the main Facebook screen: Touch the Menu icon and choose the Settings command.

Choose Refresh Interval to specify how often the Android tablet checks for Facebook updates. If you find the one-hour value too long for your active Facebook social life, choose something quicker. To disable Facebook notifica-tions, choose Never.

The following two options determine how your tablet reacts to Facebook updates:

Vibrate: Vibrates the tablet

Notification Ringtone: Plays a specific ringtone

For the notification ringtone, choose the Silent option when you want the tablet not to make noise upon encountering a Facebook update.

Touch the Back icon to close the Settings screen and return to the main Facebook screen.

The Tweet Life

Twitter is a social networking site, similar to Facebook but far briefer. On Twitter, you write short spurts of text that express your thoughts or observations, or you share links. Or you can just use Twitter to follow the thoughts and Twitterings, or *Tweets,* of other people.

- A message posted on Twitter is a *Tweet.*

- A Tweet can be no more than 140 characters long, including spaces and punctuation.

- You can post messages on Twitter and follow others who post messages.

- They say that of all the people who have accounts on Twitter, only a small portion of them actively use the service.

- I'm not a big fan of Twitter. It has some good news feeds and local information, but a lot of it doesn't interest me.

Setting up Twitter

The best way to use Twitter on the Android tablet is to already have a Twitter account. Start by going to `http://twitter.com` on a computer and following the directions there for creating a new account.

After you've established a Twitter account, obtain the Twitter app for your Android tablet. The app can be obtained from the Google Play Store. Get the Twitter app from Twitter Inc. (The Play Store features lots of Twitter apps, or *clients.*) Refer to Chapter 15 for additional information on downloading apps to your Android tablet.

When you start the Twitter app for the first time, touch the Sign In button. Type your Twitter user name or e-mail address and then type your Twitter password. After that, you can use Twitter without having to log in again — until you turn off the tablet or exit the Twitter app.

Figure 8-3 shows the Twitter app's main screen, which shows the current Tweet feed.

See the next section for information on *Tweeting,* or updating your status using the Twitter app.

Figure 8-3: The Twitter app.

Tweeting

The Twitter app provides an excellent interface to the many wonderful and interesting things that Twitter does. Of course, the two most basic tasks are reading and writing Tweets.

To read Tweets, choose the Home category, as shown in Figure 8-3, to view the timeline. Recent Tweets are displayed in a list, with the most recent information at the top. Scroll the list by swiping it with your finger.

To Tweet, touch the New Tweet icon (refer to Figure 8-3). Use the New Tweet screen, shown in Figure 8-4, to compose your Tweet.

Touch the Tweet button to share your thoughts with the Twitterverse.

✏ You have only 140 characters, including spaces, for creating your Tweet.

✏ The character counter in the Twitter app lets you know how close you're getting to the 140-character limit.

✏ Twitter itself doesn't display pictures, other than your account picture. When you send a picture to Twitter, you use an image-hosting service and then share the link, or URL, to the image. All that complexity is handled by the Twitter app.

✏ The Twitter app appears on various Share menus in other apps on your Android tablet. You use those Share menus to send to Twitter whatever you're looking at.

I should have typed something brilliant
here before I took the screen shot   Share the Tweet

Characters left

Take a picture   Share your location
    Share a picture   Mention someone

Figure 8-4: Creating a Tweet.

Even More Social Networking

The Internet is brimming with social networking opportunities. Facebook may be the king, but lots of landed gentry are eager for that crown. It almost seems as though a new social networking site pops up every week. Beyond Facebook and Twitter, other social networking sites include, but are not limited to

- ✔ Google+
- ✔ LinkedIn
- ✔ Meebo
- ✔ Myspace

I recommend first setting up the social networking account on a computer, similar to the way I describe earlier in this chapter for Facebook and Twitter. After that, obtain an app for the social networking site using the Google Play Store. Set up and configure that app on your Android tablet to connect with your existing account.

- ✔ See Chapter 15 for more information on the Google Play Store.
- ✔ As with Facebook and Twitter, your social networking apps might appear on various Share menus on the Android tablet. That way, you can easily share your pictures and other types of media with your online social networking pals.

Jeremiah Gookin
● nxkxogmkumm@gmail.com 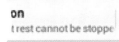 **9** on
t rest cannot be stoppe 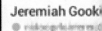 Jeremiah Gookin
● nxkxogmkumm@gmail.com

Like a Phone Does

*I*s it just me, or are telephones becoming less and less significant? Even on a typical cell phone, the job of making calls is handled by a Phone or Dialer app. It's as if making phone calls is only one small part of the phone's capabilities.

Android tablets are not phones. Despite that fact, it's possible to use your tablet to make a phone call. Depending on the apps installed on your tablet, you can text chat, voice chat over the Internet, call your Aunt Edna's landline that she's had since 1957, and even make video phone calls.

Can We Google Talk?

One of the ways that you can fool your Android tablet into acting more like a phone is to use the Google Talk app. It offers features to accommodate text chat, voice chat, and video chat. The only downside to the app is that you can communicate with only your Google contacts. You can fix that problem by reading the section, "Getting friends on Google Talk."

 If I were a gambling man, I would wager that Google Talk will eventually be replaced by the Messenger feature of Google+. They're both similar, but presently Google+ serves a smaller audience.

Using Google Talk

Get started with Google Talk by opening the Talk app on your Android tablet. Like all the apps, it's located on the Apps screen, though you may be lucky and find a Talk app shortcut right on the main Home screen.

When you start the Talk app the first time, you're prompted to sign in using your Google account: Touch the Sign In button. Follow the directions on the screen to complete the painful setup.

After signing in, you see the main Talk screen, shown in Figure 9-1. Your Google contacts who have activated Google Talk, either on their computer or on a mobile gizmo such as the Android tablet, appear in the Friends list on the screen.

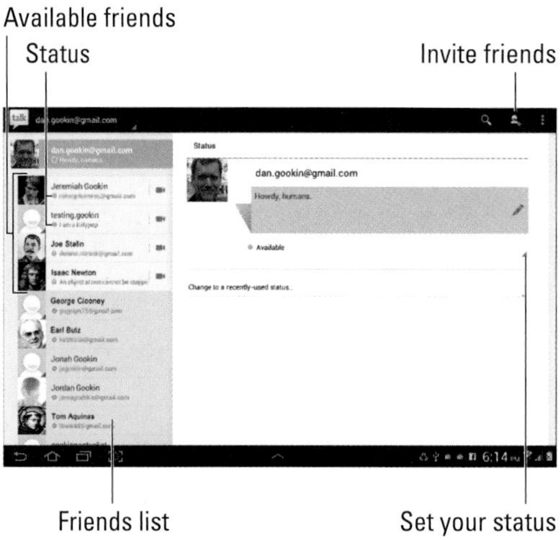

Figure 9-1: Google Talk.

To stop using Google Talk, touch the Menu icon in the upper-right corner of the screen and choose the Sign Out command.

If you don't sign out, Google Talk continues to run on the tablet, which is good if you want to catch incoming chat notifications.

Setting your status and message

Two items associated with your account in the Talk app are found on the Friends list as well: your status and the status message.

The status tells other Google Talk users whether or not you've available for a conversation. The status message is just a bit of text that appears below your name when you're online. You set either option in the same way: Touch your account name at the top of the Friends list.

To set your status, touch the green Menu icon by your account picture and choose Available, Busy, or Invisible. There's also a Sign Out option, which sets your status to Offline. If you're available, the status appears as a green dot, shown in Figure 9-1. Friends who are not logged in sport a gray X.

To set your status message, touch the status message and type a status. If I'm not always available to chat, I write, "Give it a try, I may answer."

When you're done setting your status or status message, touch the Back icon to return to the main Talk screen.

Getting friends on Google Talk

Yeah, it happens: You don't have any friends. Well, at least you don't have any friends showing up in the Friends list in Google Talk. You can easily fix that problem: Touch the Invite Friends icon (labeled in Figure 9-1). Type the friend's e-mail address and touch the Done button to send that person an invite.

You can send and receive invitations on a mobile device running the Talk app or on a computer with the Gmail web page open. When you receive an invitation, you find it listed in the Friends list. Invitations have the heading *Chat Invitation*.

To accept an incoming invitation, touch the Chat Invitation item in your Friends list. You see the Accept Invitation window. Touch the Accept button to confirm your friendship and, eventually, chat with that person.

Spam robots are out there who will entice you to chat. If you don't know the person or don't recognize the e-mail address, don't accept the invitation. Touch the Decline button to politely dismiss the request. If you're certain the person is a spambot, touch the Block button.

Your friends can be on a computer or mobile device to use Google Talk; it doesn't matter which. But they must have a camera available to enable video chat.

Typing at your friends

The most basic form of communications with the Talk app is text chatting. That means typing at another person, which is probably one of the oldest forms of communications on the Internet. It's also the most tedious, so I'll be brief.

You start text chatting by touching a contact in the Friends list. Type your message in the Type Message box, as shown in Figure 9-2. Touch the Send button to send your comment.

Voice chat

App icon   Video chat

Current chat friend   Conversation

Send message

Figure 9-2: Text chatting.

You type, your friend types, and so on until you get tired or the tablet runs out of battery juice.

At any time, you can touch the App icon to return to the main screen (your Friends list). Or you can just choose another friend from the list and chat with that friend instead.

Resume any conversation by choosing that same contact in the Friends list.

To end a chat, touch the Menu icon and choose the End chat command.

Chatting with multiple people is possible: During a chat, touch the Menu icon and choose the Add to Chat command. Invite a friend by choosing his or her account name from the list (only available friends are shown).

Talking and video chat

Take the conversation up a notch by touching the Voice or Video icon in the text chat window (labeled in Figure 9-2.) When you do, your friend receives an invite pop-up and a talk notification. Or if a friend is asking you to voice or video chat, you see the pop-up. Touch the Accept button to begin talking.

Figure 9-3 shows what video chat may look like. The person you're talking with appears in the big window; you're in the smaller window. With the connection made and the invite accepted, you can begin enjoying video chat.

Effects menu

Speaker menu

Mute the microphone

App icon   Exit video chat

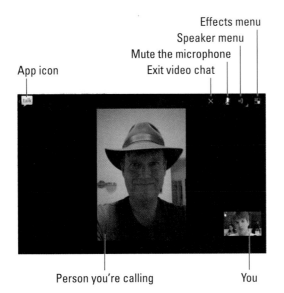

Person you're calling   You

Figure 9-3: Video chat on the Android tablet.

The onscreen controls (upper-right corner in Figure 9-3) may vanish after a second; touch the screen to see the controls again.

To end the conversation, touch the Close (X) icon. Well, say "Goodbye" first and then touch the X.

- ✔ When you're nude or just don't want to video chat, touch the Decline button for the video chat invite. Then choose that contact and reply with a text message or voice chat instead.

- ✔ The controls you see on the screen (refer to Figure 9-3) may change over time as Google updates the app. I've seen a Mute icon appear, and also a Speaker menu from which you can configure sound in the Talk app. I've also seen an Effects menu that lets you alter your appearance.

- ✔ Touching the smaller of the two preview windows swaps that window's content with the larger window.

- ✔ The tablet's front-facing camera is at the top center on either the long or the short edge of the tablet. If you want to make eye contact, look directly into the camera, though when you do you won't be able to see the other person on the screen.

Connect to the World with Skype

Perhaps the most versatile app for converting your "It's not a phone!" Android tablet into a phone is Skype. It's one of the most popular Internet communications programs, allowing you to text, voice, or video chat with others on the Internet as well as use the Internet to make real, honest-to-goodness phone calls.

Obtaining a Skype account

Get started with Skype by creating an account. I recommend visiting www.skype.com on a computer, where you can enjoy the full-size screen and keyboard goodness offered by that device. (If you can't find a computer, you can always use the tablet's web browser app.)

At the Skype website, click the Join Skype button or, if the page has been updated since this book went to press, find and click a similar sounding button. Sign up according to the directions offered on the website.

After you have a Skype account, the next step is to obtain a copy of the Skype app for your tablet, as covered in the next section.

✔ As with other web services, you create a Skype name to log in to your user account. The Skype name is also used to identify yourself to others who use Skype.

✔ If you want to use Skype to place phone calls, you need to stuff some cash into your account. Log in to the Skype website and follow the directions for getting Skype Credit.

✔ There's no charge for using Skype to chat with other Skype users. As long as you know the other party's Skype name, connecting and chatting is simple. See the later section, "Chatting with another Skype user."

Getting Skype for your tablet

Some Android tablets come with the Skype app; some don't. If you don't find the Skype app (or Skype Mobile) on the Apps screen, visit the Google Play Store and download it. If you find multiple Skype apps, get the one that's from the Skype company itself.

Using Skype

After installing Skype on your tablet, follow these steps to get started:

1. **Start the Skype app.**
2. **Read through the initial, informational screens.**

Executive summary: You can't make emergency calls using Skype.

3. Type your Skype name and password.

4. Touch the Sign In button.

You may be asked to accept the terms of agreement; do so. If you are presented with a tour that previews how Skype works, feel free to skip it.

One of the biggest questions you're asked when you first run the Skype app is whether you want to synchronize your contacts. I recommend choosing the preset option, Sync with Existing Contacts. Touch the Continue button.

The main Skype screen is shown in Figure 9-4. It lists people and phone numbers you've connected with on Skype. The next section, "Building your Skype Contacts list," describes how to get more contacts than just Skype Test Call.

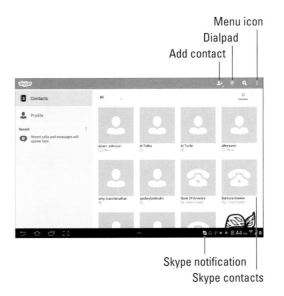

Menu icon
Dialpad
Add contact

Skype notification
Skype contacts

Figure 9-4: Skype's main screen.

The Skype app stays active the entire time your Android table is on. If you desire to sign out of Skype, follow these steps:

1. Touch the Menu icon on the Skype app's main screen.

Refer to Figure 9-4.

2. Choose Sign Out.

3. Touch the Yes button.

You're prompted to sign back in to Skype the next time you run the app.

- ✔ To quickly access Skype, touch the Skype notification icon, shown in the margin.

- ✔ Don't worry about getting a Skype number, which costs extra. Only if you expect to receive calls using Skype is that necessary.

Building your Skype Contacts list

Text, voice, and video chat on Skype over the Internet are free. If you can use a Wi-Fi connection, you can chat without incurring a loss of your cellular plan's data quota. Before you can talk, however, you need to connect with another Skype user.

Yes, the other person must have a Skype account. Further, the person must agree to your request to become a Skype contact.

The Skype app can scan your tablet's address book for any potential Skype subscribers you may have missed. The operation can take some time — like over an hour — but it's worthwhile. To find your friends on Skype, follow these steps:

1. **Touch the Contacts icon on the left side of the Skype app's main screen.**

2. **Touch the Add Contact icon.**

   Refer to Figure 9-4.

3. **Choose Add Contacts.**

4. **Type the name, e-mail address, or Skype user name of the person you want to add.**

   I just type the person's name. As you type, matches appear on the screen.

5. **Choose a contact.**

   This is the scary part! You can't be sure whether the contact found is really the person you're looking for. If you're lucky, the person is already a Skype user and you can see his or her picture. Otherwise, be polite and ask if the person knows you.

6. **Type a message in the Instant Message text box.**

   For example, type an introduction, something like, "Are you the Tina I remember from Hussongs?"

7. **Touch the Add Contact button.**

The contacts are added to the Contacts tab, but they sport a question mark status until they agree to accept your Skype invitation.

No matter how you add people to your list, you see the question mark icon as a person's status until he or she agrees to accept your request.

- You can always e-mail people you know and ask them whether they're on Skype.

- Some people may not use Skype often, so it takes a while for them to respond to your friend request.

- If you accidentally add unusual or odd Skype contacts, my advice is to delete them. To remove a contact, long-press that contact's name in the list and choose the Remove Contact command from the pop-up menu.

- You can block contacts by long-pressing their entry and choosing the Block Contact command from the pop-up menu.

- If the Skype app crashes during a contact-searching operation, it's probably because you've collected some bogus Skype contacts. It happens. A good way to get out of this situation is to use the Skype program on a computer to clean up and remove unwanted contacts. You may also need to uninstall and then reinstall the Skype app. See Chapter 15 for information on uninstalling apps.

Chatting with another Skype user

Text chat with Skype works similarly to texting on a cell phone. The big difference is that the other person must be a Skype user. So in that respect, Skype text chat works a lot like Google Talk, covered elsewhere in this chapter.

To chat, follow these steps:

1. **At the main Skype screen, choose Contacts.**

2. **Choose a contact.**

3. **Choose the Send IM option.**

   (IM stands for instant message.)

4. **Type your text in the text box.**

   The box is found at the bottom of the screen, just above the keyboard, as shown in Figure 9-5.

5. **Touch the Enter or Return key on the onscreen keyboard to send the message.**

   Providing that your Skype friend is online and eager, you'll be chatting in no time.

Add contacts to the conversation
Voice chat
Video chat

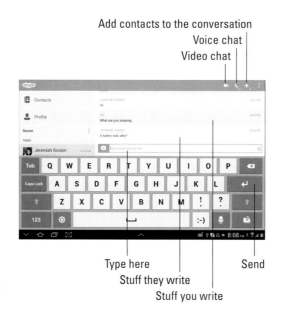

Type here   Send
Stuff they write
Stuff you write

Figure 9-5: Chatting on Skype.

At the far right end of the text box you'll find a Smiley icon. You can touch that icon to insert a cute graphic into your text — if that's what you're into.

- The Skype Chat notification, shown in the margin, appears when some-one wants to chat with you. It's handy to see, especially when you may have switched away from the Skype app to do something else on the Android tablet. Choose that notification to get into the conversation.

- You can add more people to the conversation, if you like: Touch the Menu icon and choose the Add command. Select the contacts you want to join with your chat session, and then touch the Add Selected button. It's a gang chat!

- To stop chatting, touch the Back icon. The conversation is kept in the Skype app, even after the other person has disconnected.

Sending a text message with Skype

When your Skype contact isn't online, you can try pestering the person with a text message, also known as an SMS. It works, providing you have the con-tact's cell phone, and that cell phone can receive a text message, and the person actually enjoys sending and receiving text messages.

To send a text message, summon one of your Skype contacts who has cell phone information listed. You should see a text box at the bottom of the screen that says *Type SMS Here.* Type your text message and touch the Enter or Return key on the onscreen keyboard. The message should be delivered promptly or however long text messages take to send.

Lamentably, you'll find a few downsides with text messaging on Skype.

The first drawback is that not every version of the Skype app supports the SMS feature.

The second is that the person to whom you're sending the message probably won't recognize the incoming phone number. My advice is to identify yourself in the message.

The third drawback is that the person may not be able to text you back. The person can try, but you have no guarantee of receiving the reply.

The final drawback is that text messaging costs you some Skype credit. As this book goes to press, the fee is just a hair over 11 cents per message.

✔ To get Skype credit, touch the Profile icon on the main Skype screen. Touch the Skype Credit item and follow the directions on screen to buy more credit.

✔ *SMS* stands for Short Message Service. Most people just say "text message."

Speaking on Skype (voice chat)

Perhaps the number-one reason for getting Skype is to transmogrify your Android tablet into a phone. The trick works: As long as your pal has a Skype account, you can chat it up all you want, pretending all the while that the tablet is a phone. Follow these steps:

1. **Touch the Contacts icon on the Skype app's main screen.**

2. **Choose a contact.**

   Chatting works best when the contact is available: Look for a check mark icon by his or her name.

3. **Touch the Skype Call icon atop the screen.**

   The Skype Call icon looks like a phone and is labeled *Voice chat* in Figure 9-5.

4. **If prompted, choose the contact's Skype account, not the contact's phone number.**

In a few Internet seconds, the other person picks up, and you're speaking with each other. You see the in-call screen, which is just too plain to illustrate in this book.

5. Talk.

Blah-blah-blah. There's no time limit, though Internet connection problems may inadvertently hang you up.

To disconnect the call, touch the red End Call button on the tablet's touchscreen.

When someone calls you on Skype, you see the Skype incoming call screen, which like the in-call screen is just too boring for me to illustrate in this book. Touch the big green Answer button to accept the call and start talking. Touch the big red Decline to dismiss the call, especially when it's someone who annoys you.

- ✔ Voice chat on Skype over the Internet is free. When you use a Wi-Fi connection, you can chat without incurring a loss of your cellular plan's data minutes.

- ✔ You can chat with any user in your Skype Contacts list by using a mobile device, a computer, or any other gizmo on which Skype is installed.

- ✔ The Skype incoming call screen appears even when the tablet is sleeping. The incoming call wakes up your Android tablet.

- ✔ If you plan to use Skype a lot, get a good headset.

Seeing on Skype (video call)

Placing a video call with Skype on your Android tablet is easy: After choosing a contact — one that's not only available but has the ability to do video chat — choose the Video Chat item from the contact's information page, shown in Figure 9-5. The call rings through to the contact, and if they're available, they'll pick up in no time and you'll be talking and looking at each other.

- ✔ You can touch the Video Chat icon at any time during a text chat to activate the tablet's camera.

- ✔ Some tablets may suppress the capability to video chat.

- ✔ Video chat uses a lot more data than text or even voice chat. I highly recommend that you switch to Wi-Fi when doing a video chat on your Android tablet.

Placing a Skype phone call

Ah. The big enchilada: Skype can be used to turn the Android tablet into a cell phone. It's an amazing feat. And it works quite well. Heed these steps:

1. **Ensure that you have Skype credit.**

   You can't make a "real" phone call unless you have Skype credit on your account. You add Skype credit by touching the Profile button on the main Skype screen and choosing Skype Credit.

2. **From the Skype app's main screen, choose a contact to dial or use the Dialpad icon to type in a number.**

3. **Choose or type the phone number to dial.**

   When typing a number, always input the full phone number when making a Skype phone call, including the country code (which is +1 for the United States) and the area code.

4. **Touch the big green Call button to place the call.**

   This step works just like using a cell phone. Indeed, at this point, your tablet has been transformed by the Skype app into a cell phone (albeit a cell phone that uses Internet telephony to make the call).

5. **Talk.**

   You'll see a per-minute price listed below the contact's name in the upper-left corner of the screen. That's a good reminder that the real phone call you're making is costing you money — not a lot, but something to be aware of.

6. **To end the call, touch the End Call button.**

7. **If the number you dialed isn't a current Skype contact, touch the Add Contact icon to create a Skype contact for that person.**

   Skype contacts are separate from your tablet's address book contacts. By touching the Add Contact icon, you create a phone number contact for the number you just dialed.

Lamentably, you can't receive a phone call using Skype on your Android tablet. The only way to make that happen is to pay for a Skype online number. In that case, you can use Skype to both send and receive regular phone calls. This book doesn't cover the Online Number option.

- ✔ I recommend getting a good headset if you plan on using Skype often to place phone calls.

- ✔ In addition to the per-minute cost, you may be charged a connection fee for making the call.

✔ You can check the Skype website at www.skype.com for a current list of call rates, for both domestic and international calls.

✔ Unless you've paid Skype to have a specific phone number, the phone number shown on the recipient's Caller ID screen is something unexpected, often merely the text *Unknown*. Because of that, you might want to e-mail the person you're calling and let him or her know that you're placing a Skype call. That way, the call won't be skipped because the Caller ID isn't recognized.

Part III
Omni Tablet

Build up your tablet's apps by creating a wish list in the article "The Google Play Store Wish List" online at www.dummies.com/extras/androidtablets.

uction! Adobe Reader AK Notepad Amazon Kindle   Amazon MP3

In this part . . .

- Discover your location, find interesting things nearby, and never be lost again.
- Augment your digital photo album by capturing images and recording video.
- Learn how to record an image's location and then find that location again by using the Maps app.
- Transfer music from your computer and enjoy it on your Android tablet.
- Schedule your personal and professional life by using the tablet's Calendar app.
- Enjoy an e-book on the road or wherever you take your tablet.

ry Birds Angr Calculator

endar Ca Clock

rrents Cut the Rope Downloads Dropbox Earth

There's a Map for That

I'm hoping that teleportation becomes a reality someday. It would be so convenient to travel instantly, to get where you're going without sitting in a cramped cabin. In fact, the only mystery will be whether teleportation has the same knack of losing your luggage as air travel.

One thing our fortunate descendants probably won't complain about is being lost. That's because their Android tablets and the Maps app will tell them exactly where they are. They'll be able to find all sorts of things, from tacos in pill form to used flying cars to Hello Kitty light sabers. Because it's the future, they might even be able to use the futuristic version of an Android tablet to find their lost luggage.

A Map That Needs No Folding

You can find your location, as well as the location of things near and far, by using the Maps app on your Android tablet. Good news: You run no risk of improperly folding the Maps app. Better news: The Maps app charts the entire country, including freeways, highways, roads, streets, avenues, drives, bike paths, addresses, businesses, and points of interest.

Using the Maps app

You start the Maps app by choosing Maps from the Apps screen. If you're starting the app for the first time or it has been recently updated, you can read its What's New screen; touch the OK button to continue.

Your tablet communicates with global positioning system (GPS) satellites to hone in on your current location and display it on a map, similar to Figure 10-1. (See the later sidebar, "Activate your locations!") The position is accurate to within a given range, as shown by a faint blue circle around your location.

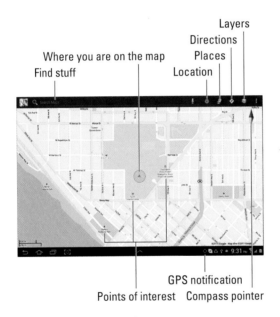

Figure 10-1: Your location on a map.

Here are some fun things you can do when viewing the basic street map:

Zoom in: To make the map larger (to move it closer), double-tap the screen or spread your fingers on the touchscreen.

Zoom out: To make the map smaller (to see more), pinch your fingers on the touchscreen.

Pan and scroll: To see what's to the left or right or at the top or bottom of the map, drag your finger on the touchscreen; the map scrolls in the direction you drag.

Rotate: Using two fingers, rotate the map clockwise or counterclockwise. Touch the Compass Pointer icon (labeled in Figure 10-1) to reorient the map with north at the top of the screen.

 Location: Touch the Location icon to zero in on your current location.

Perspective: When viewing your current location, touch the Location icon to switch to perspective view, where the map is shown at an angle. Touch the Location icon again (though now it's really the Perspective icon) to return to flat-map view or, if that doesn't work, touch the Compass Pointer icon.

The closer you zoom in on the map, the more detail you see, such as street names, address block numbers, businesses, and other sites — but no tiny people.

- ✔ The blue triangle (shown in the center of Figure 10-1) shows in which general direction the tablet is pointing.

- ✔ When the tablet's direction is unavailable, you see a blue dot as your location on the map.

- ✔ When all you want is a virtual compass, similar to the one you lost as a kid, get a Compass app from the Google Play Store. See Chapter 15 for more information about the Google Play Store. Search for "Compass."

- ✔ You can enter perspective view for only your current location.

Adding layers

You add details from the Maps app by applying *layers:* A layer can enhance the map's visual appearance, provide more information, or add other fun features to the basic street map. For example, the Satellite layer is shown in Figure 10-2.

The key to accessing layers is to touch the Layers icon (labeled in Figure 10-2). Choose an option from the Layers menu to add that information to the Map app's display.

You can add another layer by choosing it from the Layers menu, but keep in mind that some layers obscure others. For example, the Terrain layer overlays the Satellite layer so that you see only the Terrain layer.

Touch to exit perspective view

Layers button

Your approximate location and direction

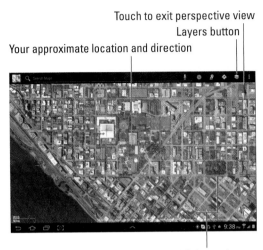

Main roads

Figure 10-2: The Satellite layer.

To remove a layer, choose it from the Layers menu; any active layer appears with a green check mark to its right. When a layer isn't applied, the street view appears.

↳ When you orient your Android tablet vertically, the Layers icon disappears from the screen. To access Layers, touch the Menu icon and then choose Layers.

↳ Most of the features found on the Layers menu originated in Google Labs. To see new features that may be added to the Maps app, visit Labs by touching the Menu icon in the Maps app. Choose Settings, and then Labs to pore over potential new features.

↳ Your Android tablet warns you when various apps access the tablet's Location features. The warning is nothing serious — the tablet is just letting you know that an app is accessing the device's physical location. Some folks may view this action as an invasion of privacy; hence the warnings. I see no issue with letting the tablet know where you are, but I understand that not everyone feels that way. If you'd rather not share location information, simply decline access when prompted.

Activate your locations!

The Maps app works best when you activate all of your tablet's location technology. I recommend that you turn on all available location settings. From the Apps screen, open the Settings app. Choose Location Access or Location Services. In the next screen, ensure that check marks appear by each item. If any on-off switches are present, activate them by switching them to the On position.

Some common location settings include

✔ **Use Wireless Networks:** Allows a cellular tablet to use signals from cell towers to triangulate your position and refine the data received from GPS satellites.

✔ **Use GPS Satellites:** Allows the tablet to access GPS satellites. However, this setting is not that accurate, which is why you need to activate more than this service to fully use the tablet's location capabilities.

✔ **Wi-Fi Location:** Supplements GPS and cell tower location services with Google's own capability to help locate your position.

✔ **Location and Google Search:** Provides information from Google to help hone in on your present location. (It may also be another name for the Wi-Fi Location setting.)

It Knows Where You Are

It's common to use a map to find out where you're going. New is the concept of using a map to find out where you are. You no longer need to worry about being lost. With your tablet's Maps app, you can instantly find out where you are and what's nearby. You can even send a message to someone in the tablet's address book to have that person join you — or rescue you.

Finding out where you are

The Maps app shows your location as a compass arrow or blue dot on the screen. But *where* is that? I mean, if you need to phone a tow truck, you can't just say, "I'm the blue triangle on the gray slab by the green thing."

Well, you *can* say that, but it probably won't do any good.

To find your current street address, or any street address, long-press a location on the Maps screen. Up pops a bubble, similar to the one shown to the right in Figure 10-3, displaying your approximate address.

Information about your current location

Touch the bubble to see more info

Long-press a location to see the address

Figure 10-3: Finding an address.

If you touch the address bubble, you see a pop-up window full of interesting
things you can do, also shown in Figure 10-3.

✔ This trick works only when the tablet has Internet access. If Internet
access isn't available, the Maps app can't communicate with the Google
map servers. See the section, "Taking the map offline."

✔ When you're searching for a location, distance and general direction are
shown in the pop-up window. Otherwise, as shown in Figure 10-3, the
distance and direction information isn't necessary.

✔ The What's Nearby command displays a list of nearby businesses or
points of interest, some of them shown on the screen and others available if you touch the What's Nearby command.

✔ Choose the Search Nearby item to use the Search command to locate
businesses, people, or points of interest near the given location.

✔ What's *really* fun to play with is the Street View command. Choosing this
option displays the location from a 360-degree perspective. In street view,
you can browse a locale, pan and tilt, or zoom in on details — to familiarize yourself with an area if, for example, you're planning a burglary.

Helping others find your location

It's possible to use the Maps app to send your current location to a friend.
If your pal has a mobile device (phone or tablet) with smarts similar to your
Android tablet, he can use the coordinates to get directions to your location.
Maybe he'll even bring some tacos in pill form!

To send your current location in an e-mail message, obey these steps:

1. **Long-press your current location on the Map.**

   You see a pop-up bubble.

2. **Touch the pop-up bubble.**

   A pop-up window with more details appears (refer to Figure 10-3).

3. **Choose the Send Location to Others command from the pop-up window.**

4. **Choose either the Gmail or Email item from the Share This Place menu.**

   The Gmail or Email app starts, with a preset subject and message. The subject is your street address or the address of the bubble you touched in Step 2. The message content is the address again, but it's also a link to the current location.

5. **Type one or more recipients in the To field.**

6. **Touch the Send button to whisk off the message.**

When the recipients receive the e-mail, they can touch the link to open your location in the Maps app — providing that they have an Android tablet or some other Android device. When the location appears, they can follow my advice in the later section, "Getting directions," for getting to your location. And don't loan them this book either; have them purchase their own copies. Thanks.

Taking the map offline

It's possible to get information from the Maps app without having Internet access or a Wi-Fi signal. You just need to remember to save a location's information before you get there. To do that, heed these steps:

1. **Use the Maps app to visit the location.**

2. **Touch the Menu icon and choose the Make Available Offline command.**

   A blue rectangle appears on the map. The rectangle indicates which chunk of the map is saved for offline viewing.

3. **Adjust the map's position so that the area you want to have available offline is within the blue rectangle.**

   Pan and zoom the map to include whatever chunk of the map you want to keep available.

4. **Touch the Done button to save the map information.**

The rectangular chunk of planet Earth you save can be viewed in the Maps app even when your tablet isn't connected to the Internet. See the later section "Making a favorite place," for information on recalling previously saved offline maps for use.

Find Things

The Maps app can help you find places in the real world, just like the Google Search app helps you find places on the Internet. Both operations work basically the same.

Open the Maps app and type something to find in the Search Maps text box (shown in the top left in Figure 10-1). You can type a variety of terms in the Search Maps box, as explained in this section.

Looking for a specific address

To locate an address, type it in the Search Maps box. For example:

```
1313 N. Harbor Blvd., Anaheim, CA 92803
```

Touch the Search key on the onscreen keyboard, and that location is shown on the map. The next step is getting directions, which you can read about in the later section, "Getting directions."

  ✔ You don't need to type the entire address. Oftentimes, all you need is the street number and street name and then either the city name or the zip code.

  ✔ If you omit the city name or zip code, the tablet looks for the closest matching address near your current location or the location displayed on the Maps app screen.

Finding a business, restaurant, or point of interest

You may not know an address, but you know when you crave sushi or Hungarian or perhaps the exotic flavors of Wyoming. Maybe you need a hotel or a gas station, or you have to find a place that buys old dentures. To find a business entity or a point of interest, type its name in the Search Maps box. For example:

```
Movie theater
```

This command flags movie theaters on the current Maps screen or nearby.

Specify your current location, as described earlier in this chapter, to find locations near you. Otherwise, the Maps app looks for places near the area you see on the screen.

Or you can be specific and look for businesses near a certain location by specifying the city name, district, or zip code, such as

```
Booze 02554
```

After typing this command and touching the Search key, you see a smattering of tippling establishments found in or near Nantucket, Massachusetts, similar to the ones shown in Figure 10-4.

Search text

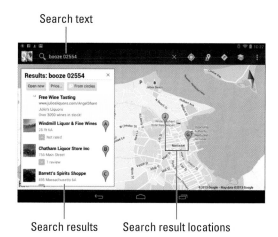

Search results   Search result locations

Figure 10-4: Finding booze in and near Nantucket, Massachusetts.

To see more information about a result, touch it. You can touch either the item in the search result list or the pin dropped on the map, such as item J shown in Figure 10-4. You'll see a pop-up cartoon bubble, which you can touch to get even more specific information.

You can touch the Directions icon on the location's details screen to get directions; see the later section, "Getting directions."

    ✔ Every letter or dot on the screen represents a search result (refer to Figure 10-4).

    ✔ Spread your fingers on the touchscreen to zoom in on the map.

✔ You can create a contact for the location, keeping it as a part of your Contacts list: After touching the location balloon, touch the Menu icon and choose the Add as a Contact command. The contact is created using data known about the business, including its location and tablet number and even a web page address — if that information is available.

Making a favorite place

Just as you can have favorite contacts, favorite web pages, and favorite politicians, you can also mark some of the places you go as favorites.

Well, maybe you don't have a favorite politician, but to flag a location as a favorite, you summon its details screen, similar to what's shown in Figure 10-3. Touch the Favorite icon and the location is saved as one of your favorite places.

To review your favorite places, touch the Maps icon and choose the My Places command. You can instantly view any favorite place on the map by choosing it from the My Places window that appears.

✔ Two special places are known as Home and Work. You can set those places from the My Places window by choosing one and then typing the location's address. The Home and Work places are flagged by special icons on the map.

✔ The Starred list shows your favorite locations. Mark a location as a favorite by touching the Favorite icon when you view the location's details. If the Favorite icon doesn't appear, touch the Menu icon and choose the Add Star command.

✔ The Recent list allows you to peruse items you've located or searched for recently.

✔ The Offline list shows those portions of the map you've selected and stored so that you can peruse their details in the Maps app when an Internet connection isn't available.

Locating a contact

You can hone in on where your friends dwell by using the Maps app. This trick works when you've specified an address for the contact — home, work, prison, or another location — in the tablet's address book app. If so, the tablet can easily help you find that location or even give you directions.

The secret? Just touch the contact's address in the address book app. In mere moments, you'll see the contact's location.

- ✔ The first time you're presented with locating a contact's address, you may see a Complete Action Using window. My advice is to choose the Maps app. Touch the Always button and you'll never be bothered with the prompt again.

- ✔ The tablet's address book is covered in Chapter 5. The app could be named Contacts, People, or something completely unexpected.

Android the Navigator

Finding something is only half the job. The other half is getting there, or sending someone else there if it's an unpleasant place. Your Android tablet is ever-ready, thanks to the various direction and navigation features nestled in the Maps app.

If you use your tablet in your auto, I strongly recommend that someone else hold it and read the directions. Or use voice navigation and, for goodness sake, don't look at the tablet while you're driving!

Getting directions

One command associated with locations on the map is Directions or Get Directions. Here's how to use it:

1. **Touch a location's cartoon bubble displayed by an address, a contact, or a business or as a result of a map search.**

   A pop-up window appears, offering more information (refer to Figure 10-3).

2. **Touch the Directions icon in the location's cartoon bubble.**

   After touching the Directions icon (shown in the margin), you'll see a pop-up window, shown in Figure 10-5. It's preset to help you get to the location you chose in Step 1 from your current location. You can change the My Location item to any other address, or swap the items as illustrated in the figure.

3. **Ensure that the starting location and destination are what you want.**

   If they're backwards, touch the Swap icon (refer to Figure 10-5). You can touch the Bookmark icon to choose a favorite place, a contact, or a specific map location.

4. **Choose a method of transportation.**

   The options available vary, depending on your location. In Figure 10-5 the items are (left-to-right): Car, Public Transportation, Bicycle, and On Foot.

Starting location   Change location

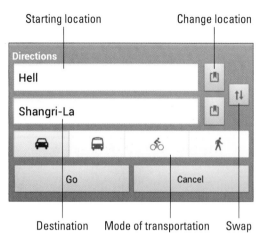

Destination   Mode of transportation   Swap

Figure 10-5: Getting where you want to go.

5. **Touch the Go button.**

A list of directions appears on the left side of the screen. On the right side of the screen you see your route plotted as a blue line on the map.

6. **Follow the blue line.**

Google doesn't provide a cheerful song to sing while you follow the blue line.

 You can modify your journey by dragging the blue line around with your finger. Touch one of the waypoints, shown in the margin, to drag the route to other streets or nearby highways. The journey distance and travel time adjust as you change your route.

➤ The blue line appears only on the tablet screen, not on streets in the real world.

➤ The Maps app alerts you to any toll roads on the specified route. As you travel, you can choose alternative, non-toll routes if available. You're prompted to switch routes during navigation; see the next section.

➤ You may not get perfect directions from the Maps app, but it's a useful tool for places you've never visited.

Navigating to your destination

Maps and lists of directions are so 20th century. I don't know why anyone would bother, especially when your Android tablet features a digital copilot in the form of voice navigation.

To use navigation, choose the Navigation option from any list of directions. Or touch the Navigation icon, shown in the margin. You can also enter the Navigation app directly by choosing it from the Apps screen, though then you must type (or speak) your destination, so it's just easier to start in the Maps app.

In navigation mode, the tablet displays an interactive map that shows your current location and turn-by-turn directions for reaching your destination. A digital voice tells you how far to go and when to turn, and gives you other nagging advice — just like a backseat driver, albeit an accurate one.

After choosing Navigation, sit back and have the tablet dictate your directions. You can simply listen, or just glance at the tablet for an update of where you're heading.

To stop navigation, touch the Menu icon and choose the Exit Navigation command.

- ✓ To remove the navigation route from the screen, exit navigation mode and return to the Maps app. Touch the Menu icon and choose the Clear Map command.

- ✓ When you tire of hearing the navigation voice, touch the Menu icon and choose the Turn Off Voice command.

- ✓ I refer to the navigation voice as *Gertrude*.

- ✓ The neat thing about the navigation feature is that whenever you screw up, a new course is immediately calculated.

- ✓ In navigation mode, the Android tablet consumes a lot of battery power. I highly recommend that you plug the tablet into your car's power adapter (cigarette lighter) for the duration of the trip. Any Android cell phone power adapter works, or any adapter with a micro-USB connector.

Adding a navigation widget to the Home screen

When you visit certain places often — such as a Turkish bathhouse — you can save yourself the time you would spend repeatedly inputting navigation information. All you need to do is create a navigation widget on the Home screen. Here's how:

1. **Summon the Apps screen.**

2. **Choose Widgets from the top of the screen.**

3. **Long-press the Directions & Navigation widget and position it to a location on the Home screen.**

   You need to scroll over a few pages to find the Directions & Navigation widget.

4. **Type a destination, a contact name, an address, or a business in the text box.**

   As you type, suggestions appear in a list. You can choose a suggestion to save yourself some typing.

5. **Choose a traveling method.**

   Your options are Car, Public Transportation, Bicycle, and On Foot.

6. **Type a shortcut name.**

7. **Choose an icon for the shortcut.**

   You may have to touch the Back icon to dismiss the onscreen keyboard and see the shortcut icons.

8. **Touch the Save button.**

   The navigation shortcut is placed on the Home screen.

9. **Touch the Home icon to return to the Home screen.**

To use the shortcut, simply touch it on the Home screen. Instantly, the Maps app starts and enters navigation mode, steering you from wherever you are to the location referenced by the shortcut.

See Chapter 19 for additional information on adding widgets to the Home screen. Information on Turkish bathhouses can be found on the Internet at www.dummies.com.

Everyone Say, "Cheese!"

In This Chapter
▶ Taking a still picture
▶ Deleting the image you just shot
▶ Turning on the flash
▶ Snapping different types of images
▶ Shooting video
▶ Recording yourself
▶ Using the LED lamp for video

I have no idea why people say "Cheese" when they get their picture taken. Supposedly it's to make them smile. Even in other countries, where the native word for *cheese* can't possibly influence the face's smile muscles, they still say it when a picture is taken. Apparently it's a tradition that's present everywhere. Well, except for maybe the moon, where it's rumored that Buzz Aldrin said "Green cheese."

When you hear folks say "Cheese" around your Android tablet, it will most likely be because you're taking advantage of the tablet's photographic and video capabilities. Or I suppose you could use the tablet as a festive cheese platter. But when you opt to take pictures or shoot video, turn to this chapter for helpful words of advice.

Android Tablet Camera 101

An Android tablet isn't the world's best camera. And I'm sure that Mr. Spock's tricorder wasn't the best camera in the *Star Trek* universe, either, but it could take pictures. That comparison is kind of the whole point: Your Android tablet is an incredible gizmo that does many things. One of those things is to take pictures, as described in this section.

✔ The tablet's primary camera is the rear-facing camera. The secondary camera, found on nearly all Android tablets, faces you as you look at the touchscreen.

✔ Not all Android tablets feature a rear-facing camera. If yours doesn't, the tablet most likely didn't come with an app that can shoot pictures or videos.

Snapping a pic

Picture-taking duties on your Android tablet are handled by the Camera app. It controls both the main camera, which is on the tablet's butt, and the front-facing camera, which is not on the tablet's butt. Like all apps on the tablet, you can find and start the Camera app by touching its icon on the Apps screen.

After starting the Camera app, you see the main Camera screen, which most likely has features similar to those illustrated in Figure 11-1.

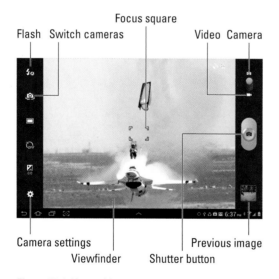

Figure 11-1: Your tablet as a camera.

To take a picture, first ensure that the Camera app is in still picture mode: Check the Camera/Video icon, shown in Figure 11-1, to confirm that it's in the Camera position. Then point the camera at the subject and touch the Shutter button.

After you touch the Shutter button, the camera focuses, you may hear a mechanical shutter sound play, and the flash may go off. You're ready to take the next picture.

To preview the image you just snapped, touch the previous picture image that appears on the screen, as shown in Figure 11-1.

- ✔ The camera focuses automatically, though you can drag the focus square around the touchscreen to specifically adjust the focus (refer to Figure 11-1). Not every Camera app features a focus square.

- ✔ Some tablet cameras sport a zoom lens; if yours does, you'll find a zoom control on the screen. Slide the button up or down (or left or right) to zoom in or out. You may also be able to use the tablet's Volume button to zoom in and out.

- ✔ You can take as many pictures with your Android tablet as you like, as long as you don't run out of space for them in the tablet's internal or removable storage.

- ✔ If your pictures appear blurry, ensure that the camera lens on the back of the tablet isn't dirty.

- ✔ Use the Gallery app to preview and manage your pictures. See Chapter 12 for more information about the Gallery.

- ✔ The Android tablet not only takes a picture but also keeps track of where you were located on planet Earth when you took it. See the section "Setting the image's location," later in this chapter, for details. Also refer to Chapter 12 for information on reviewing a photograph's location.

Deleting an image immediately after you take it

Sometimes, you just can't wait to delete an image. Either an irritated person is standing next to you, begging that the photo be deleted, or you're just not happy and feel the urge to smash into digital shards the picture you just took. Hastily follow these steps:

1. **Touch the image preview that appears in the lower-right corner of the screen.**

   The image preview is shown in the bottom right in Figure 11-1. After touching the preview, you see the full-screen image.

2. **Touch the Trash icon on the screen.**

   You may see a Delete command instead of the Trash icon. If so, touch it.

3. **Touch the OK button to erase the image.**

   The image has been banished to bit hell.

If necessary, touch the Back icon to return to the Camera app. If the Back icon has disappeared, tap the screen to see it.

If you don't see a preview, you can always remove the image by using the Gallery app. See Chapter 12.

Setting the flash

The camera on the Android tablet has three flash settings, as shown in Table 11-1.

Table 11-1		Android Tablet Camera Flash Settings
Setting	*Icon*	*Description*
Auto		The flash activates during low-light situations but not when it's bright out.
On		The flash always activates.
Off		The flash never activates, even in low-light situations.

To change or check the flash setting, look for the Flash icon on the Camera app's screen; it's shown on the left side of the screen in Figure 11-1. The icon confirms the current flash setting, which is Auto in the figure. Choose the Flash setting from the pop-up menu that appears.

✓ The Flash setting might also be found on a sliding control drawer or by first touching a Settings icon to see the Camera app's settings.

✓ A good time to turn on the flash is when taking pictures of people or objects in front of something bright, such as Aunt Ellen showing off her prized peach cobbler in front of a nuclear explosion.

✓ Some Android tablets lack flash hardware for the rear camera. On those devices, you cannot set the flash in the Camera app.

Doing a self-portrait

Who needs to pay all that money for a mirror when you have an Android tablet? Well, forget the mirror. Instead, think about taking all those self-shots without having to second-guess whether the camera is pointed at your face.

To take your own mug shot, start the Camera app and touch the Switch Cameras icon (labeled on the left in Figure 11-1). When you see yourself on the screen, you're doing it properly.

Smile. Click. You got it.

Touch the Switch Cameras icon again to direct the Android tablet to use the main camera again.

Changing the resolution

The Camera app lets you set the image's resolution, which allows for more detail in an image or less detail. More detail would be required for images you plan on editing or printing. Less detail is fine for posting images on Facebook or in situations where fuzzy images make people look attractive.

Your tablet's Camera app may feature a resolution setting on the screen. If so, use it to set the resolution. Otherwise, touch the Settings icon (refer to Figure 11-1) and choose the Resolution command to select a resolution.

The higher the resolution values, the higher the resolution (and detail) stored in the image. That high resolution also means that the image occupies more storage space in your tablet.

- ✔ The tablet's front-facing camera may feature a fixed resolution, in which case you can't set a new resolution value. Or, if you're lucky, you may be able to set the front-facing camera's resolution: Switch to that camera, and then set the resolution as described in this section.

- ✔ A picture's *resolution* describes how many pixels, or dots, are in the image. The more dots, the better the image looks and prints.

- ✔ See the later section, "Setting video quality," for information on the Video Resolution setting, which applies only to shooting video with the Android tablet.

Taking a panoramic shot

Your Android tablet's Camera app may feature a panoramic mode. A *panorama* is a wide shot, like a landscape, a beautiful vista, or a family photograph where everyone is all spread out because they don't like each other.

The method for achieving a panoramic shot may vary subtly from tablet to tablet, but generally it works like this:

1. **Start the Camera app.**

2. **Touch the Panoramic mode icon.**

   If the Camera app lacks a specific icon for taking a panoramic shot, look for a shooting mode or similar icon. The panoramic feature may be a submenu item on a main menu.

3. **Hold your arms steady.**

4. **Touch the Shutter button.**

   A colored frame appears on the screen, approximating the current shot. Arrows point in the directions in which you can pan.

5. **Pivot slightly to your right (or in whatever direction, but you must continue in the same direction).**

   As you move the camera, the colored frame adjusts to your new position. The tablet beeps as the next image in the panorama is snapped automatically. All you need to do is keep moving.

6. **Continue pivoting as subsequent shots are taken, or touch the Shutter button again to finish the panorama.**

   After the last image is snapped, wait while the image is assembled.

The Camera app sticks the different shots together, creating a panoramic image.

✓ To exit panoramic mode, choose Single Shot or whichever option returns the Camera app to its standard shooting mode.

✓ The Android tablet camera automatically captures the panoramic shot. You touch the Shutter button only when you're done.

Setting the image's location

Your Android tablet not only takes pictures but also keeps track of where you're located when you take the picture — if you've turned on that option. The feature is called geo-tag or GPS-tag, and here's how to ensure that it's on:

1. **While using the Camera app, touch the Settings icon.**

2. **Choose the Geo-Tag or GPS Tag item to turn on that item.**

3. **Touch the Back icon to close the Settings menu.**

Not everyone is comfortable with having the tablet record a picture's location, so you can turn off the option. Just repeat these steps, but choose Off in Step 2.

✔ See Chapter 12 for information on reviewing a photograph's location.

✔ The geo-tag information is stored in the picture itself. That means that other devices, apps, and computer programs can read the GPS information to determine where the image was taken.

Adjusting the camera

Android tablet Camera apps vary in the quantity and quality of features offered. Some apps feature only the basics; others come with a variety of interesting effects, modes, and other settings. Two options to look for are Scene and Special Effects.

Scene: This item, or something similar, configures the camera for taking certain types of pictures. Choose an option that describes the type of images you're capturing, such as Sports for quick action, Night for low-light situations, or Text for copying documents. A Best or None setting directs the camera to choose the best scene by guessing.

Special Effects: This item, also called Effects, enhances the image in a number of interesting and unusual ways. For example: None for no effects; Grayscale to shoot in monochrome; Sepia for that old-time look; Negative, which is how people who watch too much politics on television see the world; and others, depending on the Camera app.

Live, It's Tablet Video!

When the action is hot — when you need to capture more than a moment (and maybe the sounds) — switch the tablet's camera into video mode. Doing so may not turn you into the next Christopher Nolan, however, because I hear he uses an iPhone to make his films.

Recording video

Video chores on the Android tablet are handled by the same Camera app that takes still images, as discussed earlier in this chapter. The secret is to switch the Camera app into video mode. You do that by flipping the Camera/Video switch, shown on the right in Figure 11-2.

Video mode for your tablet's Camera app may look subtly different than the interface shown in Figure 11-2, but the basic elements are there; start shooting the video by touching the Record button.

While the tablet is recording, the Record button changes to a Stop button. A time indicator appears in the upper-right corner of the screen, telling you the video shot duration.

Adjust white balance
Switch cameras   Activate video camera
Light on/off   Maximum recording time

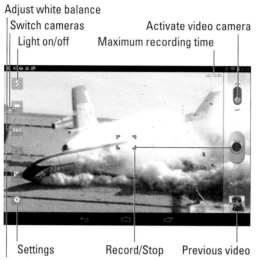

Settings   Record/Stop   Previous video
Self timer

Figure 11-2: Your tablet is a video camera.

To stop recording, touch the Stop button.

✔ Hold the tablet steady! The camera still works when you whip the tablet around, but wild gyrations render the video unwatchable.

✔ The Camera app may restart itself in video mode if that was the active mode when you last quit.

✔ The video's duration depends on its resolution (see the next section) as well as on the storage available on your tablet. The maximum recording time is shown on the screen before you shoot (refer to Figure 11-2). While you record, the elapsed time appears.

✔ If the Camera app features zoom controls for shooting still images, it also has them for shooting video. The controls appear on the screen or, on some tablets, you can adjust the zoom with the Volume button.

✔ Visual effects (the cheap kind, not the Hollywood CGI kind) can be applied to the video. The Effects icon may be on the screen, or you can access that item through the Settings icon.

✔ Chapter 12 covers the Gallery app, used to view and manage videos stored on your tablet. Directions for sharing your video on YouTube are in Chapter 14.

Setting video quality

You might guess that setting the highest video quality would always be best. Not so! For example, video you shoot for YouTube need not be of top quality.

Multimedia text messaging, or Multimedia Messaging Service (MMS) video should be of very low quality or else the video doesn't attach to the message. Also, high-resolution video uses up a heck of a lot more storage space on your Android tablet.

To set the video quality while using the Camera app, touch the Settings icon. Or if you see a Resolution or an Image Quality item, choose it instead.

✔ The range of video resolutions available depends on what the tablet's camera is physically capable of recording.

✔ The tablet's front-facing camera may have a limited selection of video quality settings. To change its resolution, switch to the front-facing camera and then use the Resolution command to set the resolution.

✔ Check the video quality *before* you shoot! Especially if you know where the video will end up (on the Internet, on a TV, or in an e-mail message), it helps to set the quality first.

Shedding some light on your subject

You don't need a flash when recording video, but occasionally you need a little more light. You may be able to manually turn on the tablet's LED flash to help: Look for a Lamp or Light setting, similar to what's shown in Figure 11-2.

✔ The light comes on only when you start recording your video.

✔ I've not seen a light for shooting video with the front-facing camera, although I wouldn't be surprised if some tablet offered that feature.

✔ Turning on the LED light consumes a hefty portion of battery power. Use it sparingly.

Shooting yourself

Put away your crossbow, blow gun, and rubber bands. When I refer to "shooting yourself," I'm writing about an Android tablet's capability to let you record your own image — your face — by using the front-facing video camera. It's cinchy.

The secret to shooting yourself is to touch the Switch Cameras icon, shown earlier in Figure 11-2. As soon as you see your punum on the touchscreen, you've done things properly.

Also see Chapter 9 for information on video chat, which is a live version of shooting yourself.

Digital Photo Album

In This Chapter

▶ Viewing images and videos

▶ Finding an image's location

▶ Setting an image for a contact or as wallpaper

▶ Editing images

▶ Working with Picasa

▶ Printing an image

▶ Publishing a video on YouTube

▶ Sharing images and videos

*W*hat's the point of the tablet having a camera unless you can eventually review, peruse, browse, and chortle at those various images and videos? To solve that problem, your tablet features a digital photo album. You use it to view, manage, and manipulate the images stored in your Android tablet. Further, you can import other images, including photos stored on your computer or found on the Internet. It sounds easy, and I wish I could promise you that, but I've written this chapter anyway.

Where Your Pictures Lurk

Some people hang their pictures on the wall. Some put pictures on a piano or maybe on a mantle. In the digital realm, pictures are stored electronically, compressed and squeezed into a series of ones and zeroes that mean nothing unless you have an app that lets you view those images. On your Android Tablet, that app is the *Gallery*.

Visiting the Gallery

Start the Gallery app by choosing its icon from the Apps screen. Or you might find a Gallery app shortcut icon on the Home screen.

When the Gallery app opens, you see your visual media (pictures and videos) organized into piles, or albums, as shown in Figure 12-1. What you see may not be exactly what's shown in the figure. That's because of all the apps on Android tablets, the Gallery tends to be the most customized between the various manufacturers.

Go to Main

View menu   Album name   Play slideshow   Image name
                            Go to Album   Share icon

Main   Album   Picture

Figure 12-1: Image organization in the Gallery's app.

Touch an album, such as the flower thumbnail in Figure 12-1 (left), to open it and view the pictures or videos it contains. Touch the App icon in the upper-left corner of the screen to return to the main screen.

Touching an album in the Gallery app displays that album's contents in a grid of thumbnail previews. Peruse the images and videos in an album by swiping the screen left and right.

To view an image or play a video, touch a thumbnail image. Images appear full size on the screen, similar to what's shown on the right in Figure 12-1. You can rotate the tablet horizontally or vertically to see the image in another orientation. Later sections describe in more detail what you can do when viewing an image.

Videos play when you choose them. The video-playing screen is illustrated in Figure 12-2. To see the controls shown in the figure, touch the screen while the video is playing.

Video playing

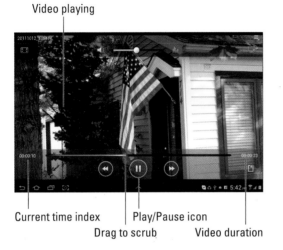

Current time index | Play/Pause icon

Drag to scrub | Video duration

Figure 12-2: Watching a video.

> ✓ The albums in the Gallery app feature names related to the image's source. The Camera album contains video you've shot using the tablet, the Download album contains images downloaded from the Internet, and so on.

> ✓ Albums labeled with the Picasa Web icon have been synchronized between Picasa Web on the Internet and your Android tablet. See the section "Using your Picasa account," later in this chapter.

> ✓ Various apps may also create their own albums in the Gallery app.

> ✓ Images synchronized with a computer may appear in their own albums.

> ✓ Some versions of the Gallery app let you create albums and organize your images; some versions do not.

> ✓ Your tablet's Gallery app may feature a View menu. Use that menu to control how the images and videos are displayed in the gallery. For example, images can be displayed by album or date.

> ✓ When a picture preview features a tiny Play icon, similar to what's shown in the margin, the preview is a video. Otherwise, the thumbnails represent still images.

> ✔ To view all the images in an album, touch the Slideshow icon, labeled in Figure 12-1. Playing a slideshow turns your Android tablet into a fancy, animated picture frame. To stop the slideshow, touch the screen.

Finding out where you took a picture

Your Android tablet can save location information when it takes a picture. The information is often called a geo-tag. To use that information in the Gallery app, heed these steps:

1. **View the image.**

2. **Touch the Menu icon.**

3. **Choose the Show on Map command.**

   When this command is unavailable, your tablet either lacks the geo-tag feature or the image wasn't saved with a geo-tag. Otherwise, the Maps app starts, showing the approximate location where the picture was taken, as illustrated in Figure 12-3.

Image viewed in the Gallery app

Image location on the map

Figure 12-3: Finding where an image was taken.

Videos shot with an Android tablet can also store location information, though this information may not be accessible by using the steps outlined in this section.

Refer to Chapter 11 for information on how to turn the geo-tag on or off when taking pictures.

Assigning an image to a contact

There's no tolerating those generic silhouette images for your pals in the tablet's address book. To dispense with that nonsense, assign a picture from the Gallery app to a contact. It can be any picture, even something appropriately embarrassing. Follow these steps:

1. **View an image in the gallery.**

2. **Touch the Menu icon.**

3. **Choose Set Picture As.**

   If the Set Picture As command doesn't appear, you can't use that image; not every album allows its images to be set for contacts.

4. **Choose Contact Photo.**

5. **Scroll through the address book and choose a particular contact.**

   You can use the Find Contacts command to easily locate a contact when you have an abundance of them.

6. **Crop the image.**

   Refer to the later section, "Cropping an image," for detailed instructions on working the crop-thing.

7. **Touch the OK or Done button.**

   Or touch the Cancel button to chicken out or change your mind.

The contact's image is set. It appears any time you deal with the contact, such as when receiving an e-mail message.

Images changed for a Google contact are instantly synchronized with your Google account on the Internet.

Setting an image as wallpaper

You can set the tablet's Home screen background or wallpaper to be any picture in the Gallery app. Basically, you follow the same steps as outlined in the preceding section, but in Step 4, choose the Wallpaper, Home Screen Wallpaper, or Lock Screen Wallpaper item instead of Contact Photo. Crop or otherwise orient the wallpaper image and you're done.

✔ The lock screen is the background image you see when the tablet is locked; the wallpaper is the background displayed behind icons and widgets on the Home screen.

   ✔ Touch the Home icon to see the new wallpaper.

   ✔ You can also change wallpaper by long-pressing the Home screen and choosing a Wallpapers category. See Chapter 19 for details.

Edit and Manage the Gallery

The best tool for image editing is a computer amply equipped with photo-editing software, such as Photoshop or a similar program that's also referred to as "Photoshop" because the term is pretty much generic. Regardless, you can use the Gallery app to perform some minor photo surgery. This section covers that topic, as well as general image management.

   ✔ Some versions of the Gallery app offer more photo-editing features than others. I've seen commands to remove red eye, add special effects, and even make homely people look pretty. This section covers the most common commands.

   ✔ The Galley app may restrict editing on images imported from Internet photo-sharing sites. It's best to edit and manage those images on the hosting service's website directly.

Cropping an image

One of the few, true image-editing commands available in the Gallery app is Crop. You use the Crop tool to slice out portions of an image, such as when removing ex-spouses and convicts from a family portrait. To crop an image, obey these directions:

1. **Summon the image you want to crop.**

2. **Touch the Menu icon.**

   If you can't see the icon, touch the screen and the icon will reappear.

3. **Choose Crop.**

   If the Crop command is unavailable, you have to choose another image. (Not every album lets you modify images.)

4. **Work the crop-thing.**

   You can drag the rectangle around to choose which part of the image to crop. Drag an edge of the rectangle to resize the left and right or top and bottom sides. Or drag a corner of the rectangle to change the rectangle's size proportionally. Use Figure 12-4 as your guide.

Resize rectangle   Cancel
Move rectangle   Crop

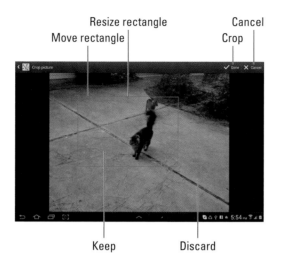

Keep   Discard

Figure 12-4: Working the crop-thing.

Some versions of the Galley app may display a tool palette when you're prompted to crop an image. Don't mess with the palette! Just crop the image.

If you screw up cropping, cancel the operation and start over: Touch the Cancel button or the Back icon.

5. **Touch the OK or Apply Crop button when you're done cropping.**

Only the portion of the image within the colored rectangle is saved; the rest is discarded.

There's no way to undo a crop action after you've confirmed the changes (Step 5).

If you're lucky, some versions of Gallery app keep the original image and create a new image with your crop edits. Not all Gallery app variations are so forgiving, however, so be careful when you crop!

Rotating pictures

Showing someone else an image on your Android tablet can be frustrating, especially when the image is a vertical picture that refuses to fill the screen when the tablet is in a vertical orientation. You can fix that issue by rotating the picture. Heed these steps in the Gallery app:

1. **Choose an image to rotate.**

2. **Touch the Menu icon.**

3. **Choose Rotate Left to rotate the image counterclockwise; choose Rotate Right to rotate the image clockwise.**

If these easy steps don't work, your tablet's Gallery app offers more advanced editing features. To rotate an image, touch the Menu icon. If you don't see any Rotate commands, choose the Edit command, and then choose Modify. You'll eventually find a Rotate command or tool.

Some versions of the Rotate command reorient images in 90-degree increments. Others are more free-form. Again, the command's behavior depends on how your tablet's manufacturer has implemented the Gallery app.

To undo an image rotation, just use the opposite Rotate command.

Deleting images and videos

It's entirely possible, and often desirable, to remove unwanted, embarrassing, or questionably legal images from the Gallery.

So how do you know what you can delete? Simple: If you see the Trash icon atop the screen when viewing an image, you can delete that image. Touch the Trash icon, and then touch the OK or Confirm Delete button. The image is gone.

The procedure for deleting a video might work the same as for deleting an image. When it doesn't, you'll have to select the video in its album and then delete it. See the next section.

- ✔ You can't undelete an image you've deleted. There's no way to recover such an image using available tools on the Android tablet.

- ✔ To delete images from Picasa, visit Picasa Web on the Internet at

  `http://picasaweb.google.com`

- ✔ Some images can't be deleted, such as images brought in from social networking sites or from online photo-sharing albums.

- ✔ You can delete a whole swath of images by selecting them as a group. See the next section.

Selecting multiple pictures and videos

You can apply the Delete command, as well as a smattering of editing commands, to a slew of items in the Gallery at once. To do so, you must know the secret, which I carefully divulge in these steps:

1. **Open the album you want to mess with.**

2. **Long-press an image or video to select it.**

   Instantly, you activate image-selection mode. (That's my name for it.) The screen changes to look like Figure 12-5.

3. **Continue touching images and videos to select them.**

   Or you can choose the Select All command, if it's available. Look for it on the menu if you can't find it on the screen.

4. **Perform an action on the group of images or videos.**

   Other sections describe specifically what you can do, though generally your options are limited to sharing the images, deleting them, or using the Menu icon to view other commands, such as Rotate Left and Rotate Right.

To deselect items, touch them again. To deselect everything, touch the Back icon.

Delete images
Share

Selected items

Figure 12-5: Choosing images to mess with.

Set Your Pictures Free

Keeping your precious moments and memories in your tablet is an elegant solution to the problem of lugging around photo albums. But when you want to show your pictures to the widest possible audience, you need a much larger stage. That stage is the Internet, and you have many ways to send and save your pictures, as covered in this section.

Using your Picasa account

Part of your Google account includes access to Picasa Web, the online photo-sharing website. If you haven't yet been to Picasa Web on the Internet, use your computer to visit the `http://picasaweb.google.com` website.

Configure things by logging into your Google account on that website.

Your Picasa account is automatically synchronized with your Android tablet. Any pictures you put on Picasa are also found on your tablet, accessed through the Gallery app. If not, follow these steps to ensure that Picasa is being property synced:

1. **On the Home screen, touch the Apps icon.**

2. **Open the Settings icon.**

3. **Access your Google account.**

   Choose your Google account below the Accounts heading. If there is no Accounts heading, choose Accounts & Sync and then choose your Google account from the list under Manage Accounts.

4. **Ensure that there's a check mark by the Sync Picasa Web Albums item, although it might be titled Google Photos.**

   That's pretty much it.

Any images you have on Picasa Web are automatically copied to your Android tablet from now on.

If you prefer not to have Picasa synchronize your images, repeat the steps in this section but remove the check mark in Step 4.

- ✓ Picasa albums feature the Picasa logo, as shown in the margin.

- ✓ Images stored on Picasa can be viewed on your tablet, but not edited. To edit or otherwise manage the images, go to the Picasa Web website on the Internet.

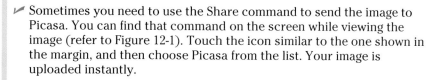 Some tablets feature an Instant Upload icon (shown in the margin) when you view an image. Touch that icon to immediately send the image you're viewing to the Internet, saving it in your Picasa account's Instant Upload album.

✏ The Instant Upload command might also be accessed by touching the Menu icon.

 ✏ Sometimes you need to use the Share command to send the image to Picasa. You can find that command on the screen while viewing the image (refer to Figure 12-1). Touch the icon similar to the one shown in the margin, and then choose Picasa from the list. Your image is uploaded instantly.

✏ If the Instant Upload button disappears from the screen while viewing an image, touch the screen to bring it back.

✏ The idea here is to fill up your Picasa album with images. That way you'll have those images available on your Android tablet, other mobile Android devices, as well as any computer with Internet access.

Printing pictures

It's entirely possible to print any image stored in the Gallery app. Don't go looking for a printer cable; you print wirelessly using the tablet's Bluetooth radio. The only problem you need to solve is ensuring that you have a Bluetooth printer handy, that the printer is *paired* with the tablet, and that the printer is stocked with the proper kind of photo paper.

When you have the tablet and a Bluetooth printer paired and on speaking terms, obey these steps to print an image in the gallery:

1. **Ensure that the tablet's Bluetooth wireless radio is on.**

   Refer to Chapter 16 for information about Bluetooth.

2. **Ensure that the Bluetooth printer is on, that its Bluetooth radio is on, and that the printer is stocked with ink and paper, ready to print.**

3. **Open the Gallery app and browse to find the image you want to enshrine on paper.**

 4. **Touch the Bluetooth icon.**

   If you don't see a Bluetooth icon, touch the Share icon or choose the Bluetooth (or Share) command from the Menu icon's menu.

5. **Choose the Bluetooth printer from the Bluetooth Device Chooser window.**

6. **If prompted by the printer, confirm that the image upload is okay.**

   Not every Bluetooth printer has such a prompt; some just go ahead and print the image.

Bluetooth printing isn't perfect. For example, your Android tablet may not recognize the Bluetooth printer. It happens. As an alternative, you can attach an image to an e-mail message, send it to yourself, and then print it from your computer.

Posting your video to YouTube

The best way to share a video is to upload it to YouTube. As a Google account holder, you also have a YouTube account. You can use the YouTube app on your tablet along with your account to upload your videos to the Internet, where everyone can see them and make rude comments about them. Here's how:

1. **Ensure that the Wi-Fi connection is activated.**

   The best way to upload a video is to turn on the Wi-Fi connection, which doesn't incur data surcharges like the digital cellular network does. In fact, if you opt to use the 4G LTE network for uploading a YouTube video, you'll see a suitable reminder about the data surcharges.

2. **Start the Gallery app.**

3. **Open the album containing the video you want to upload.**

4. **Touch the screen if you need to see the icons.**

5. **Touch the Share icon.**

6. **Choose YouTube.**

   The Upload Video window appears, listing all sorts of options and settings for sending the video to YouTube.

7. **Type the video's title.**

8. **Set other options, such as Privacy, and add tags (text descriptions of the video).**

9. **Touch the Upload button.**

   You return to the Gallery, and the video is uploaded. It continues to upload even if the tablet falls asleep.

An uploading notification appears while the video is being sent to YouTube. Feel free to do other things with your tablet while the video uploads. When the upload has completed, the notification stops animating and becomes the Uploads Finished icon.

To view your video, open the YouTube app. It's found on the Apps screen and discussed in detail in Chapter 14.

> ✐ YouTube often takes awhile to process a video after it's uploaded. Allow a few minutes to pass (longer for larger videos) before the video becomes available for viewing.

> ✐ *Upload* is the official term to describe sending a file from your Android tablet to the Internet.

Sharing with the Share menu

Occasionally, you stumble across the Share command when working with photos in the Gallery app. This command is used to distribute images from your Android tablet to your pals in the digital realm.

The menu that appears when you touch the Share icon contains various options for sharing media. The number and variety of items that appear depend on the apps installed on your tablet, which Internet services you belong to (Facebook and Twitter, for example), and which type of media is being shared.

Here's a quick summary of the various items you may find on the Share menu, as well as how they work:

Bluetooth: You can use the wireless Bluetooth networking standard to send images to a Bluetooth printer or to upload the images to a Bluetooth-enabled computer. Printing with Bluetooth is covered earlier in this chapter, in the section "Printing pictures."

Facebook, Google+, Twitter: Sharing pictures on a social networking site is simple. You just choose the image and then choose the social networking site from the Share menu. Fill in the information on the next screen, and soon the image is shared with all your friends and followers. See Chapter 8 for more information on social networking on an Android tablet.

Email and Gmail: Choosing Email or Gmail for sharing sends the media file from your Android tablet as a message attachment. Fill in the To, Subject, and Message text boxes as necessary. Touch the Send button to send the media.

Picasa: The Picasa photo-sharing site is one of those free services you get with your Google account. See the previous section, "Using your Picasa account," for details on sharing images with Picasa.

YouTube: The YouTube sharing option appears when you choose to share a video from the Gallery app. See the previous section, "Posting your video to YouTube."

Music, Music, Music

*Y*our Android tablet's amazing arsenal of features includes its capability to play music. So it effectively replaces any gramophone that you've been lugging around, which is the whole idea behind such an all-in-one gizmo like an Android tablet. You can cheerfully and adeptly transfer all your old Edison cylinders and 78 LPs over to the tablet for your listening enjoyment. More specifically, this chapter explains how to listen to music, get more music, and manage that music on your tablet.

Listen Here

All Android tablets come with at least one music-playing app. It may be called Music or Music Player. A second app that might appear is aptly named Play Music. That's Google's own music-playing app, and it might be the only music app on your tablet.

This chapter assumes that you're using the Play Music app. Other music apps are similar, although I believe you'll find the Play Music app to be far more beneficial, especially if you own other Android gizmos.

Browsing your music library

The Play Music app is your source of musical delight on your Android tablet. You can find it on the Apps screen, or perhaps you'll see a shortcut icon plastered on the Home screen.

After you start the Play Music app, you see a screen similar to Figure 13-1. If you're displeased with the quantity of music available, refer to the later section, "Add Some Music to Your Life." It explains how to get more tunes.

App icon   Albums   Google Play Store
    Category menu   Search music

Current song   No album art   Imported album art

Figure 13-1: The Play Music app, Album category.

The music stored on your Android tablet is presented in the Play Music app by category. Each category appears atop the screen (refer to Figure 13-1). Change categories by swiping the screen left and right.

Here are the categories you may find in the Play Music app:

Playlists: Music you've organized into playlists that you create. Choose a playlist name to view songs organized in that playlist. Included are recently played songs, songs from the Internet, and other preset categories.

Recent: Songs and albums are listed in the order in which you've imported them from your computer or purchased them online. Scroll the list up or down to find recent items.

Artists: Songs are listed by recording artist or group. Choose Artist to see those songs listed by album.

Albums: Music is organized by album, as shown in Figure 13-1. Choose an album to list its songs.

Songs: All music (songs and audio) is listed individually in alphabetical order.

Genres: Audio is organized by categories such as Alternative, County, and Rock.

These categories are merely ways the music is organized — to make the music easier to find when you may know, for example, an artist's name but not an album title. The Genres category is for those times when you're in the mood for a certain type of music but don't know or don't mind who recorded it.

A *playlist* is a list you create yourself to organize songs by favorite, theme, mood, or whatever other characteristic you want. The section "Organize Your Music," later in this chapter, discusses playlists.

✔ Music is stored on the tablet's internal memory, as well as on the removable microSD card. It's also possible to keep music on the Internet at

   play.google.com/music

✔ Your tablet's storage capacity limits the total amount of music that can be stored. Also, consider that storing pictures and videos horns in on some of the space that can be used to store music.

✔ Two types of album artwork are used by the Play Music app. For purchased music, the album artwork represents the original album. That may also happen for music copied (imported) from your computer. Otherwise, the Play Music app slaps down a generic album cover, as shown in Figure 13-1.

✔ When the Android tablet can't recognize an artist, it uses the title Unknown Artist. This usually happens with music you copy manually to your tablet and audio recordings you make yourself.

Playing a tune

To listen to music by locating a song in the Play Music app library, as described in the preceding section, touch the song title. The song plays, as shown in Figure 13-2.

While the song plays, you're free to do anything else on the tablet. In fact, the song continues to play even when the tablet is locked or goes to sleep.

After the song has finished playing, the next song in the list plays. The order depends on how you start the song. For example, if you start a song from the album view, all songs in that album play in the order listed.

Album cover artwork   Song info

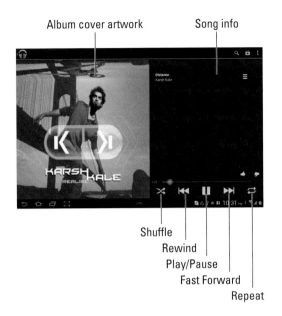

Shuffle
Rewind
Play/Pause
Fast Forward
Repeat

Figure 13-2: A song is playing.

The next song in the list doesn't play if you have activated the Shuffle icon (labeled in Figure 13-2). In that case, the Play Music app randomly chooses another song from the same list. Who knows which one is next?

The next song also might not play when you have the Repeat option on: The three repeat settings are illustrated in Table 13-1, along with the Shuffle settings. To change settings, simply touch either the Shuffle or the Repeat icon. If those icons disappear from the screen, touch the screen briefly and they'll show up again.

Table 13-1		Shuffle and Repeat Icons
Icon	*Setting*	*What Happens When You Touch the Icon*
	No Shuffle	Songs play one after the other
	Shuffle	Songs are played in random order
	No Repeat	Songs don't repeat

Icon	Setting	What Happens When You Touch the Icon
	Single Repeat	The same song plays over and over
	List Repeat	All songs in the list play over and over

To stop the song from playing, touch the Pause icon (labeled in Figure 13-2).

A notification icon (shown in the margin) appears while music is playing on your tablet. To quickly summon the Play Music app, touch that notification. The notification itself shows controls to pause the song or to skip forward or backward.

 ✔ Volume is set by using the Volume switch on the side of the tablet.

 ✔ While browsing the Play Music app's library, the currently playing song is displayed at the bottom of the screen (refer to Figure 13-1).

 ✔ Some of the music on your Android tablet is Google music, originating from the Internet. It's not available to play unless the tablet has a Wi-Fi connection. See the later section "Making music available full-time" for a tip on how to remedy this situation.

 ✔ To choose which songs play after each other, create a playlist. See the section "Organize Your Music," later in this chapter.

 ✔ After the last song in the list plays, the Play Music app stops playing songs — unless you have the List Repeat option set, in which case the list plays again.

 ✔ You can use the Android tablet's search capabilities to help locate tunes in your Music library. You can search by artist name, song title, or album. The key is to touch the Search icon when you're using the Play Music app. Type all or part of the text you're searching for and then touch the Search icon on the onscreen keyboard. Choose the song you want to hear from the list that's displayed.

Being the life of the party

You need to do four things to make your Android tablet the soul of your next shindig or soirée:

 ✔ Connect it to a stereo.

 ✔ Use the Shuffle command.

 ✔ Set the Repeat command.

 ✔ Provide plenty of drinks and snacks.

"What's this song?"

A special widget available at the Google Play Store, or perhaps already installed on your tablet, is called What's This Song. Use this widget to identify music playing within earshot of your tablet.

For example, while listening to music, touch the widget. After a few seconds, the song is recognized and its title and other information are displayed. You can choose to buy the song at the Google Play Store or touch the Refresh icon and start over.

The What's This Song widget works best (I would argue exclusively) with recorded music. Try as you might, you cannot sing into the thing and have it recognize a song. Humming doesn't work either. I've tried playing the guitar and piano, and — nope — that didn't work either. But for listening to ambient music, it's a pretty good tool for identifying what you're listening to.

Hook the tablet into any stereo that has a standard line input. You need, on one end, an audio cable that has a mini-headphone jack and, on the other end, an audio input that matches your stereo. Look for such a cable at Radio Shack or any stereo store.

After you connect your tablet, start the Play Music app and choose the party playlist you've created. If you want the songs to play in random order, touch the Shuffle icon.

You might also consider choosing the List Repeat command (see Table 13-1) so that all songs in the playlist repeat.

To play all songs saved on your Android tablet, choose the Songs category and touch the first song in the list. You should also consider creating a playlist, just in case not everyone likes *all* your tunes. See the later section, "Organize Your Music."

Enjoy your party, and please drink responsibly.

Add Some Music to Your Life

Consider yourself fortunate if your Android tablet came with some tunes preinstalled. That may happen, courtesy of Google Play on the Internet.

Otherwise, none of my favorites were in there! What to do? Why, add more music! This section goes over a few ways to get music into your tablet.

Borrowing music from a computer

The computer is the equivalent of the 20th-century stereo system — a combination tuner, amplifier, and turntable — plus all your records and CDs. If you've already copied your music collection to your computer, or if you use your computer as your main music storage system, you can share that music with your Android tablet.

Many music-playing, or jukebox, programs are available. On Windows, the most common program is Windows Media Player. You can use this program to synchronize music between your PC and the Android tablet. Here's how it works:

1. **Connect the Android tablet to your PC.**

   Use the USB cable that comes with the tablet.

   Over on the PC, an AutoPlay dialog box appears in Windows, prompting you to choose how best to add the Android tablet to the Windows storage system.

2. **Close the AutoPlay dialog box.**

   The AutoPlay dialog box might not appear. If it doesn't, that's okay.

3. **Start Windows Media Player.**

4. **Click the Sync tab or Sync toolbar button.**

   The Android tablet appears in the Sync list on the right side of the Windows Media Player, as shown in Figure 13-3. If not, click the Next Device link or button until it shows up.

5. **Drag to the Sync Area the music you want to transfer to your tablet (refer to Figure 13-3).**

6. **Click the Start Sync button to transfer the music from your PC to the Android tablet.**

   The Sync button may be located atop the list, as shown in Figure 13-3, or it might be found on the bottom.

7. **Close the Windows Media Player when you're done transferring music.**

   Or you can keep it open — whatever.

8. **Unplug the USB cable.**

   Or, you can leave the tablet plugged in.

Galaxy Tab "drive"   Android tablet
                       Click to sync │ Sync tab

Drag music to here   Music to sync

Figure 13-3: Windows Media Player meets Android tablet.

The next time you start the Play Music app, you'll find your music right there in the library. Now you can enjoy your computer's music anywhere you take the Android tablet.

✔ Also see Chapter 17 for more information about connecting your tablet to a computer.

✔ A small chance exists that the Play Music app won't recognize music copied from your PC. Specifically, audio files used by the Windows Media Player may not work. I've seen only one tablet where such a problem exists; otherwise the transfer should work just peachy.

✔ The Android tablet can store only so much music! Don't be overzealous when copying your tunes. In Windows Media Player (refer to Figure 13-3), a capacity-thermometer thing shows you how much storage space is used and how much is available on your tablet. Pay heed to the indicator!

✔ You can't use iTunes to synchronize music with the Android tablet.

✔ Okay, I lied in the preceding point: You *can* synchronize music using iTunes but only when you install the *iTunes Agent* program on your computer. You then need to configure the iTunes Agent program to use your Android tablet with iTunes. After you do that, iTunes recognizes the Android tablet and lets you synchronize your music. Yes, it's technical; hence the icon in the margin.

Buying music at the Google Play Store

It's possible to get your music for your Android tablet from the same source where you get apps for your Android tablet — the Google Play Store. Getting apps is covered in Chapter 15. Getting music is covered right here:

1. **Open the Play Store app.**

   You can find the app on the Home screen or, like all apps, on the Apps screen. You can also get to the Google Play Store by touching the Play Store icon in the Play Music app (labeled in Figure 13-1).

2. **Choose the Music category.**

   The Music category is shown at the main screen. If you visited the Google Play Music store from the Play Music app, you're already viewing the Music category.

3. **Use the Search command to locate music you want, or just browse the categories.**

   Keep an eye out for free music offers at the Play Store. It's a great way to pick up some tunes.

   Eventually you'll see a page showing details about the song or album. Choose a song from the list to hear a preview. The button next to the song or album indicates the purchase price, or it says Free for free music.

4. **Touch the price icon to purchase a song or album.**

   Don't worry — you're not buying anything yet.

5. **Choose your credit card or payment source.**

   If a credit card or payment source doesn't appear similar to what's shown in Figure 13-4, choose the Add Card option to add a payment method. Sign up with Google Checkout and submit your credit card or other payment information.

6. **Touch the Accept & Buy button.**

   If the Accept & Buy button isn't available (refer to Figure 13-4) you'll have to touch the check box to agree to the Payments terms.

   The album or song is downloaded to your tablet.

Your purchase   Touch to buy

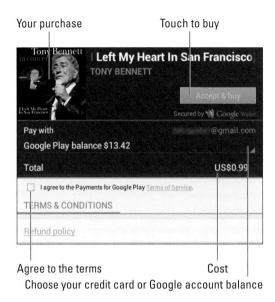

Agree to the terms   Cost
Choose your credit card or Google account balance

Figure 13-4: Buying some music.

A notification appears when the transfer of the album or song has completed. You can then use the Play Music app to listen to the new music; you'll find it quickly by choosing the Recent category from the Play Music app's main screen.

- ✔ All music sales are final. Don't blame me; I'm just writing down Google's current policy for music purchases.

- ✔ If you plan on downloading an album or multiple songs, connect to a Wi-Fi network. That way you won't run the risk of a data surcharge on your cellular plan. See Chapter 16 for information on activating the tablet's Wi-Fi.

- ✔ The Google Play Music notification icon is the same icon that appears when you download a new app for your tablet. The notification name, however, is Google Play Music.

- ✔ You'll eventually receive a Gmail notice regarding the purchase. The Gmail message is your receipt.

- ✔ For more information on the Google Play Store, see Chapter 15.

Using the Internet to access your tunes

Music you purchase from the Google Play Music Store is available on any mobile Android device with the Play Music app installed, providing you use the same Google account on that device. You can also listen to your tunes by visiting the `music.google.com` site on any computer connected to the Internet.

As long as you log into your Google account on a computer connected to the Internet, you can use Google Play on the Internet to buy music, listen to music, and even upload music from your computer to your Google Play music library.

Organize Your Music

The Play Music app categorizes your music by album, artist, song, and so forth, but unless you have only one album and enjoy all the songs on it, that configuration probably won't do. To better organize your music, you can create *playlists*. That way, you can hear the music you want to hear, in the order you want, for whatever mood hits you.

Reviewing your playlists

Any playlists you've already created or that have been preset on the tablet appear in the Playlists category. To see the playlists, choose Playlists from the category menu in the Play Music app. (Refer to Figure 13-1.) Playlists you've created are displayed on the screen, as shown in Figure 13-5.

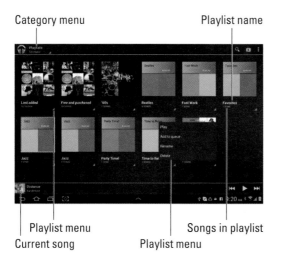

Category menu   Playlist name

Playlist menu   Songs in playlist
Current song   Playlist menu

Figure 13-5: Playlists in the Play Music app.

To see which songs are in a playlist, touch the playlist's album icon. To play the songs in the playlist, touch the first song in the list. Or you can choose the Play command from the playlist's menu, as shown in Figure 13-5.

A playlist is a helpful way to organize music when a song's information may not have been completely imported into your Android tablet. For example, if you're like me, you probably have a lot of songs labeled Unknown. A quick way to remedy that situation is to name a playlist after the artist and then add those unknown songs to the playlist. The next section describes how it's done.

Creating your own playlists

Making a new playlist is easy, and adding songs to the playlist is even easier. Follow these steps:

1. **Choose the Playlist category in the Play Music app.**

2. **Touch the Menu icon in the upper-right corner of the screen.**

3. **Choose New Playlist.**

4. **Type a name for your playlist.**

    Short and descriptive names are best.

5. **Touch the OK button to create the playlist.**

    The new playlist is created and placed on the Playlists screen, similar to what's shown in Figure 13-5.

But the playlist is empty! To add songs, you need to go out and fetch them. Here's how you do that:

1. **Hunt down the song you want to add to a playlist.**

    You don't need to play the song; simply display the song in the Play Music app.

    Likewise, you can hunt down albums, artists, or even genres. The technique described in this set of steps works for every category in the Play Music app.

2. **Touch the menu triangle by the song (or album or artist).**

3. **Choose the command Add to Playlist.**

4. **Choose a playlist.**

    The song (or album or artist) is added to the playlist's repertoire of music.

Repeat this set of steps to continue adding songs to playlists.

You can have as many playlists as you like on the tablet and stick as many songs as you like in them. Adding songs to a playlist doesn't noticeably affect the tablet's storage capacity.

- To remove a song from a playlist, open the playlist and touch the menu triangle by the song. Choose the command Remove from Playlist.

- Removing a song from a playlist doesn't delete the song from your tablet's music library.

- Songs in a playlist can be rearranged: While viewing the playlist, use the tab on the far left end of a song title to drag that song up or down in the list.

- To delete a playlist, touch the menu triangle in the playlist icon's lower-right corner. Choose the Delete command. Touch OK to confirm.

Making music available full-time

As long as you have a Wi-Fi connection with your Android tablet, you can play the music you've stored on Google Play Music on the Internet. When you don't have a connection, the music doesn't play. That is, unless you follow these steps:

1. **Locate the song, artist, or album you want to keep stored on the tablet.**

2. **Touch the Menu icon to the right of the song, artist, or album.**

3. **Choose the Keep on Device command.**

   Your tablet ensures that the music is transferred to the tablet from the Internet, and therefore is available to play all the time.

A quick way to select multiple songs, albums, or artists for download from the Internet is to touch the Menu icon and choose the command Choose On-Device Music. Touch the Pushpin icon next to the songs you want to keep on the tablet. Touch the Done button (upper left on the screen) when you're done.

If you want to check which songs are available on the device, touch the Menu icon and choose the On Device Only option. After doing so, only the music copied to your Android tablet appears in the Play Music app. Choose the On Device Only command again to see all your music, stored locally or online.

Removing unwanted music

Depending on the source, you have two ways to deal with unwanted music on your Android tablet.

The first way is to visit Google Play on the Internet at the `music.google.com` site. Click the Menu icon by a song and choose the Delete command. Click the Delete Song button to confirm.

The steps for removing music stored directly on the Android tablet are similar: Touch the Menu icon by a song and choose the Delete command. Touch the OK button to confirm.

- ✔ When you don't see the Delete command on the Android tablet, the song cannot be removed locally. You'll need to visit Google Play on the Internet to remove the song.

- ✔ There is no way to recover a song you delete on the Android tablet.

- ✔ Removing music stored on the tablet occupies the Android tablet's internal storage. If that's a concern, refer to the previous section on keeping music stored locally. You can repeat the steps listed to remove the Keep On Device option for music, which frees up storage space.

Music from the Stream

Although they're not broadcast radio stations, some sources on the Internet — *Internet radio* sites — play music. If you're lucky, your tablet came with some Internet radio apps. If you're not so lucky, or you want to expand your options, you can look into obtaining these two apps:

- ✔ TuneIn Radio
- ✔ Pandora Radio

The TuneIn Radio app gives you access to hundreds of Internet radio stations broadcasting around the world. They're organized by category, so you can find just about whatever you want. Many of the radio stations are also broadcast radio stations, so odds are good you can find a local station or two, which you can listen to on your Android tablet.

Pandora Radio lets you select music based on your mood and customizes, according to your feedback, the tunes you listen to. The app works like the Internet site www.pandora.com, in case you're familiar with it. The nifty thing about Pandora is that the more you listen, the better the app gets at finding music you like.

All these apps are available at the Google Play Store. They're free, though paid versions might also be available.

- ✔ You need a Wi-Fi connection if you plan on listening to music streaming from the Internet.

- ✔ See Chapter 15 for more information about the Google Play Store.

- ✔ Internet music of the type delivered by the apps mentioned in this section is referred to by the nerds as *streaming music*. That's because the music arrives on your Android tablet as a continuous download from the source. Unlike music you download and save, streaming music is played as it comes in and not stored long-term.

Other Amazing Feats

In This Chapter

▶ Waking up to your Android tablet
▶ Making tablet calculations
▶ Keeping your appointments
▶ Scheduling new events
▶ Reading digital books
▶ Playing games
▶ Watching junk on YouTube
▶ Buying or renting films and TV shows

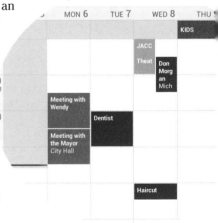

Your Android tablet is bursting with potential, limited only by the apps installed. Despite the variety of things it can do, you will find some limitations. For example, you cannot use an Android tablet as a Yoga block. It makes a poor kitchen cutting board. And despite efforts by European physicists, the Android tablet just cannot compete with the Large Hadron Collider. Still, for more everyday purposes, I believe you'll find your tablet more than up to the task.

This chapter corrals many (but not all) of the things you can do on your Android tablet. Among the devices it replaces are your alarm clock, calculator, day planner, game machine, e-book reader, and even your TV set. That's not even the full list, but rather everything I could legally cram into this chapter without violating the *For Dummies* chapter length regulations.

It's a Clock

Your Android tablet keeps constant, accurate track of the time, which is displayed at the top of the Home screen as well as on the lock screen. That's handy, but it just isn't enough, so the tablet ships with an app that tells the time and also may double as an alarm clock.

The app may be called Clock or Alarm, but either one does the same thing: Displays the time and wakes you up.

To employ the Clock or Alarm app as an alarm clock, you need to create and set an alarm. The method varies, depending on the app. Generally the steps work like this:

1. **Touch the Add Alarm icon.**

   The Set Alarm screen appears.

2. **Fill in the information about the alarm.**

   Set the alarm's time, decide whether it repeats daily or only on certain days, choose a ringtone, set the vibration mode, and make any other settings.

3. **Touch the Label text box to give the alarm a name.**

   The name you choose appears on the tablet's screen when the alarm goes off, so be clever. For example, *Wake up, Get to the airport,* and *Annoy my spouse* are excellent examples of good, descriptive labels.

4. **Touch the OK or Done button to create the alarm.**

   You'll see your alarm in the list in the Alarms window.

5. **Ensure that a check mark appears next to the alarm; the check mark sets the alarm.**

Alarms must be set or else they don't trigger. How you set the alarm depends on the app: It can be set when it's created or, more commonly, you place a check mark by the specific alarm when all the alarms are selected.

When the alarm goes off, you can touch the Dismiss button to tell the tablet, "Okay! I'm up!" Or you can touch the Snooze button to be annoyed again after a few minutes.

- ✔ Your tablet keeps the clock accurate by using the Internet connection. You never have to set the time.

- ✔ Information about a set alarm appears on the Clock app's screen as well as the tablet's lock screen.

- ✔ When an alarm is set, an Alarm notification appears in the status area atop the screen. That notification is your clue that an alarm is set and ready to trigger.

✔ Turning off an alarm doesn't delete the alarm. To remove an alarm, long-press it and choose the Delete Alarm option from the menu. Touch the OK button to confirm.

✔ The alarm doesn't work when you turn off the Android tablet. However, the alarm does go off when the tablet is locked or sleeping.

It's a Large Calculator

Why are you still lugging around a calculator? Even one of those teensy solar-powered calculators that banks used to give away. Remember when banks actually gave stuff away? Man, I am dating myself.

The next time you crave a calculator, start the Calculator app by choosing its icon from the Apps screen. Each tablet's Calculator app looks subtly different, though Figure 14-1 shows more-or-less how they all appear.

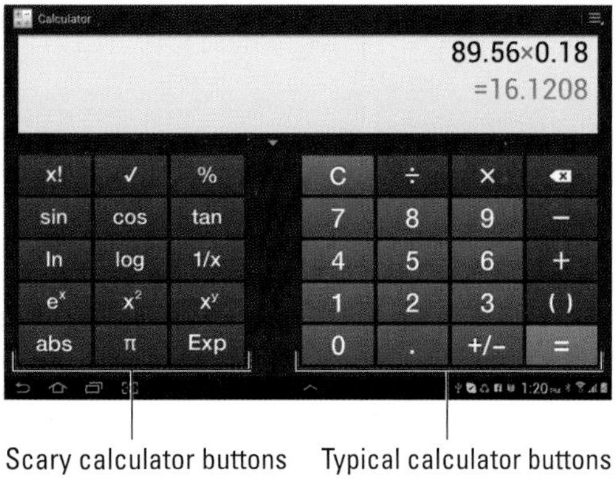

Scary calculator buttons   Typical calculator buttons

Figure 14-1: The Calculator app.

Type your equations using the various keys on the screen. Parenthesis keys can help you determine which part of a long equation gets calculated first. Use the Clr or C key to clear input.

✔ Long-press the calculator's text (or results) to cut or copy the results.

✔ The Clr (Clear) key changes to a Delete key when you type a number. That way, you can delete your input without clearing the entire calculation.

✔ I use the Calculator app most often to determine my tip at a restaurant. In Figure 14-1, a calculation is being made for an 18 percent tip on an $89.56 tab.

It's a Calendar

Feel free to take any datebook you have and throw it away. You never need to buy another one again. That's because your Android tablet is the ideal datebook and appointment calendar. Thanks to the Calendar app and the Google Calendar service on the Internet, you can manage all your scheduling right on your Android tablet. It's almost cinchy.

✔ Google Calendar works with your Google account to keep track of your schedule and appointments. You can visit Google Calendar on the web at

`http://calendar.google.com`

✔ You automatically have a Google Calendar; it comes with your Google account.

✔ I recommend that you use the Calendar app on your Android tablet to access Google Calendar. It's a better way to access your schedule than using the Chrome app to reach Google Calendar on the web.

✔ Before you throw away your datebook, copy into the Calendar app future appointments and recurring info, such as birthdays and anniversaries.

Browsing your schedule

To see what's happening next, to peruse upcoming important events, or just to know which day of the month it is, summon the Calendar app. It's located on the Apps screen along with all the other apps that dwell on your Android tablet. You may also find a shortcut to the Calendar app on the Home screen — maybe even a Calendar widget as well.

Figure 14-2 shows the Calendar app's three views: month, week, and day. There's also an agenda view, which displays only upcoming events. Some Calendar apps feature a 4-day view as well.

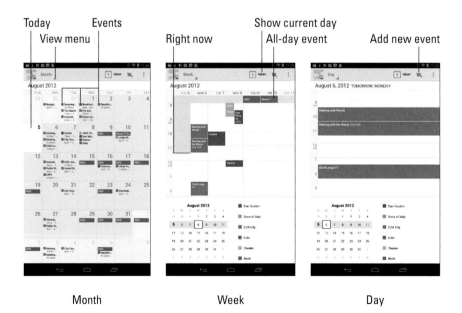

Month   Week   Day

Figure 14-2: The Calendar app.

Be sure to note how the current day is highlighted on the calendar. In Figure 14-2, the current day is shown as August 5.

✔ Use month view to see an overview of what's going on, and use week or day view to see your appointments.

✔ I check week view at the start of the week to remind me of what's coming up.

✔ To scroll from month to month, swipe the screen up or down. In the week and day views, scroll left to right. To return to the current day, touch the Today button, though that may also be a menu item. In Figure 14-2 it's a button.

✔ Different colors flag your events, as seen in Figure 14-2. The colors represent a calendar category to which the events are assigned. See the later section, "Creating an event," for information on calendar categories.

Reviewing appointments

To see more detail about an event, touch it. When you're using month view, touch the date with the event on it to see the week view. Then choose an event to see its details, similar to what's shown in Figure 14-3.

The information you see depends on how much information was recorded when the event was created. Some events have only a minimum of information; others may have details, such as a location for the event. When the event's location is listed, you can touch that location, and the Maps app pops up to show you where the event is being held.

Touch the Back icon to dismiss the event's details.

Touch to see event location on the Maps app
Delete event
Event details
Edit event

Lodge Meeting
Friday, September 14, 6:00pm – 8:30pm
Monthly
St. George's Cathoic Church Post Falls

REMINDERS

15 minutes — Notification — ✕

Add reminder

Review or change reminder warning
Change to Gmail reminder
Remove reminder

Figure 14-3: Event details.

✔ Birthdays and a few other events on the calendar may be pulled in from the People app or even from some social networking apps. That probably explains why some events could be listed twice; they're pulled in from two sources.

✔ The best way to review upcoming appointments is to choose the Agenda item from the Views menu.

Creating an event

The key to making the calendar work is to add events: appointments, things to do, meetings, or full-day events such as birthdays or colonoscopies. To create an event, follow these steps in the Calendar app:

1. **Select the day for the event.**

   Or if you like, you can switch to day view, where you can touch the starting time for the new event.

2. **Touch the Add New Event icon (refer to Figure 14-2).**

   The New Event or Add Event screen appears. Your job now is to fill in the blanks to create the new event.

3. **Add information about the event.**

   The more information you supply, the more detailed the event, and the more you can do with it on your Android tablet as well as on Google Calendar on the Internet. Here are some of the many items you can set when creating an event:

   - **Time/Duration:** If you followed Step 1, you don't have to set a starting time. Otherwise, specify the time the meeting starts and stops, or choose to set an all-day event such as a birthday or your mother-in-law's visit that was supposed to last for an hour.

   - **Event Name or Title:** This item can be a meeting name, a flight number, or perhaps the person you're meeting.

   - **Location:** Adding an event location not only tells you where the event will be located but also hooks that information into the Maps app. My advice is to type information in the event's Where field just as though you're typing information to search for in the Maps app. When the event is displayed, the location is a link; touch the link to see where it is on a map.

   - **Repeat:** Use this item to configure a recurring schedule. For example, if your meeting is every month on the third Wednesday, touch the Menu icon by the Repetition item and choose that option.

     When you have events that repeat twice a month, say on the first and third Monday, you need to create two separate events, one for the first Monday and another for the third. Then have each event repeat monthly.

   - **Reminder:** Some versions of the Calendar app allow you to set a reminder before an event begins. If you prefer not to have a reminder, touch the X button by the Reminders item to remove the reminder. Otherwise, specify the time before the meeting you'd like to be notified, and whether you want a tablet notification, a Gmail message reminder, or both.

- **Calendar Category:** Touch the colored calendar text atop the screen to choose a calendar category.

Calendar categories are handy because they let you organize and color-code your events. They're confusing because Google calls them "calendars." I think of them more as categories. So I have different calendars (categories) for my personal schedule, work, government duties, clubs, and so on.

4. Touch the Done or Save button to create the new event.

The new event appears on the calendar, reminding you that you need to do something on such-and-such a day with what's-his-face.

- ✏ You can change an event at any time: Simply touch the event to bring up more information and then touch the Choose the Edit icon to modify the event, similar to what's shown in Figure 14-3.

- ✏ To remove an event, touch the event to bring up more information and touch the Delete icon at the top right of the screen. Touch the OK button to confirm.

- ✏ Setting an event's time zone is necessary only when the event takes place in another time zone or when you have an event that spans time zones, such as an airline flight. In that case, the Calendar app automatically adjusts the starting and stopping times for events depending on where you are.

- ✏ If you forget to set the time zone and you do end up hopping around the world, your events will be set according to the time zone in which they were created, not the local time.

It's an E-Book Reader

The latest craze in publishing: e-books, or electronic books. Books printed on paper are just so 14th century.

An *e-book* is essentially a digital version of the material you would normally read on paper. The words, formatting, figures, pictures — all that stuff is stored digitally so that you can read it on some sort of e-book reader. For an Android tablet, you need e-book software. That comes in the form of the Play Books app as well as the Amazon Kindle eBook reader app.

✔ The primary advantage of an e-book reader is that you can keep an entire library of books with you. So rather than hire a Sherpa to haul around your collection, it's much easier to shop online and carry e-books in your tablet.

✔ It's important to know that e-books is pronounced "ee-books," not "eb-ooks," which makes no sense but, given technological jargon, who really knows?

✔ I load up on new e-books before I leave for a trip. It's better than stewing over the collection at those airport book kiosks, especially when the salted nuts are so tempting.

✔ It's easy and free to build up your e-book library with classics and older books. Most of those titles are free, though some compilations have a modest price tag, such as 99 cents.

Using the Play Books app

Google wants you to enjoy your digital reading experience by using the Play Books app. Locate that app on the Home screen or on the Apps screen. If you don't find it, you can obtain a copy from the Google Play Store, as described in Chapter 15.

After first running the Play Books app, you may be prompted to turn on synchronization, touch the Turn On Sync button.

The Play Books app organizes the books into a library and displays the books for reading, similar to what's shown in Figure 14-4. The library lists any titles you've obtained for your Google Books account. Or when you're returning to the Play Books app after a break, you see the current page of the e-book you were last reading.

Scroll through the library by swiping the screen left or right. To begin reading, touch a book to open it. The next section covers how you read a book using the Play Books app.

Buy more books at the Google Play Store

Scroll library left and right

Figure 14-4: The Play Books library.

✔ If you don't see a book in the library, touch the Menu icon and choose the Refresh command.

✔ To ensure that your reading material is always available, touch the Menu icon and choose the Make Available Offline command. That way, the tablet doesn't have to access the Internet to synchronize and download books from the library. I choose that command specifically before I leave on a trip where an Internet signal may not be available (such as on an airplane).

✔ To remove a book from the library, long-press the cover and choose the Remove from My Library command. There is no confirmation: The book is instantly removed.

✔ Synchronization allows you to keep copies of your Google Books on all your Android devices, as well as on the http://books.google.com website.

Reading a Play Books e-book

The e-book experience on an Android tablet should be familiar to you, especially if you're reading this text in a real book. The entire page-turning and reading operation works the same. The only major difference is that you can read a physical book without batteries and in direct sunlight, but I won't dwell on that.

Touch a book in the Play Books app library to open it. If you've opened the book previously, you're returned to the page you last read. Otherwise, the first page you see is the book's first page.

Figure 14-5 illustrates the basic book-reading operation in the Play Books app. You turn pages by swiping left or right, but

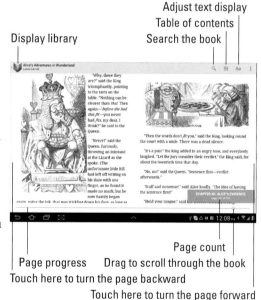

Adjust text display
Table of contents
Display library   Search the book

Page count
Page progress   Drag to scroll through the book
Touch here to turn the page backward
Touch here to turn the page forward

Figure 14-5: Reading an e-book in the Play Books app.

probably mostly left. You can also turn pages by touching the far left or right sides of the screen.

The Play Books app works in both vertical and horizontal orientations, whichever you prefer; the text jumbles around in most e-books to accommodate either presentation.

- ✔ If the onscreen controls (shown in Figure 14-5) disappear, touch the screen to see them again.

- ✔ The Aa button is used to adjust the display. Touching that button displays a palette of options for adjusting the text on the screen and the brightness.

- ✔ To return to the library, touch the Play Books app icon in the upper-left corner of the screen or touch the Back icon.

Getting more Google Play books

Nothing is more delightful for an author to write about than buying books, especially when he's urging someone else to do it. For the Play Books app, you obtain new titles — free or paid — from the Google Play Store, the same place you visit to obtain apps for your tablet.

To quickly visit the Google Play Store's online bookstore, touch the Google Play icon on the Play Books app's main screen (labeled in Figure 14-4). You can also start the Play Store app and choose Books from the main screen.

Search for books, browse the categories, or use the Search icon to locate a specific title, topic, or author.

- ✔ Books with a price button must be purchased using your Google Checkout account. The process is the same as for buying an app: See Chapter 15 for the specifics.

- ✔ Free books have a Free button.

- ✔ Books you obtain from the Google Play Store, free or paid, can be synchronized with any Android device you have where the Play Books app is installed. Use the Refresh command, discussed in the earlier section, "Using the Play Books app," to synchronize books between your various Android gizmos.

- ✔ Not every title is available as an e-book.

Using the Amazon Kindle app

Another e-book reader worthy of consideration is the Amazon Kindle app. As the name implies, it provides access to the Kindle eLibrary of books right there on your Android tablet — the same library you'd have if you owned a Kindle e-book reader, but you were smarter than that.

You can pick up a copy of the Amazon Kindle app free at the Google Play Store; see Chapter 15 for details on how to get new apps for your tablet.

When you start the Amazon Kindle app for the first time, you may be asked to register or sign in to your Amazon account. Do so. By signing in, you can instantly coordinate your Kindle e-book library with any previous purchases you may have made.

After everything is set up, you can enjoy reading Kindle e-books just as you would any other e-book reader on an Android tablet; they all work basically the same, although some interesting features are available on the Amazon Kindle app that aren't available on other e-books readers, such as Play Books. For example, you can highlight text and perform web searches in a Kindle e-book. That's pretty swanky.

> ✔ Kindle e-books are obtained from the Amazon Kindle store. You must use the Kindle app to access that store to purchase your e-books.
>
> ✔ Some tablets may block access to the Amazon Kindle store. Yeah, that's a cheap shot, but I've seen it happen. If you can't buy Kindle e-books using your tablet, you can always access your Amazon Kindle account on the Internet (probably on a computer) and buy books that way. Visit
>
> `kindle.amazon.com`

It's a Game Machine

Nothing justifies your expensive, high-tech investment in electronics like playing games. Don't even sweat the thought that you have too much "business" or "work" or other important stuff you can do on an Android tablet. The more advanced the mind, the more the need for play, right? So indulge yourself.

Your Android tablet's manufacturer may have tossed in a few sample games to whet your appetite. The games are most likely teasers or samples of paid games. Don't fret! You can obtain an abundance of games, free or not, from the Google Play Store. Look for the Lite versions of games, which are free. If you like the game, you can fork over the 99 cents or whatever the full version costs.

See Chapter 15 for details on shopping at the Google Play Store.

It's Your Video Entertainment

Someday it may be possible to watch "real" TV on your Android tablet, but why bother? You'll find plenty of video apps available on your tablet to sate your television-watching desires. Two of the most common are YouTube and Play Movies. So while you may not be able to pick up and enjoy the local Action News team every day at 5:00 PM, you're not bereft of video enjoyment on your tablet.

Enjoying YouTube

YouTube is the Internet phenomenon that proves that real life is indeed too boring and random for television. Or is that the other way around? Regardless, you can view the latest YouTube videos by using the YouTube app on your Android tablet.

The main YouTube screen is depicted in Figure 14-6.

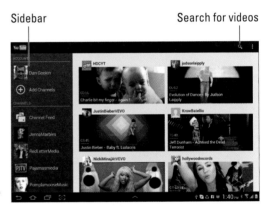

Sidebar   Search for videos

Use the sidebar to choose from your favorite channels or view recommended or popular videos.

To view a video, touch its name or icon in the list.

Search for videos by touching the Search icon. Type the video name, a topic, or any search terms to locate videos. Zillions of videos are available.

Figure 14-6: YouTube.

Touch the Back icon to return to the main YouTube screen after watching a video or if you tire of a video and need to return to the main screen out of boredom.

- ✔ Refer to Chapter 12 for information on adding a video you've recorded on your Android tablet to your account on YouTube.

- ✔ Use the YouTube app to view YouTube videos, rather than use the tablet's web browser app to visit the YouTube website.

- ✔ Because you have a Google account, you also have a YouTube account. I recommend that you log in to your YouTube account when using YouTube on your Android tablet: Touch the Menu icon and choose the

Sign In command. Log in if you haven't already. Otherwise, you see your account information, your videos, and any video subscriptions.

✔ Not all YouTube videos are available for viewing on mobile devices.

✔ If your Android tablet features NFC, you can use the Android Beam feature to instantly share YouTube videos with other Android users. Just touch the back of your Android tablet to their mobile device. When prompted, touch the text on the screen to send your friend the video.

Buying and renting movies

The Google Play Store lets you not only buy apps and books for your Android tablet but also rent movies. Open the Play Movies app, found on the All Apps screen, to boost your tablet's video potential.

Renting or purchasing a movie is done at the Google Play Store. Choose a movie or TV show to rent or buy. Touch the price button, and then choose your method of payment. The process works just like getting an app for your tablet, which is described in Chapter 15.

Movies and shows rented at the Play Store are available for viewing for up to 30 days after you pay the rental fee. After you start the movie, you can pause and watch it again and again during a 24-hour period.

✔ Not every film or TV show is available for purchase. Some are rentals only.

✔ You can use the Personal Videos category in the Play Movies app to view any videos stored on your Android tablet.

✔ One of the best ways to view movies on your Android tablet is to connect it to an HDMI monitor or TV set. That way, you get the big screen experience and can share the movie with several friends without crowding around the tablet. This trick works when your tablet features an HDMI connection and you've purchased the appropriate HDMI cable. If your tablet doesn't have an HDMI connection, you might be able to add one by plugging into a docking stand with HDMI output.

15

More Apps

In This Chapter

▶ Shopping at the Google Play Store

▶ Downloading or buying an app

▶ Installing an app remotely

▶ Sending an app suggestion to a friend

▶ Updating your apps

▶ Removing an app

*Y*our Android tablet's capabilities aren't limited to the paltry assortment of preinstalled apps. No way! A digital cornucopia of apps is available — hundreds of thousands of them, from productivity apps to references to educational to finance to games. The variety is almost unlimited. Those apps can be found at a single location, the Google Play Store.

Not only does the Play Store offer apps, but it's the place to go for e-books, music, videos, and sometimes even magazines. Other chapters throughout this book discuss obtaining those items at the Play Store; this chapter offers more detailed descriptions of how the Play Store works.

★★★☆ 164,012
00,000+ downloads

EDITORS' CHOICE

VIEW

Hello, Google Play Store

People love to shop when they're buying something they want or when they're spending someone else's money. You can go shopping for your Android tablet, and I'm not talking about buying a docking stand or a combination keyboard cover. I'm talking about apps, music, magazines, movies, TV shows, and books.

Yes! Some people still read books. I find that they're the most handsome people around.

The Google Play Store may sound like the place where you can go buy outdoor wear for Internet-savvy children, but it's really an online place where you go to pick up new digital stuff for your Android tablet. You can browse, you can get free items, or you can pay. It all happens at the Play Store app.

- ✔ Officially, the store is called the Google Play Store. It may also be referenced as Google Play. The app, however, is named Play Store.

- ✔ The Google Play Store was once known as the Android Market, and you may still see it referred to as the Market.

- ✔ This section is about getting apps for your tablet. For information on getting music, see Chapter 13. Refer to Chapter 14 for information on books and video available at the Play Store.

- ✔ *App* is short for application. It's a program, or software, you can add to your Android tablet to make it do new, wondrous, or useful things.

- ✔ Because your tablet uses the Android operating system, it can run nearly all apps written for Android.

- ✔ The Play Store is available only when the tablet has an Internet connection.

- ✔ The Play Store app is frequently updated, so its look may change from what you see in this chapter. Updated information on the Google Play Store is available on my website, at

  www.wambooli.com/help/tablets

Browsing the Google Play Store

You access the Google Play Store by opening the Play Store app, found on the Apps screen and possibly also on the main Home screen.

After opening the Play Store app, you see the main screen, similar to the one shown on the far left in Figure 15-1. You can browse for apps, games, books, movie rentals, and so on.

Touch a top-level item to view more details. You can swipe the screen left or right to see different categories, featured items, and best-sellers. Scroll down to peruse the entire list.

After choosing an individual item, you see a screen detailing the specifics, as shown in the far right in Figure 15-1. Scroll down to glean more information.

When you have an idea of what you want, such as an app's name or even what it does, searching works fastest: Touch the Search icon at the top of the Play Store screen. Type all or part of the app's name or perhaps a description.

My Apps icon   App icon   Scroll categories   Share app

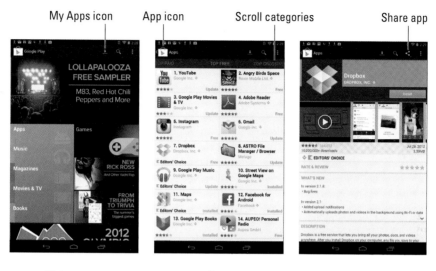

Main screen   Apps   Individual app

Figure 15-1: The Google Play Store.

Return to the previous screen by touching the App icon in the upper-left corner of the screen.

- The first time you enter the Google Play Store, or after the Play Store app is updated, you have to accept the terms of service. To do so, touch the Accept button.

- You can be assured that all apps that appear in the Google Play Store can be used with your Android tablet. There's no way to download or buy something that's incompatible.

- Pay attention to an app's ratings. Ratings are added by people who use the apps — people like you and me. Having more stars is better. You can see additional information, including individual user reviews, by choosing the app.

- Another good indicator of an app's success is how many times it's been downloaded. Some apps have been downloaded more than ten million times. That's a good sign.

- In addition to getting apps, you can download widgets for the Home screen as well as wallpapers for your tablet. Just search the Play Store for *widget* or *live wallpaper*.

- See Chapter 19 for more information on widgets and live wallpapers.

Obtaining an app

After you locate the app you've always dreamed of, the next step is to download it, copying it from the Google Play Store on the Internet into your Android tablet. The app is then installed automatically, building up your collection of apps and expanding what your Android tablet can do.

Good news: Most apps are available free. Better news: Even the apps you pay for don't cost dearly. In fact, it seems odd to sit and stew over whether paying 99 cents for a game is "worth it."

I recommend that you download a free app first to familiarize yourself with the process. Then try your hand at a paid app.

Free or not, the process of obtaining an app works pretty much the same. Follow these steps:

1. **If possible, activate the Wi-Fi connection to avoid incurring data overages.**

   See Chapter 16 for information on connecting your Android tablet to a Wi-Fi network.

2. **Open the Play Store app.**

3. **Find the app you want and open its description.**

   The app's description screen looks similar to what's shown on the far right in Figure 15-1.

   The difference between a free app and a paid app is the blue button you use to obtain the app. For a free app, the button says Install. For a paid app, the button shows the app's price.

   You may find three other buttons next to an app: Open, Update, and Uninstall. The Open button opens an app already installed on your Android tablet, the Update button updates an already installed app, and the Uninstall button removes an already installed app. See the later sections, "Updating an app" and "Removing downloaded apps" for more information on using the Update button and Uninstall button, respectively.

4. **Touch the Install button to get a free app; for a paid app, touch the button with the price on it.**

   Don't fret if you touched a price button! You're not buying anything yet.

   You see a screen describing the app's permissions. The list isn't a warning, and it doesn't mean anything bad. The Play Store is just telling you which of your tablet's features the app uses.

5. **For a paid app, choose your payment method.**

Account balance and credit card information appears in the Purchase & Allow Access window. The card must be on file with Google Checkout. If you don't yet have a card on file, choose the option Add Card and then fill in the fields on the Credit Card screen to add your payment method to Google Checkout.

If you have any Google Credit, choose your Google Play balance from the credit card list.

6. **Touch the Accept & Download button for a free app; touch the Accept & Buy button for a paid app.**

For a paid app, you may have to place a blue check mark by the item I Agree to the Payments for Google Play. Only after doing that does the Accept & Buy button become available.

If you chicken out, touch the Back icon. Otherwise, the Downloading notification appears as the app is downloaded. You're free to do other things on your Android tablet while the app is downloaded and installed.

7. **Touch the Open button to run the app.**

Or, if you were doing something else while the app was downloading and installing, choose the Successfully Installed notification, as shown in the margin. The notification features the app's name with the text Successfully Installed beneath it.

At this point, what happens next depends on the app you've downloaded. For example, you may have to agree to a license agreement. If so, touch the I Agree button. Additional setup may involve setting your location, signing in to an account, or creating a profile.

After you complete initial app setup, or if no setup is necessary, you can start using the app.

- Apps you download are added to the All Apps screen, made available like any other app on your tablet.

- Some apps may install shortcut icons on the Home screen after they're installed. See Chapter 19 for information on removing the icon from the Home screen, if that is your desire.

- For a paid app, you'll receive an e-mail message from the Google Play Store, confirming your purchase. The message contains a link you can click to review the refund policy should you change your mind on the purchase.

- Be quick on that refund: Some apps allow you only 15 minutes to get your money back. You know when the time is up because the Refund button on the app's description screen changes its name to Uninstall.

- Peruse the list of services an app uses (in Step 3) to look for anything unusual or out of line with the app's purpose. For example, an alarm clock app that uses your contact list and the text messaging service would be a red flag, especially if it's your understanding that the app doesn't need to text messages to any of your contacts.

- Also see the section "Removing downloaded apps," later in this chapter.

- Chapter 23 lists some Android apps that I recommend, all of which are free.

Installing apps from a computer

You don't ever need to use an Android tablet to install apps. Using a computer, you can visit the Google Play website, choose software, and have that app installed remotely. It's kind of cool, but yet kind of scary at the same time. Here's how it works:

1. **Use a computer's web browser to visit the Google Play store on the Internet at**

   ```
   https://play.google.com/store
   ```

   Bookmark that site!

2. **If necessary, click the Sign In link to log in to your Google account.**

   Use the same Google account you used when setting up your Android tablet. You need to have access to that account so that Google can remotely update your various Android devices.

3. **Browse for something.**

   You can hunt down apps, books, music — the whole gamut. It works just like browsing the Play Store on your tablet.

Never buy an app twice

Any apps you've already purchased in the Google Play Store, say for an Android phone or other mobile device, are available for download to your Android tablet at no charge. Simply find the app and touch the Install button.

You can review any already purchased apps in the Play Store: Touch the My Apps button from the top of the screen. In the All category, apps you've already purchased at the Google Play Store appear next to the text *Purchased*. Choose that item to reinstall the paid app.

4. **Click the Install or Buy button.**

5. **Choose your Android tablet from the Send To menu.**

The Send To menu lists all your Android devices, or at least those compatible with what you're getting.

Your Android tablet may be listed using its technical name, not the brand name you're used to.

6. **For a free app, click the Install button. For a paid app, click the Continue button, choose your payment source, and then click the Buy button.**

Installation proceeds.

As if by magic, the app is installed on your Android tablet — even though you used a computer to do it. Heck, the tablet need not even be within sight of you, and the app still remotely installs.

You probably won't be using the Internet on a computer to install most of the software on your tablet. However, it's a great trick to know, especially when you're using the computer and discover some new goodies you may desire for your Android tablet. In that case, you can remotely install the app, music, book, or whatever. It's handy.

App Management

The Play Store app is not only where you buy apps — it's also used for performing app management. That task includes reviewing apps you've downloaded, updating apps, organizing apps, and removing apps you no longer want or that you severely hate.

Reviewing your apps

To peruse the apps you've downloaded from the Google Play Store, follow these steps:

1. **Start the Play Store app.**

2. **Touch the My Apps icon, found at the top of the screen.**

Refer to Figure 15-1 for the icon's location. It looks similar to the Downloading notification.

3. **Peruse your apps.**

You'll see two categories for your Play Store apps: Installed and All, similar to what's shown in Figure 15-2. Installed apps are found on your tablet; All apps include apps you have downloaded but which may not currently be installed. Swipe the screen left or right to switch between the categories, although some tablets may just have you touch the Installed or All categories atop the screen.

Update button

Apps in need of an update

Installed apps   All your apps

Figure 15-2: The My Apps list.

In Figure 15-2, you see three apps that are in need of an update. The Google Voice app is listed separately because it requires a manual update. The rest of the apps, starting at the bottom of the screen, are installed and up-to-date.

The All Your Apps screen lists any app you've ever installed on any Android device, even if it's not installed on the Android tablet. Apps flagged as Installed are, in fact, installed on the tablet. Apps listed as Free or Purchased are not installed, but can be simply by touching their icons.

See the later section "Updating an app," on how the update process works.

Sharing an app

When you love an app so much that you just can't contain your glee, feel free to share that app with your friends. You can easily share a link to the app in the Google Play Store by obeying these steps:

1. **In the Google Play Store, choose the app to share.**

   You can choose any app, but you need to be at the app's details screen to share the app.

2. **Touch the Share icon.**

   A menu appears listing various apps and methods for sharing the app's Play Store link with your pals.

3. **Choose a sharing method.**

   For example, choose Gmail to send a link to the app in an e-mail message.

4. **Use the chosen app to send the link.**

   What happens next depends on which sharing method you've chosen.

The end result of these steps is that your friends receive a link. They can touch that link on their Android device and be whisked instantly to the Google Play Store, where they can easily install the app.

Methods for using the various items on the Share menu are found throughout this book.

Updating an app

The Play Store notifies you of new versions of your apps. Whenever a new version is available, you see it flagged for updating, as shown in Figure 15-2. Updating the app to get the latest version is cinchy.

Some apps are updated automatically; there's no need for you to do anything. Other apps must be updated manually. You can update a group of apps by touching an Update button (labeled in Figure 15-2). For manual updates, choose the item in the list, and then touch the Update button.

To make updating easier, you can place a blue check mark by the item Allow Automatic Updating. Find that button by choosing an app and viewing its description screen.

The updating process often involves downloading and installing a new version of the app. That's perfectly fine; your settings and options aren't changed by the update process.

Even though automatic updating may be configured for some apps, they still require a manual update. Don't ask me why because I'd just make up a reason.

Removing downloaded apps

I can think of a few reasons to remove an app. It's with eager relish that I remove apps that don't work or somehow annoy me. It's also perfectly okay to remove redundant apps, such as when you're trying to find a decent music-listening app and you end up with a dozen or so that you never use.

Whatever the reason, remove an app by following these directions:

1. **Start the Play Store app.**

2. **Touch the My Apps icon at the top of the screen.**

   The My Apps icon button looks like the Downloading notification.

3. **In the Installed list, touch the app that offends you.**

4. **Touch the Uninstall button.**

5. **Touch the OK button to confirm.**

   The app is removed.

The app continues to appear on the All list even after it's been removed. After all, you downloaded it once. That doesn't mean that the app is still installed.

✔ In most cases, if you uninstall a paid app right away, your credit card or account is fully refunded. The definition of "right away" depends on the app and is stated on the app's description screen. It could be anywhere from 15 minutes to 24 hours.

✔ Removing an app does free a modicum of storage inside the tablet. Just a modicum.

✔ You can always reinstall paid apps that you've uninstalled. You aren't charged twice for doing so.

✔ Some apps are preinstalled on your tablet, or they're part of the Android operating system. They cannot be removed. I'm sure there's probably a technical way to uninstall those apps, but seriously: Just don't use the apps if you can't remove them.

Part IV
Nuts and Bolts

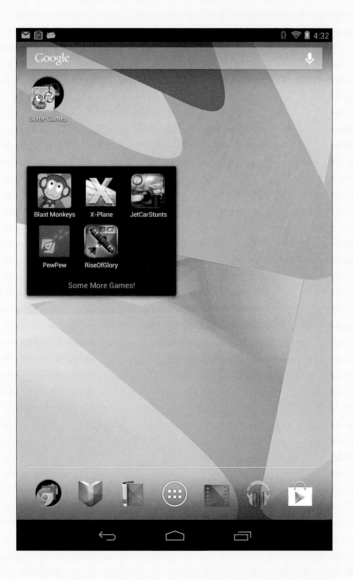

 Augment your ability to store icons on the tablet's Home screen by building folders in the article "Building App Folders" online at www.dummies.com/extras/androidtablets.

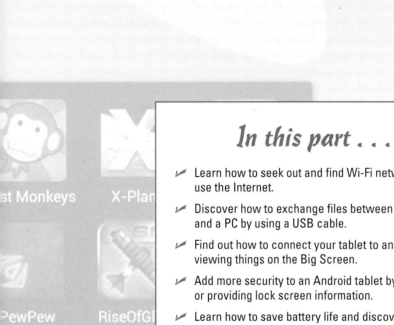

In this part . . .

- Learn how to seek out and find Wi-Fi networks, connect, and use the Internet.

- Discover how to exchange files between your Android tablet and a PC by using a USB cable.

- Find out how to connect your tablet to an HDTV or monitor for viewing things on the Big Screen.

- Add more security to an Android tablet by applying a password or providing lock screen information.

- Learn how to save battery life and discover which items on the tablet are using the most battery juice.

It's a Wireless Life

In This Chapter

▶ Accessing a Wi-Fi network
▶ Using Bluetooth
▶ Pairing with a Bluetooth peripheral
▶ Printing with your Android tablet
▶ Transferring information with Android Beam

A long time ago, progress was judged by how many wires something had. Newsreels showcased telephone poles and power lines marching across the countryside like victorious troops. Truly, the more wires, the better.

Today things are not quite so promising for wires. The new theme is to be entirely wireless. Tablets epitomize the wireless paradigm by operating a free and unbound existence; there is no wire for networking, no wire communicating with peripherals, and no decorative wires to make a fashion statement. Beyond a single cable to both charge the battery and communicate with a computer, your Android tablet truly is a wireless gizmo.

The Wonderful World of Wireless

You know that wireless networking has hit the big time when you see people asking Santa Claus for a wireless router at Christmas. Such a thing would have been unheard of years ago because routers were used primarily for woodworking back then.

The primary reason for wireless networking is to connect your Android tablet to the Internet. For exchanging and synchronizing files, refer to Chapter 17.

Using the cellular data network

Not every Android tablet is designed to be used with the digital cellular network. When your tablet is so blessed, it can use that network to connect to the Internet. The digital cellular signal is the same type used by cell phones and cellular modems to wirelessly connect to the Internet, and the signal is available almost everywhere.

Several types of digital cellular networks are available:

4G LTE/HSPA: The fourth generation of wide-area data network is as much as ten times faster than the cruddy old 3G network. It's the latest craze in cellular networking. The cellular providers are busily covering the country in a coat of 4G LTE or HSPA paint; if the signal isn't available in your area now, it will be soon.

3G: The third generation of wide-area data networks is several times faster than the previous generation of data networks. This type of wireless signal is the most popular in the United States.

1X: Several types of original, slower cellular data signals are available. They all fall under the 1X banner. It's slow, but it still works.

Your Android tablet always uses the best network available. So, if the 4G LTE network is within reach, that network is used for Internet communications. Otherwise, a slower network is chosen.

✔ A notification icon for the type of network being used appears in the status area.

✔ Accessing the digital cellular network isn't free. Your cellular tablet most likely has some form of subscription plan for a certain quantity of data. When you exceed that quantity, the costs can become prohibitive.

✔ See Chapter 18 for information on how to avoid cellular data overcharges when taking your Android tablet out and about.

✔ A better way to connect your tablet to the Internet is to use the Wi-Fi signal, covered in the next section. The digital cellular network signal makes for a great fallback because it's available in more places than Wi-Fi is.

✔ If you opt out of the cellular data plan, you can always use a cellular Android tablet as a Wi-Fi tablet. You cannot, however, adapt a Wi-Fi tablet to access the digital cellular network.

Understanding Wi-Fi

Android tablets use the same Wi-Fi networking standards as other wireless Internet devices, such as a laptop computer. So as long as Wi-Fi networking is set up in your home, office, or in the lobby at your proctologist, it's the same.

To make Wi-Fi work on an Android tablet requires two steps. First, you must activate Wi-Fi, by turning on the tablet's wireless radio. The second step is connecting to a specific wireless network. That network gives the tablet access to the Internet.

Wi-Fi stands for *wireless fidelity.* It's also known by various famous numbers, including 802.11g and 802.11n.

Activating and deactivating Wi-Fi

Activating Wi-Fi networking on your Android tablet works in two different ways, depending on whether you have the Jelly Bean or Ice Cream Sandwich version of the Android operating system on your tablet. If you're unsure as to which is which, peruse both sets of directions before sending me an angry e-mail.

For Jelly Bean tablets, activating Wi-Fi works along these lines (use Figure 16-1 as your guide):

1. **Touch the Apps icon.**

2. **Open the Settings app.**

3. **Ensure that the button by Wi-Fi is in the On position.**

    If not, touch the button. It changes from Off to On and changes color; blue is shown in Figure 16-1.

For Ice Cream Sandwich tablets, follow these general steps to activate the Wi-Fi radio (use Figure 16-2 as your guide):

1. **Touch the Apps icon.**

2. **Open the Settings app.**

3. **Choose the Wi-Fi item.**

    The Wi-Fi window appears on the right side of the screen, shown in Figure 16-2.

4. **Slide the button by the Wi-Fi item to the right.**

Settings screen   Wi-Fi screen

Figure 16-1: Activating the Wi-Fi radio for Android Jelly Bean.

After the tablet's Wi-Fi radio is activated, it can connect a Wi-Fi network. If the tablet has already been configured to connect to an available wireless network, it's connected automatically. Otherwise, you have to choose an available network, which is covered in the next section.

To turn off Wi-Fi, repeat the steps in this section. Turning off Wi-Fi disconnects the tablet from any wireless networks.

✔ Using Wi-Fi to connect to the Internet doesn't incur data usage charges.

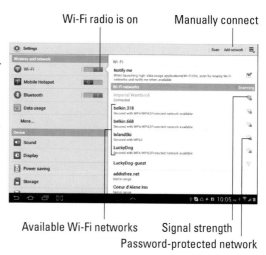

Figure 16-2: Activating the Wi-Fi radio for Android Ice Cream Sandwich.

> ✔ It's perfectly okay to keep the tablet's Wi-Fi radio on all the time. It does drain the battery, but you really need that Internet access to get the most from your Android tablet.

Connecting to a Wi-Fi network

After you've activated the Android tablet's Wi-Fi radio, you can connect to an available wireless network. The method can vary, depending on whether or not the wireless router features WPS authentication.

WPS routers feature the WPS icon, which is labeled in Figure 16-1. If you see that icon on the router — and, yes, you need to see and access the router to use WPS access — obey these steps to connect to the Wi-Fi network:

1. **Touch the Apps icon on the Home screen.**

2. **Open the Settings app.**

3. **Choose Wi-Fi.**

   The Wi-Fi settings screen appears, as shown on the right in both Figures 16-1 and 16-2.

4. **Touch the WPS icon on the screen.**

5. **After being prompted by the tablet, touch the WPS button (it sports the WPS icon) on the wireless router to connect the devices.**

   That's it. You're done.

For all other types of wireless routers (and even WPS routers that you can't physically access), follow these steps to connect to the wireless network:

1. **Touch the Apps icon on the Home screen.**

2. **Open the Settings app.**

3. **Choose Wi-Fi.**

   The Wi-Fi settings screen appears (refer to Figures 16-1, right, and 16-2, right).

4. **Choose a wireless network from the list.**

   When no wireless networks are listed, you're sort of out of luck regarding wireless access from your current location.

5. **If prompted, type the network password.**

   Touch the Show Password check box so that you can see what you're typing; some of those network passwords can be *long.*

6. **Touch the Connect button.**

   The network is connected immediately. If not, try the password again.

When the tablet is connected to a wireless network, you see the Wi-Fi Connected status icon, similar to what's shown in the margin. This icon means that the tablet's Wi-Fi is on, connected, and communicating with a Wi-Fi network.

Some wireless networks don't broadcast their names, which adds security but also makes connecting more difficult. In those cases, touch the Manually Connect icon (labeled in Figures 16-1 and 16-2) to add the network. You need to type the network name, or *SSID,* and choose the type of security. You also need the password if one is used. You can obtain this information from the girl with the pink hair who sold you coffee or from whomever is in charge of the wireless network at your location.

- ✔ Not every wireless network has a password. Still:

- ✔ Be careful when connecting to a non-password-protected network. It's possible that the Bad Guys can monitor such a network, stealing passwords and other information.

- ✔ WPS stands for Wi-Fi Protected Setup. Not every Wi-Fi router features such a button.

- ✔ Some public networks are open to anyone, but you have to use the Chrome app to find a login web page that lets you access the network: Simply browse to any page on the Internet, and the login web page shows up.

- ✔ The Android tablet automatically remembers every Wi-Fi network it has ever been connected to and automatically reconnects upon finding the same network again.

- ✔ To disconnect from a Wi-Fi network, simply turn off Wi-Fi. See the preceding section.

- ✔ A Wi-Fi network's broadcast signal goes only so far. My advice is to use Wi-Fi whenever you plan to remain in one location for a while. If you wander away, your tablet loses the signal and is disconnected.

Share the Cellular Connection

It's good to have a cellular tablet and be able to use the Internet wherever you roam. It's so good that people around you, those without a mobile data connection, will seethe with jealousy. You'll even be able to hear the seething. It's maddening.

Rather than endure endless seething, you can take advantage of a technology called Internet connection sharing. As a gesture of goodwill, you can stifle the seething and share your Android tablet's cellular connection, described in this section.

Creating a mobile hotspot

The best way to share a digital cellular connection with the most people is to set up your own Android tablet wireless mobile hotspot. Carefully heed these steps:

1. **Turn off the tablet's Wi-Fi radio.**

   You can't be using a Wi-Fi connection when you create a Wi-Fi hotspot. Actually, the notion is kind of silly: If the tablet can get a Wi-Fi signal, other gizmos can too, so why bother creating a Wi-Fi hotspot in the first place?

   See the earlier section, "Activating and deactivating Wi-Fi," for information on disabling Wi-Fi.

2. **If you can, plug in your Android tablet.**

   It's okay if you don't find a power outlet, but running a mobile hotspot draws a lot of power.

3. **From the Apps screen, open the Settings app.**

4. **Choose Mobile Hotspot.**

   The item may also be titled Tethering & Mobile Hotspot, and it may also be lurking on the More menu. If you don't see that item, or it can't be readily found, your tablet most likely lacks the capability to form a Wi-Fi hotspot.

   If you can't find a Mobile Hotspot item on the Settings screen, also look for a Mobile Hotspot app.

5. **Activate the mobile hotspot.**

   You may have to slide a switch or touch an icon or a button to activate the setting.

You can continue to use the tablet while it's sharing the digital cellular connection, but other devices can now use their Wi-Fi radio to access the shared connection.

To turn off the mobile hotspot, repeat the steps in this section, but disable the Mobile Hotspot in Step 5.

✔ You can change the mobile hotspot configuration by touching the Configure button at the top of the Mobile Hotspot window.

✔ The range for the mobile hotspot is about 30 feet.

✔ Some cellular providers may not allow you to create a mobile hotspot unless you pay an extra service fee on your cellular contract.

✔ Don't forget to turn off the mobile hotspot when you're done using it. Those data rates add up quickly!

Sharing the Internet via tethering

A personal way to share your Android tablet's digital cellular connection is *tethering.* This operation is carried out by connecting the tablet to another gizmo, such as a laptop computer, via its USB cable. Then you activate USB tethering, and the other gizmo is suddenly using the tablet like a modem.

To set up tethering, obey these steps:

1. **Turn off the tablet's Wi-Fi radio.**

   You cannot share a connection with the Wi-Fi radio on; you can share only the digital cellular connection.

2. **Connect the tablet to a PC using its USB cable.**

   Specifically, the PC must be running Windows or some flavor of the Linux operating system.

3. **At the Home screen, touch the Apps icon.**

4. **Open the Settings app.**

5. **Look for a Tethering item.**

   It might be named Tethering and Mobile Hotspot. The item may also be found by touching the More button below Data Usage. If so, choose the Tethering option when it appears.

   If you can't find the Tethering option, your tablet isn't capable of tethering the cellular connection. It happens.

6. **Place a check mark by the USB Tethering option.**

7. **On the PC, choose Public when prompted to specify the type of network to which you've just connected.**

While tethering is active, a Tethering notification appears. It reminds you that the tablet is sharing its cellular signal. You can choose that notification to turn off tethering: Simply remove the check mark by the USB Tethering option.

 ✔ Sharing the digital network connection incurs data usage charges against your cellular data plan. Be careful with your data usage when you're sharing a connection.

 ✔ You may be prompted on the PC to locate and install software for the tablet. Do so: Accept the installation of new software when prompted by Windows.

 ✔ You cannot share the Internet connection on a PC running Windows XP.

The Bluetooth World

Computer nerds have long had the desire to connect high-tech gizmos to one another. The Bluetooth standard was developed to sate this desire in a wireless way. Although Bluetooth is wireless communication, it's not quite the same as wireless networking. It's more about connecting peripheral devices, such as keyboards, mice, printers, headphones, and other gear. It all happens in a wireless way, as described in this section.

Bluetooth devices are often marked with the Bluetooth icon, shown in the margin. It's your assurance that the peripheral can work with other Bluetooth devices.

Activating Bluetooth

To make the Bluetooth connection, turn on the tablet's Bluetooth radio. Obey these directions:

1. **Touch the Apps icon on the Home screen.**

2. **Open the Settings icon.**

3. **Ensure that the button next to the Bluetooth item is set to On.**

Refer to Figure 16-1 for the location of the Bluetooth item in Android Jelly Bean. Figure 16-2 illustrates its position for Android Ice Cream Sandwich.

When Bluetooth is on, the Bluetooth status icon appears, which looks like a little Bluetooth logo (refer to the preceding section).

To turn off Bluetooth, repeat the steps in this section: Touch the On button to reset it back to Off in Step 3.

- See Chapter 19 for information on installing the Power Control widget. Using that widget, you can quickly turn on or off Bluetooth right from a Home screen.

- You'll also find a Bluetooth switch in the Quick Settings for your tablet. Display the Quick Settings shade or access the Quick Settings part of the Notifications shade to look for the Bluetooth switch.

Pairing with a Bluetooth peripheral

After ensuring that the tablet's Bluetooth radio is on, the next step to connecting a Bluetooth peripheral is to pair the devices. Your tablet and the

Bluetooth gizmo must start wirelessly holding hands. Pairing is required before the tablet can use the device, and you must pair the tablet to each Bluetooth peripheral you want to use.

To pair your Android tablet with a Bluetooth device, follow these steps:

1. Ensure that Bluetooth is on.

Refer to the preceding section.

2. Turn on the Bluetooth gizmo or ensure that its Bluetooth radio is on.

Some Bluetooth devices have separate power and Bluetooth switches. Your goal here is to make the Bluetooth device *discoverable*.

3. On the Android tablet, touch the Apps icon on the Home screen and open the Settings app.

4. Choose Bluetooth.

You'll see the Bluetooth screen. Figure 16-3 illustrates the Bluetooth screen as it may appear on tablets with Android Jelly Bean; Figure 16-4 illustrates how the screen may look on Android Ice Cream Sandwich tablets.

The Bluetooth screen shows any devices already paired with the tablet, such as the printer shown in Figure 16-3 or the keyboard shown in Figure 16-4. Also shown in the list are any other Bluetooth devices available for pairing.

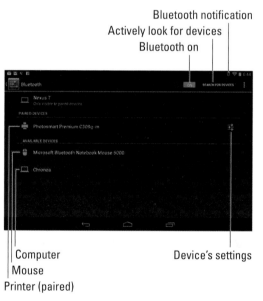

Figure 16-3: Finding Bluetooth gizmos (Jelly Bean).

5. If the Bluetooth device has an option to become visible or discoverable, select it.

For example, some Bluetooth gizmos have a tiny button to press that makes the device visible to other Bluetooth gizmos.

After making the Bluetooth device visible, it should appear on the Bluetooth screen, as shown in Figures 16-3 and 16-4. If it doesn't, touch the Search for Devices button.

6. **Choose the Bluetooth device from the list.**

7. **If necessary, input the device's passcode or otherwise acknowledge the connection.**

   Not every device has a passcode. If prompted, acknowledge the passcode on either the Android tablet or the other device.

After you acknowledge the passcode (or not), the Bluetooth gizmo and your Android tablet are connected and communicating. You can begin using the device.

Bluetooth is on   Check for Bluetooth gizmos

Available Bluetooth printer

Make the tablet visible

Paired device's settings

Figure 16-4: Finding Bluetooth gizmos (Ice Cream Sandwich).

Connected devices appear on the Bluetooth Settings window, under the heading Paired Devices.

To break the connection, you can either turn off the gizmo or disable the Bluetooth radio on your Android tablet. Because the devices are paired, when you turn on Bluetooth and reactivate the device, the connection is instantly reestablished.

  ✔ How you use the device depends on what it does. For example, a Bluetooth keyboard can be used for text input, a computer using Bluetooth can be accessed for sharing files, and a printer can be used for printing documents or pictures, which is covered in the next section.

  ✔ See Chapter 17 for information on using Bluetooth to transfer files between the Android tablet and a computer.

  ✔ You can unpair a device by touching its Settings icon, found on the far right next to a paired device. Choose the Unpair command to break the Bluetooth connection and stop using the device.

  ✔ You need to unpair devices you don't plan on using again in the future. Otherwise, simply turn off the Bluetooth device when you're done.

Printing to a Bluetooth printer

The common way to print information from your Android tablet is to use a paired and connected Bluetooth printer. The secret is to find and use the

Share button or command, choose Bluetooth, and then select your printer. Of course, here are some more detailed steps:

1. **View the document, web page, or image you want to print.**

   You can print from the Chrome app, Gallery app, Maps app, or a number of apps you can install on your Android tablet.

2. **Choose the Share command.**

   If a Share icon isn't visible in the app, touch the Menu icon to look for the Share command.

3. **Choose Bluetooth from the menu.**

4. **Choose your Bluetooth printer from the list of items on the Bluetooth Device Chooser screen.**

5. **If a prompt appears on the printer, confirm that the Android tablet is printing a document.**

   The document is uploaded (sent from the tablet to the printer), and then it prints. You can view the uploading status by checking the notifications in the lower-right corner of the screen.

Not everything on your Android tablet can be printed on a Bluetooth printer. When you can't find the Share command or the Bluetooth item isn't available on the Share menu, you can't print using Bluetooth.

- Bluetooth printers sport the Bluetooth logo somewhere.

- To print from the Maps app, view a location's information and choose the Share This Location command. Choose Bluetooth.

Android, Beam It to Me

A recent addition to the wireless radio pantheon is NFC, or Near Field Communications. It allows your tablet to communicate with other NFC devices, primarily for the quick transfer of information. The technology is called Android Beam.

Before you can use Android Beam, ensure that it's been activated. Follow these steps:

1. **At the Home screen, touch the Apps icon.**

2. **Choose the Settings icon to open the Settings app.**

3. **Touch the More command found below the Wireless & Networks heading.**

4. **Ensure that a check mark appears next to the NFC item.**

   If not, touch the box to add a check mark.

With NFC activated, you can use your tablet to communicate with other NFC devices. Simply touch your tablet to another NFC device, such as another Android tablet or a smartphone.

When the two Android Beam devices touch — usually back-to-back — you'll see a Touch to Beam prompt on the screen. Touch the screen and the item you're viewing is immediately sent to the other device. That's pretty much it.

  ✔ Use Android Beam to swap contacts, web pages, map locations, pictures, and lots of other things. Generally speaking, if the app features a Share icon, you can probably use Android Beam.

  ✔ Both devices present the Touch to Beam prompt when they get close. If the other person touches his or her screen at the same time you do, information is swapped between both devices.

Connect, Share, and Store

In This Chapter

▶ Making the USB connection

▶ Setting the connection type

▶ Hooking up to a Mac

▶ Transferring files to and fro

▶ Connecting with Bluetooth

▶ Performing basic file management

▶ Connecting to an HDMI TV

A s much as it tries, your Android tablet just can't be completely wireless. Unless you have a wireless charging pad for the tablet, you're going to need the USB cable to resupply the battery with juice. But the USB cable is more than a power cord; it's also a method of communications — specifically, file transfer between your tablet and a computer. This chapter carefully describes how that transfer works. Also discussed is the anxiety-laden issue of storage and sharing, which is presented in a deceptively cheerful manner.

The USB Connection

The most direct way to connect an Android tablet to a computer is by using a wire — specifically, the wire nestled at the core of a USB cable. You can do lots of things after making the USB connection, but everything starts with connecting the cable.

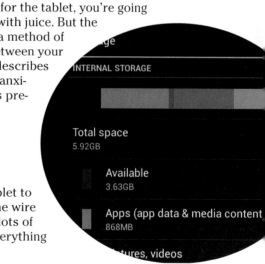

INTERNAL STORAGE

Total space
5.92GB

Available
3.63GB

Apps (app data & media content
868MB

tures, videos

Connecting the tablet to a computer

The USB cable that came with your Android tablet can be used to physically connect both the tablet and a computer. It's cinchy, thanks to three-dimensional physics and the following two important pieces of advice:

- One end of the USB cable plugs into the computer.
- The other end plugs into the Android tablet.

The connectors on either end of the USB cable are shaped differently and cannot be plugged in incorrectly. If one end of the cable doesn't fit, try the other end. If it still doesn't fit, try plugging it in another way.

What happens after you connect the tablet and the computer is described in the following sections.

- The tablet may show a USB connection status icon when the connection is made. The icon looks similar to what's shown in the margin. Not all tablets display this icon.
- By connecting the Android tablet to your computer, you are adding, or *mounting*, its storage to your computer's storage system. That process allows file transfers to take place.

- Even if you don't use the USB cable to communicate with the computer, the Android tablet's battery charges when it's connected to a computer's USB port — as long as the computer is turned on, of course.

Dealing with the USB connection on a PC

Upon successful connection between an Android tablet and a computer running Microsoft Windows, a number of things happen. Don't let any of these things cause you undue alarm.

First, you may see a connection screen on the tablet. That screen indicates that the tablet is attempting to synchronize files with the computer. The screen may describe the connection, using acronyms such as MTP or PTP, or it may not show anything at all.

Second, you may see some activity on the PC, some drivers being installed and such. That's normal behavior any time you first connect a new USB gizmo to a Windows computer.

Third, you may witness the Windows AutoPlay dialog box. That dialog box helps you deal with the tablet's storage, to transfer music, pictures, files, and so on. Choose an option from the AutoPlay dialog box, such as Sync Digital Media Files to This Device or Choose What Happens with This Device. From that point on, use Windows or a specific program chosen from the AutoPlay dialog box to work with the files on your tablet.

Later sections in this chapter describe specific things you can do after the connection is made.

- ✔ The AutoPlay dialog box may not appear when you connect the Android tablet to your PC. It's possible to configure Windows not to display that dialog box.

- ✔ Even if the AutoPlay dialog box doesn't appear, you can still access media and files stored on the Android tablet from your computer. The later section "Files Back and Forth" has details.

- ✔ Tablets that feature a microSD card are mounted twice into the PC's storage system, once for internal storage and a second time for the removable storage card. You'll see two AutoPlay dialog boxes, one for each storage location on the tablet.

- ✔ If you're nerdy, you can open the Android tablet's icon in the Computer window; press the Win+E keyboard shortcut in Windows to see the Computer window. You'll find the Android tablet listed as either a Portable Media Player (MTP) or a Digital Camera (PTP) connection. Open the Android tablet icon to browse the tablet's storage.

Connecting an Android tablet to a Mac

The USB connection between an Android tablet and a Macintosh computer can be straightforward: After making the connection, the tablet's storage appears as a generic drive icon on the Mac desktop. When that doesn't work, you'll have to use an alternative connection method, the Android File Transfer program.

Download the Android File Transfer program from the www.android.com/filetransfer website. Install the software. Run it. From that point on, when you connect your tablet to the Macintosh, you'll see a window listing all the folders and files on the tablet. Use that window for file management, as covered later in this chapter.

If the Mac still fails to recognize your Android tablet, you'll need to configure the USB connection as an MTP device. Refer to the next section.

Configuring the USB connection

Some tablets connect to a computer as a removable storage device, similar to plugging in a thumb drive. Other tablets may connect and pretend that they're a portable media player or a digital camera. These options are set by the tablet's manufacturer or, in some happy cases, you can choose how the computer sees the tablet after the USB connection is made.

The easiest way to configure the USB connection is to summon the Notifications shade and choose the USB item. You'll see a menu from which you can choose how the tablet presents itself to the computer — for example, as external storage, a digital camera, or a portable music player.

When you can't choose a USB notification, you'll have to trudge through these steps:

1. **At the Home screen, touch the Apps icon.**

2. **Open the Settings app.**

3. **Choose Storage.**

4. **Touch the Menu icon, and then choose the USB connection command.**

   The command's title differs from tablet to tablet, such as USB PC Connection or USB Computer Connection.

   Two common options are MTP and PTP.

5. **If the MTP option is available, choose it.**

   The only time you need to choose PTP is when the computer doesn't recognize the tablet configured as an MTP device.

   If MTP isn't available, choose the option that configures the tablet as a removable storage device, hard drive, or thumb drive.

6. **Touch the Home icon to return to the Home screen.**

MTP stands for *Media Transfer Protocol*. PTP stands for *Picture Transfer Protocol*. Do not bother memorizing these definitions.

Disconnecting the tablet from a computer

On a PC, the disconnection process is cinchy: When you're done transferring files or music, close all the programs and folders you have opened on the computer, specifically those you've used to work with the tablet's storage. Then you can disconnect the USB cable. That's it.

On a Macintosh, you have to be more careful. Eject the tablet's storage just as you would any removable storage: Drag the tablet's storage icon(s) to the Trash. Or, in any Finder window, click the Eject button by the tablet's storage icon. Only when the icon is removed from the desktop is it okay to disconnect the USB cable.

✔ If you're using the Android File Transfer program on your Mac, quit that program before you eject the tablet's storage.

✔ It's a Bad Idea to unplug the tablet while you're transferring information or while a folder window is open on your computer. Doing so could damage the tablet's internal storage, rendering some of the information kept there unreadable.

Files Back and Forth

The point of making the USB connection between an Android tablet and a computer is to exchange files. You can't just wish the files over. Instead, I recommend following the advice in this section, which also covers the ordeal of transferring files using Bluetooth.

 A good understanding of basic computer operations is necessary before you attempt file transfers between your computer and the Android tablet. You need to know how to copy, move, rename, and delete files. It also helps to be familiar with what folders are and how they work. The good news is that you don't need to manually calculate a 64-bit cyclical redundancy check on the data, nor do you need to know what a parity bit is.

Transferring files between a computer and an Android tablet

I can think of plenty of reasons why you would want to copy a file between a computer and an Android tablet, many of which are legal.

For example, you can copy pictures and videos, music and audio files, and even vCards that help you build contacts for the tablet's address book. And you can just copy random files when you're on a caffeine high and nothing is on TV.

Follow these steps to copy a file or two between a computer and an Android tablet:

1. **Connect the Android tablet to the computer by using the USB cable.**

   Specific directions are offered earlier in this chapter.

2. **Open the Android tablet's storage to display its folder window.**

   On a Windows computer, choose the option to View Files from the AutoPlay dialog box. If the AutoPlay dialog box doesn't show up, open the Computer window and then open the Android tablet's storage icon.

   On a Macintosh, the Android File Transfer program starts automatically. Otherwise, you can open the tablet's folder window on the desktop.

   The Android tablet's folder window looks like any other folder window. The difference is that the files and folders in that window are stored on the tablet, not on your computer.

3. **Locate the files you want to copy.**

   Open the folder that contains the files, or somehow have the file icons visible on the screen.

The best way to copy files is to have two folder windows open at once, one for the computer and the other for the tablet. Figure 17-1 illustrates how such an arrangement might look.

Specific folders on the tablet
Drag files to here to copy to the root folder

Files on the computer

Files on the Android tablet

Figure 17-1: Copying files to the Android tablet.

4. Drag the file icon(s) from one folder to another to copy.

When you drag a file from the computer's folder to the tablet, you're copying the file, such as a vCard file, to the tablet. Dragging a file from the tablet's folder to the computer copies files in the other direction.

You don't have to be specific where you copy the file from your computer to the tablet. You can drop the file in the *root* folder, shown in Figure 17-1. That's the tablet's main folder. If you want to be specific, drag the file to the Download folder.

5. Close the folder windows and disconnect the USB cable when you're done.

Refer to specific instructions earlier in this chapter.

Any files you've copied from the computer are now stored on the Android tablet. What you do with them next depends on the reasons you copied the files: view pictures using the Gallery (Chapter 12); import vCards using the tablet's address book app (Chapter 5); listen to music (Chapter 13), and so on.

✔ The best way to synchronize music is by using a music jukebox program on your computer. See Chapter 13.

✔ Files you've downloaded on the Android tablet are stored in the Download folder.

✔ Pictures and videos on the Android tablet are stored in the DCIM/Camera folder.

✔ Music on the Android tablet is stored in the Music folder, organized by artist.

✔ Files transferred via Bluetooth are stored in the bluetooth folder. See the next section.

✔ Your tablet may feature two storage locations. If you can't find a file in one spot, look in the other.

Using Bluetooth to copy a file

Here's a great way to give yourself a headache: Use the Bluetooth to copy a file between your Android tablet and a Bluetooth-enabled computer. It's slow, it's painful, and it might even work.

✔ Get started by pairing your tablet with the computer. See Chapter 16 for details. When your tablet and computer are paired and connected, how the file transfer works depends on whether you're using a PC or a Macintosh.

✔ Although a Bluetooth transfer can work, I've found it's not the most reliable method. It's definitely not the easiest way to transfer files.

Send a file from the PC to an Android tablet

On a PC, follow these steps to copy a file to the Android tablet:

1. **Right-click the Bluetooth icon in the Notification Area on the desktop.**

   The icon looks like the Bluetooth logo, shown in the margin. The Notification Area dwells on the far-right end of the taskbar.

2. **Choose Send a File from the pop-up menu.**

3. **Choose your Android tablet from the list of Bluetooth devices.**

   If you don't see the tablet listed, ensure that the Bluetooth radio is on for both devices and that they're paired.

4. **Click the Next button.**

5. **Click the Browse button to locate files to send to the tablet.**

6. **Use the Browse dialog box to locate and select one or more files.**

7. **Click the Open button to choose the file(s).**

8. **Click the Next button.**

   The tablet may signal a notification alert, which lets you know that a file transfer is taking place.

9. **Touch the Accept button.**

   If you don't see the Accept button, choose the Bluetooth Share: Incoming File notification.

10. **On the PC, touch the Finish button.**

    The transfer is complete.

On your Android tablet, you can pull down the notifications and choose the Bluetooth Share: Received Files notification. You'll see the Inbound Transfers screen, which lists the file(s) downloaded. Choose a file from the list to examine it using the appropriate app.

- ✔ Images sent to the Android tablet from a PC can be found in the Gallery app, in the Bluetooth album.

- ✔ Not all PCs are equipped with Bluetooth. To add Bluetooth to a PC, you need a Bluetooth adapter. Inexpensive USB Bluetooth adapters are available at most computer and office supply stores.

Send a file from an Android tablet to a PC

To send a file from the tablet to a PC, you need to use the Bluetooth item found on the Share menu in various apps. Follow these steps:

1. **On the Android tablet, locate and select the media or file you want to send to the PC.**

2. **Choose the Share command.**

3. **From the Share or Share Via menu, choose Bluetooth.**

   If you see a Bluetooth icon in the app, just touch it to summon a list of Bluetooth devices.

4. **Choose the PC from the list.**

5. **On the PC, click the Notification Area icon that appears, indicating that a Bluetooth file transfer request is pending.**

6. **On the PC, click the OK button in the Access Authorization dialog box.**

   The file is sent to the PC.

On my PC, the received files are stored in the Bluetooth Exchange Folder, found in the Documents or My Documents folder.

Send a file from a Macintosh to the tablet

To copy a file to the Android tablet by using Bluetooth on a Macintosh, follow these steps:

1. **Use the Bluetooth menu on the Mac to choose the Android tablet and then choose Send File, as shown in Figure 17-2.**

   You can find the Bluetooth menu at the far-right end of the menu bar.

2. **Use the Select File to Send dialog box to browse for and select the file on your Mac that you want to send to the Android tablet; click the Send button.**

3. **On the Android tablet, choose the Bluetooth notification.**

4. **In the File Transfer window on the tablet, touch the Accept button.**

   The file is sent from your Mac to the Android tablet. It appears in a list of Bluetooth Inbound Transfers.

Figure 17-2: Copying a file using Bluetooth on the Mac.

You can touch the file in the Inbound Transfers window to open it and do whatever interesting thing that the tablet wants to do with that file.

Sadly, I cannot get the Mac to accept a file sent to it from any Android tablet by using Bluetooth. You might have more success, but keep in mind that the USB file transfer, coupled with the Android File Transfer program, works like a charm.

Android Tablet Storage

Somewhere, deep in your Android tablet's bosom, lies a storage device or two. That storage works like the hard drive in a computer, and for the same purpose: keeping apps, music, video, pictures, and a host of other information for the long term. This section describes what you can do to manage that storage.

- Android tablets come with 8GB, 16GB, or 32GB of internal storage. In the future, models with larger storage capacities might become available.

- Removable storage in the form of a microSD card is available on some Android tablets. The capacity of a microSD card can vary between 8GB up to 64GB.

✔ A GB is a gigabyte, or 1 billion bytes (characters) of storage. A typical 2-hour movie occupies about 4GB of storage, but most things you store on the tablet — music and pictures, for example — take up only a sliver of storage. Those items do, however, occupy more storage space the more you use the tablet.

Reviewing storage stats

You can see how much storage space is available on your Android tablet's internal storage by following these steps:

1. **At the Home screen, touch the Apps icon.**

2. **Open the Settings app and choose Storage.**

   You see a screen similar to Figure 17-3. It details information about storage space on the tablet's internal storage.

You can choose a category to see more information, or to launch a program. For example, touching the Downloads category (refer to Figure 17-3) displays a list of files you've downloaded. Touching the Pictures, Videos category starts the Gallery app.

Used space   Free space

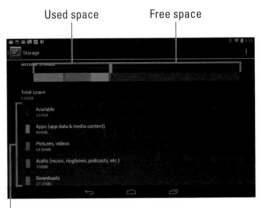

What's consuming storage

Figure 17-3: Android tablet storage information.

✔ Things that consume the most storage space are videos, music, and pictures, in that order.

✔ To see how much storage space is left, refer to the Available item.

✔ Don't complain if the Total Space value is far less than the stated capacity of your Android tablet. In Figure 17-3, it shows 5.92GB total space, even though my tablet has 8GB of storage. The missing space is considered overhead, as are several gigabytes taken by the government for tax purposes.

Managing files

You probably didn't get an Android tablet because you enjoy managing files on a computer and wanted another gizmo to hone your skills. Even so, you can practice the same type of file manipulation on the Android tablet as you would on a computer. Is there a need to do so? Of course not! But if you want to get dirty with files, you can.

Some Android tablets come with a File Management or My Files app. It's a traditional type of file management app, which means if you detest managing files on your computer, you'll experience the same pain and frustration on your tablet. Such an app is depicted in Figure 17-4.

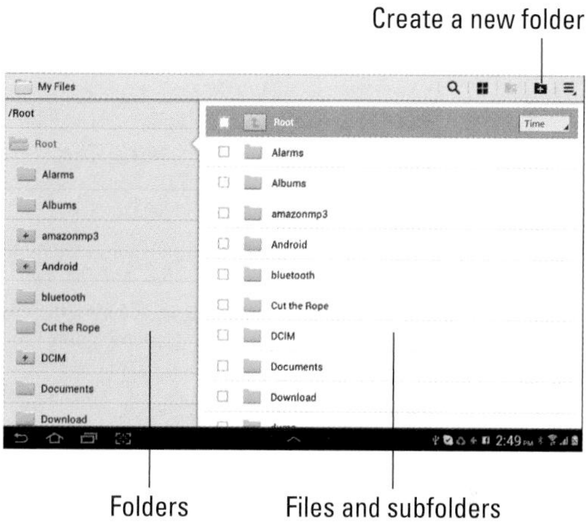

Create a new folder

Folders   Files and subfolders

Figure 17-4: A typical file management app.

When your tablet lacks a file management app, you can swiftly obtain one. You'll find an abundance of file management apps available at the Google Play Store. One that I admire and use is the Astro File Manager/Browser from Metago. See Chapter 15 for more information on the Google Play Store.

If you simply want to peruse files you've downloaded from the Internet, open the Downloads app, found on the Apps screen. Refer to Chapter 7.

The HDMI Connection

You may think having a 10-inch tablet really smokes those folks with the smaller 8-inch tablets. Ha! You're in for a surprise. That's because any tablet with HDMI output, even those doinky 7-inch models, can hook up to an 80-inch plasma HDTV screen and really show who's boss.

When your Android tablet features an HDMI connection, whether it's a 7-inch model or a 10-inch behemoth, you too can enjoy the pleasures of a larger screen. It doesn't have to be an 80-inch plasma screen, either; any monitor or HDTV with HDMI input does the job.

To make the HDMI connection, plug your tablet into an HDMI-equipped monitor or HDTV. You'll need a special HDMI cable to make the connection; such an item can be found on the Internet or wherever you purchased your tablet.

Upon success, an HDMI notification or pop-up appears on the tablet's screen. Choose it and select how to display information on the external monitor. Depending on the tablet, you can choose to run a slideshow, present videos or music, or simply mirror the information displayed on the touchscreen.

When you're finished using the HDMI connection, simply disconnect the tablet from the HDTV or monitor. The display returns to normal operation.

✔ If your tablet lacks an HDMI port, check to see whether a multimedia dock or HDMI USB dongle is available.

✔ I've used HDMI output on my tablet to rent and view a movie on a widescreen HDTV. The whole family got to enjoy it.

18

On the Road

In This Chapter

▶ Bringing the Android tablet on a trip
▶ Taking the tablet on an airplane
▶ Using an Android tablet overseas
▶ Avoiding those data roaming charges

*A*s a mobile device, your Android tablet is designed to go wherever you go. And if you throw the tablet, it can go beyond where you go, but that's not my point. Being wireless and having a generous battery, the tablet is built to go on the road. Where can you take it? How can it survive? What if it runs off by itself? These are the issues regarding taking your tablet elsewhere, each of which are covered in this chapter.

You Can Take It with You

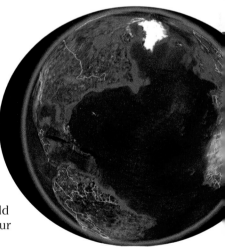

How far can you go with an Android tablet? As far as you want. As long as you can carry the tablet with you, it goes where you go. How it functions may change depending on your environment, and you can do a few things to prepare before you go, which are all covered in this section.

Preparing to leave

Unless you're being unexpectedly abducted, you should prepare several things before leaving on a trip with your Android tablet.

First and most important, of course, is to charge the thing. I plug my Android tablet in overnight before I leave the next day. The tablet's battery is nice and robust, so it should last you your entire journey.

Second, consider loading up on some reading material, music, as well as a few new apps before you go.

For example, consider getting some e-books for the road. I prefer to sit and stew over the Play Store's online library before I leave, as opposed to wandering aimlessly in some airport sundry store, trying hard to focus on the good books rather than on the salty snacks. Chapter 14 covers reading e-books on your Android tablet.

Picking up some music might be a good idea as well. Visit Chapter 13.

I usually reward myself with a new game before I go on a trip with my tablet. Visit the Play Store and see what's hot or recommended. A good puzzle game can make a nice, long international flight go by a lot quicker. See Chapter 15 for information on obtaining games from the Google Play Store.

 Another nifty thing to do is save some web pages for later reading. I usually start my day by perusing online articles and angry editorials in the local paper. Because I don't have time to read that stuff before I leave, and I do have time on the plane, and I'm extremely unwilling to pay for in-flight Wi-Fi, I save my favorite websites for later reading.

Not every web browser app is capable of saving web pages. Generally speaking, it works like this:

1. **Navigate to the page you want to save for later reading.**

2. **Touch the Menu icon.**

3. **Choose the Save for Offline Reading command.**

    The command might also read simply Save Page or Save. Either way, choosing that command downloads the page, saving it to the tablet's storage.

Repeat these steps for each web page you want to read when offline.

To view the page, open the web browser app and touch the Bookmarks icon. Choose the Saved Pages tab. You see the web page listed. If the web page name is too cryptic, just look at the thumbnail preview to get an idea of what you've saved.

Downloaded web pages might be missing some information, such as interactive features and perhaps even some images. Although this arrangement may not look pretty, at least you'll have some reading material on the plane — specifically, stuff you're used to reading that day anyway.

Going to the airport

I'm not a frequent flier, but I am a nerd. The most amount of junk I've carried with me on a flight is two laptop computers and three cell phones. I know that's not a record, but it's enough to warrant the following list of travel tips, all of which apply to taking an Android tablet with you on an extended journey:

- ✔ Take the Android tablet's AC adapter and USB cable with you. Put them in your carry-on luggage.

- ✔ Many airports feature USB chargers, so you can charge the tablet in an airport if you need to. Even though you need only the cable to charge, bring along the AC adapter anyway.

- ✔ At the security checkpoint, place your Android tablet in a bin by itself or with other electronics.

- ✔ Use the Calendar app to keep track of your flights. The event title serves as the airline and flight number. For the event time, use the takeoff and landing schedules. For the location, list the origin and destination airport codes. And, in the Description field, put the flight reservation number. If you're using separate calendars (categories), specify the Travel calendar for your flight.

- ✔ See Chapter 14 for more information on the Calendar app.

- ✔ Some airlines offer apps you can use while traveling. At the time this book went to press, American Airlines, Southwest, United, Continental, and a host of other airlines feature apps. You can use the apps to not only keep track of flights but also to check in. Eventually, printed tickets will disappear, and you'll merely show your "ticket" on the Android tablet screen, which is then scanned at the gate.

- ✔ Some apps you can use to organize your travel details are similar to, but more sophisticated than, the Calendar app. Visit the Google Play Store and search for *travel* or *airlines* to find a host of apps.

Flying with an Android tablet

It truly is the most trendy of things to be aloft with the latest mobile gizmo. Like taking a cell phone on a plane, however, you have to follow some rules. Although your Android tablet isn't a cell phone, you still have to heed the flight crew's warnings regarding cell phones and other electronics.

First and foremost, turn off the Android tablet when instructed to do so. This direction is given before takeoff and landing, so be prepared.

Before takeoff, you'll most likely want to put the tablet into airplane mode. Yep, it's the same airplane mode you'd find on a cell phone: The various scary and dangerous wireless radios on the tablet are disabled in that mode. With airplane mode active, you're free to use the tablet in-flight, facing little risk of causing the plane's navigational equipment to fail and the entire flight to end as a fireball over Wyoming.

To enter airplane mode, touch the Airplane Mode item on the Quick Settings shade. If your tablet lacks a Quick Settings shade, you can find Quick Settings on the Notifications shade.

When the Android tablet is in airplane mode, a special icon appears in the status area, similar to what's shown in the margin.

To exit airplane mode, repeat the steps in this section to deactivate the Airplane Mode item in the Quick Settings shade.

- Airplane mode might be called flight mode on some tablets.

- You will also find an Airplane Mode icon in the Settings app. It may be on the main Settings app screen, or you may have to touch the More item in the Wireless and Networks area to find it.

- An Airplane Mode item can also be found on the Tablet or Device menu: Press and hold the Power Lock button and then choose Airplane Mode from the menu.

- Officially, the Android tablet must be powered off when the plane is taking off or landing. See Chapter 2 for information on turning off the tablet.

- You can compose e-mail while the tablet is in airplane mode. Messages aren't sent until you disable airplane mode and connect again with a data network.

- Bluetooth wireless is disabled in airplane mode. Even so:

- Many airlines now feature wireless networking onboard, which you can use with the Android tablet — if you're willing to pay for the service. Simply activate Wi-Fi on the tablet, per the directions in Chapter 16, and then connect to the in-flight wireless network when it's available.

Getting to where you are

After you arrive at your destination, the tablet may update the date and time according to your new location. One additional step you may want to take is to set the tablet's time zone. By doing so, you ensure that your schedule adapts properly to your new location.

To change the tablet's time zone, follow these steps:

1. **Open the Settings app.**
2. **Choose Date and Time.**
3. **If you find an Automatic Time Zone setting, ensure that there is a check mark by that option.**

    If so, you're done; the tablet automatically updates its time references. Otherwise, continue with Step 4.

4. **Choose Select Time Zone.**
5. **Pluck the current time zone from the list.**

If you've set appointments for your new location, visit the Calendar app to ensure that their start and end times have been properly adjusted. If you are prompted to update appointment times based on the new zone, do so.

When you are done traveling or change your time zone again, make sure that the tablet is updated as well. When the Automatic Time Zone setting isn't available, follow the steps in this section to reset the tablet's time zone.

The Android Tablet Goes Abroad

You have no worries taking a Wi-Fi Android tablet abroad. Because the tablet uses Wi-Fi signals, your biggest issue is simply finding that type of Internet access so that you can use your tablet's communications capabilities. This rule also holds true for cellular tablets, which can also use Wi-Fi abroad. But for the digital cellular signal, more precautions need to take place. After all, you don't want to incur any data roaming charges, especially when they're priced in *zloty* or *pengö.*

Traveling overseas with an Android tablet

Yes, your Android tablet works overseas. The two resources you need to heed are a way to recharge the battery and a way to access Wi-Fi. As long as you have both, you're pretty much set. (Mobile data roaming is covered in the next section.)

You can easily attach a foreign AC power adapter to your tablet's AC power plug. You don't need a voltage converter — just an adapter. Once attached, you can plug your tablet into those weirdo overseas power sockets without risk of blowing anything up. I charged my Android tablet nightly while I spent time in France, and it worked like a charm.

Wi-Fi is pretty universal, and as long as your location offers this service, you can connect an Android tablet to the Internet, pick up your e-mail, browse the web, or do whatever other Internet activities you desire. Even if you have to pay for Wi-Fi access, I believe that you'll find it less expensive than paying a mobile data roaming charge.

Even when you have Wi-Fi, I recommend getting some Skype credit to make international phone calls. See Chapter 9 for more information on Skype.

Disabling data roaming

When I've taken a cellular Android tablet abroad, I've kept it in airplane mode. If you do that, there's no chance of data roaming charges, and you can still enable Wi-Fi. Even so, and just to be sure, consider disable data roaming on your Android tablet by obeying these steps:

1. **On the Home screen, touch the Apps icon.**
2. **Open the Settings app.**
3. **Choose the More command, found at the bottom of the first section of commands.**
4. **Choose Mobile Networks.**
5. **Remove the check mark by the Data Roaming option.**

Of course, you don't need to heed my advice if you want to be shocked by an outrageous cellular bill when you return from your trip. That's exactly what happens should the tablet latch onto a foreign cellular provider. Unless you've set up things ahead of time, it's roam, roam, roam. That's expensive.

- ✔ The steps in this section also apply for potential roaming charges in the United States as well. If you take the tablet out of your cellular provider's service area, you could incur roaming charges. It's not that common, but it could happen.

- ✔ Contact your digital cellular provider when you're traveling abroad to ask about overseas data roaming. A subscription service or other options may even be available, especially when you plan to stay overseas for an extended length of time.
- ✔ You can determine whether the tablet is roaming by looking at the Status screen: Run the Settings app, choose About Device or About Tablet, and then choose Status. The Roaming item in the list describes whether or not the tablet is data roaming.

Customize Your Android Tablet

*I*t's entirely possible to own an Android tablet for years and never once customize it. It's not that customization is impossible; it's that most people just don't bother. Maybe they don't know how to customize it; maybe they don't try; or maybe they're deathly afraid that the tablet will seek revenge.

Poppycock!

It's *your* tablet! Great potential exists to make the device truly your own. You can change the way it looks to the way it sounds. Revenge is not part of the equation.

Home Screen Decorating

Lots of interesting items can festoon an Android tablet's Home screen. Icons, widgets, and shortcuts adorn the Home screen like olives in a festive salad. All that stuff can change, even the background images. Directions and suggestions are offered in this section.

Hanging new wallpaper

Wallpaper is the background image you see when you use the Home screen. The lock screen also has wallpaper, and some tablets let you change the wallpaper as well.

All Android tablets offer two types of wallpaper you can choose from: traditional and live. Live wallpaper is animated. Not-so-live (traditional) wallpaper can be any image, such as a picture you've taken and stored in the Gallery app or an image included by the manufacturer for use as wallpaper.

To set new wallpaper for the Home or lock screen, obey these steps:

1. **Long-press any empty part of the Home screen.**

   The empty part doesn't have a shortcut icon or widget floating on it.

   Upon success, you'll see a Wallpaper menu.

2. **If prompted, choose whether to set the wallpaper for the Home screen or the lock screen.**

   Not every tablet provides a method of setting the lock screen wallpaper.

   You may also find an option to set both wallpapers to the same image.

3. **Choose a wallpaper type.**

   Three options are available:

   - *Gallery:* Choose a still image from the Gallery app.
   - *Live Wallpapers:* Choose an animated or interactive wallpaper from a list. (This option may be available only when setting the Home screen wallpaper.)
   - *Wallpapers:* Choose a wallpaper from a range of images preinstalled on the tablet.

4. **Choose the wallpaper you want from the list.**

   For the Gallery option, browse the albums to choose an image. Crop the image to select the portion you want included on the Home screen.

   For certain live wallpapers, a Settings icon may appear so that you customize certain aspects of the interactive wallpaper.

5. **Touch the OK or Set Wallpaper button to confirm your selection.**

   The new wallpaper takes over the Home screen.

Live wallpaper features some form of animation, which can often be interactive. Otherwise, the wallpaper image scrolls slightly as you swipe from one Home screen page to another.

- ✔ You might also be able to set wallpaper from the Settings app: Choose Display, and then choose Wallpaper.

- ✔ The Zedge app provides an über-repository of wallpaper images, collected from Android users all over the world. Check out Zedge at the Google Play Store; see Chapter 15.

- ✔ See Chapter 12 for more information about the Gallery app, including information on how to crop an image.

Adding apps to the Home screen

The first thing I did on my Android tablet was to place my most favorite apps on the Home screen. Here's how that works:

1. **Touch the Apps icon on the Home screen.**

2. **Long-press the app icon you want to add to the Home screen.**

   The app icon appears to lift from the Apps screen, and then you see a Home screen preview, similar to what's shown in Figure 19-1.

3. **Drag the app to a position on the Home screen.**

   When there's no room on the Home screen, drag the icon to the far right or far left edge of the screen to switch to another Home screen page.

4. **Position the app where you want it to go and lift your finger.**

   Don't worry if the app isn't in exactly the right spot. The later section, "Moving and removing icons and widgets," describes how to rearrange icons on the Home screen.

Drag here to move one page left

Favorites bar

Drag the icon to a position on the Home screen

Drag here to move one page right

Figure 19-1: Stick an app on the Home screen.

The app hasn't moved: What you see is a copy. You can still find the app on the Apps screen, but now the app is — more conveniently — also available on the Home screen.

TIP

✔ Keep your favorite apps, those you use most often, on the Home screen.

✔ Icons on the Home screen are aligned to a grid. You can't stuff more icons on the Home screen than will fit in the grid, so when a Home screen page is full of icons (or widgets), use another Home screen page.

Putting an app on the Favorites bar

Some Android tablets feature a Favorites bar (refer to Figure 19-1), which is a row of app icons that dwell along the bottom of the Home screen. The Favorites bar on each Home screen page shows the same app icons, so the bar makes an ideal location for those apps you use most often.

To place an icon on the Favorites bar, first move an existing icon off: Long-press the icon and drag it up to the Home screen. Then you can drag any other icon from the Home screen — or from the Apps screen — to the Favorites bar.

If you don't first move an existing icon off the Favorites bar and then try to add another icon on top of it, one of two things may happen. First, the tablet could replace the existing icon with the new one. The old icon is removed. Second, the tablet may create a folder, combining both icons into a single item.

✔ When the Home screen rotates, the Favorites bar may or may not rotate with it. If not, look for the Favorites bar on the bottom or on the right of the Home screen, depending on the tablet's orientation.

✔ Making folders is a topic provided on this book's bonus page:

www.dummies.com/extras/androidtablets

Slapping down widgets

A *widget* works like a tiny interactive or informative window, often providing a gateway to another app on the Android tablet. Just as you can add apps to the Home screen, you can also add widgets.

Android tablets come with a smattering of widgets preaffixed to the Home screen, possibly just to show you the variety. You can place even more widgets on the Home screen by following these steps:

1. Touch the Apps icon on the Home screen.

2. **Touch the Widgets category atop the Apps screen.**

   Or you can just scroll the list of apps to the left until Widgets is displayed.

   The widgets appear on the Apps screen in little preview windows.

3. **Scroll the list to find the widget you want to add.**

   Some widgets, such as the Contact widgets, are icon-sized. Others are quite large. That's okay because you can resize widgets.

4. **Long-press the widget and drag it to a Home screen panel.**

   Position the widget on the Home screen, dragging it left or right to another page if necessary.

5. **Release your finger to plop down the widget.**

6. **(Optional) Resize the widget by dragging one of its edges in or out.**

Some widgets can change their size, some cannot. To find out which, long-press the widget. If the widget can be resized, you'll see four dots on its edges. (Lift your finger after long-pressing the widget.) The dots are handles, which you can drag using your finger to resize the widget. Touch anywhere on the Home screen when you're done resizing a widget.

The variety of available widgets depends on the applications you have installed. Some applications come with widgets; some don't. Some widgets come independently of any application.

 ✔ There must be room for the widget or the tablet won't let you plop it down. Choose another page or remove icons or widgets to make room.

 ✔ To remove a widget, see the next section.

 ✔ More widgets are available at the Google Play Store. See Chapter 15.

Moving and removing icons and widgets

Icons and widgets are fastened to the Home screen by something akin to the same glue they use on sticky notes. You can easily pick up an icon or a widget, move it around, and then restick it. Unlike sticky notes, the icons and widgets never just fall off, or so I'm told.

To move an icon or a widget, long-press it. Eventually, the icon seems to lift and break free, as shown in Figure 19-2.

You can drag a free icon to another position on the Home screen or to another Home screen panel, or you can drag it to the Trash icon that appears on the Home screen. That icon may look like a trash can, similar to what's shown in Figure 19-2, or may simply be a large X.

Widgets can be moved around or deleted in the same manner as icons.

Delete icon or widget

Long-press to "lift" icon

Figure 19-2: Moving an icon about.

✔ Dragging a Home screen icon or widget to the trash ousts that icon or widget from the Home screen. It doesn't uninstall the app or widget, which is still found on the Apps screen. In fact, you can always add the icon or widget to the Home screen again, as described earlier in this chapter.

✔ When an icon, a widget, or a folder hovers over the Trash icon, ready to be deleted, its color changes to red.

✔ See Chapter 15 for information on uninstalling applications.

✔ Your clue that an icon or a widget is free and clear to navigate is that the Trash icon appears. (Refer to Figure 19-2.)

Managing Home screen pages

Some Android tablets let you add, remove, and rearrange Home screen pages. The number of pages you can add or remove depends on the tablet, and not every tablet lets you rearrange the Home screens. If you're able to manage the Home screens, the procedure works like this:

1. **Long-press the Home screen.**

   A Home screen menu appears. It can be used to add apps or widgets, change wallpaper, and manage Home screen pages.

2. **Choose the Page command.**

   After choosing the Page command, you see an overview of the Home screen pages, similar to what's shown in Figure 19-3.

3. **Work with the Home screen thumbnail images.**

   For example, drag the thumbnail pages hither and thither to rearrange their order.

To delete a page, drag it to the Delete icon, similar to the way apps and widgets are removed, but in this instance you're removing an entire Home screen page — and all its contents.

To add a Home page, touch the Plus icon (refer to Figure 19-3). On some tablets, the Plus icon may appear atop the screen. If a Plus icon doesn't appear, your tablet probably has the maximum number of pages.

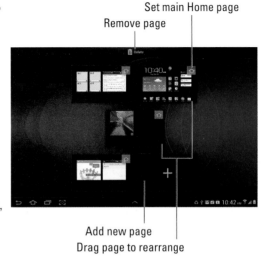

Set main Home page

Remove page

Add new page

Drag page to rearrange

4. **Touch the Done or Save button when you're done.**

Figure 19-3: Working with Home screen pages.

If such a button isn't available, touch the Back icon.

Some tablets allow you to set the primary Home screen page, which doesn't necessarily have to be the center Home screen page. I've seen different ways to accomplish that task. Most common is to touch the Home icon in a thumbnail's preview, which is what's illustrated in Figure 19-3.

If you can't locate the Page command, or the Home screen lacks a long-press menu, try pinching the Home screen: Touch the screen with two fingers and drag them together. If that doesn't work, your tablet most likely doesn't allow you to mess with the Home screen pages.

Android Tablet Security

Android tablets don't seem to have a very secure lock. That screen swipe thing is fancy, and it keeps the cat from unlocking the tablet, but it won't keep out the Bad Guys. A better form of protection is to employ a lock screen better than the standard sliding lock, covered in this section.

Finding the locks

The keys to your Android tablet's screen locks are found within the Settings app. Here's how to get there:

1. **At the Home screen, touch the Apps icon.**

2. **Open the Settings app.**

3. **Choose Security.**

   On some tablets, the item is titled Location and Security. You might also find the screen locks under the Lock Screen category.

4. **Choose Screen Lock.**

   This item might be titled Configure Lock Screen on some tablets.

5. **If a screen lock is already set, you must trace the pattern or type the PIN or password to continue.**

I call the next screen the Choose Lock screen, though your tablet may present a different title. The screen lists the variety of screen locks available. Among them you may find:

None: The screen doesn't lock. Choosing this option disables all locks.

Slide or *Swipe:* The Android tablet simply uses the standard locking screen. Slide the Unlock button or swipe the screen to unlock the tablet.

Face Unlock: Use the device's front camera to have your adorable face unlock the tablet. This option may not be available on all Android tablets.

Pattern: To unlock the tablet, you must trace a pattern on the touchscreen.

PIN: The Android tablet is unlocked by typing a personal identification number (PIN).

Password: You must type a password to unlock your tablet.

To set or remove a lock, refer to the following sections.

Removing the screen lock

The Choose Lock screen can not only set the tablet's lock but also change or remove the lock.

After visiting the Choose Lock screen, as described in the preceding section, touch the None button to remove any screen lock. Or, to restore the original screen lock, touch the Slide or Swipe button.

Unlocking the tablet with your face

The Face Unlock option allows you to get access to your Android tablet simply by looking at it. Or, well, I suppose someone could hold up a picture of you to unlock the tablet. Perhaps Google didn't think of that? Anyway, follow these steps to enable face unlock:

1. **Get to the Choose Lock screen.**

   Refer to the earlier section "Finding the locks" for specific directions.

2. **Choose Face Unlock.**

   In the directions on the screen that you probably didn't read, it says that face unlock is less secure than other forms of locking the tablet. But it's fun, so what the heck?

3. **Touch the Set It Up button.**

   Read over these next four steps before you try them.

4. **Hold up the tablet so that it's facing you at eye-level — as if you were using the Android tablet as a very expensive mirror.**

5. **Touch the Continue button.**

6. **Line up your face with the oval dots on the screen, and then hold the tablet steady as the dots change color from white to green.**

7. **Upon success, touch the Continue button.**

   Because the face unlock method isn't very reliable, you need to specify a backup method:

8. **Choose Pattern or PIN to set a backup lock for those numerous times face unlock fails.**

   Refer to later sections in this chapter for how to set up those types of locks.

9. **After confirming the pattern or PIN lock, touch the OK button.**

   The face unlock is now ready for action.

Most of the time, face unlock works fine. When it doesn't, you need to use the backup pattern or PIN lock. You'll also need to use the pattern or PIN whenever you need to change the lock, as discussed in the earlier section "Finding the locks."

Creating an unlock pattern

One of the most common ways to lock an Android tablet is to apply an *unlock pattern*. The pattern must be traced exactly as it was created to unlock the device and get access to your apps and other features. To create an unlock pattern, follow along:

1. **Summon the Choose Lock screen.**

   Refer to the earlier section, "Finding the locks."

2. **Choose Pattern.**

   If you've not yet set a pattern lock, you may see a tutorial describing the process; touch the Next button to skip over the dreary directions.

3. **Trace an unlock pattern.**

   Use Figure 19-4 as your inspiration. You can trace over the dots in any order, but you can trace over a dot only once. The pattern must cover at least four dots.

4. **Touch the Continue button.**

5. **Redraw the pattern.**

   You need to prove to the doubtful tablet that you know the pattern.

6. **Touch the Confirm button.**

   And the pattern lock is set.

On some tablets, you may be prompted to type a PIN as a backup lock. Do so: Type a four-digit (or more) combination to use in case you forget the pattern. When you're done, confirm the PIN, and then touch the OK button. Also see the next section for more details on setting a PIN lock.

Ensure that a check mark appears by the option Make Pattern Visible on the Screen or Screen Security window. The check mark ensures that the pattern shows up. For even more security, you can disable the option, but you have to be sure to remember how — and where — the pattern goes.

Pattern so far

Keep tracing

Release finger when done.

I began the pattern here

Figure 19-4: Set an unlock pattern.

- ✔ To remove the pattern lock, set either None or Slide as the type of lock, as described in the earlier section, "Finding the locks."

- ✔ Wash your hands! Smudge marks on the display can betray your pattern.

TECHNICAL STUFF

Delaying the screen lock

Your tablet features a sleep timeout, a period of inactivity after which the tablet automatically locks. You can adjust that timeout, as described in this chapter, but you can also adjust how quickly the tablet locks after the timeout. The tablet can lock immediately, or you can set a delay during which the tablet can be unlocked merely by touching the screen.

To set the screen lock timeout delay, open the Settings app and choose the Security category. Choose the Automatically Lock option. (That option appears only when a pattern, PIN, or password lock is set.) Choose a timeout value from the scrolling list. A value of 0 means that the tablet locks immediately. The standard value is 5 seconds.

Setting a PIN

I suppose that using a PIN, or personal identification number, is more left-brained than using a pattern lock. What's yet another number to memorize?

A *PIN lock* is a code between 4 and 16 numbers long. It contains only numbers, 0 through 9. To set a PIN lock for your Android tablet, follow the directions in the earlier section, "Finding the locks," to reach the Choose Lock screen. Choose PIN from the list of locks.

Use the onscreen keypad to type your PIN once, and touch the Continue button. Type the PIN again to confirm that you know it. Touch OK.

The next time you turn on or unlock the Android tablet, you'll need to type that PIN to get access.

To disable the PIN, reset the Android tablet security level as described in the section "Removing the screen lock," earlier in this chapter.

Assigning a password

The most secure way to lock an Android tablet is to apply a full-on password. Unlike a PIN, a *password* can contain numbers, symbols, and both upper- and lowercase letters.

Set a password by choosing Password from the Choose Lock screen; refer to the earlier section, "Finding the locks," for information on getting to that screen. The password you select must be at least four characters long. Longer passwords are more secure.

You're prompted to type the password whenever you unlock your Android tablet or whenever you try to change the screen lock. Touch the OK button to accept the password you've typed.

See the earlier section, "Removing the screen lock," for information on resetting the password lock.

Setting the owner info text

You can customize the lock screen by adding custom text that helps identify your Android tablet or simply displays a pithy saying for entertainment value. The feature is called Owner Info or Owner Information, so I suppose the real reason is to type your name and contact info in case the tablet gets lost or stolen.

To set the Owner Info for your Android tablet, follow these steps:

1. **Visit the Settings app.**

2. **Choose Security.**

3. **Choose Owner Info or Owner Information.**

4. **Ensure that there is a check mark next to the Show Owner Info on Lock Screen option.**

5. **Type text in the box.**

   Use the onscreen keyboard to type the text.

6. **Touch the Settings icon in the upper-left corner of the screen when you're done typing.**

Whatever text you type in the box appears on the lock screen. Therefore I recommend typing your name, address, phone number, e-mail, and so on. That way, should you lose your Android tablet and an honest person finds it, he or she can get it back to you.

The Owner Info doesn't show up on the lock screen when None is selected as a screen lock.

Various Adjustments

You'll find plenty of things to adjust, tune, and tweak on your Android tablet. The Settings app is the gateway to all those options, and I'm sure you could waste hours there if you had hours to waste. My guess is that your time is precious; therefore, this section highlights some of the more worthy options and settings.

Singing a different tune

The Sound screen is where you control which sound the Android tablet plays for its notification alert, but it's also where you can set volume and vibration options.

To display the Sound screen, choose Sound from the Settings app screen. You'll see the Sound screen. Some of the worthy options you'll find include the following, although the specific names on your tablet may be slightly different from what's shown here:

Vibration: Choose the Vibration item to set whether the tablet vibrates during a notification and, potentially, how vigorously the tablet vibrates. Touch the OK button when you're done making adjustments.

Volumes: Though you can set the Android tablet volume using the Volume buttons on the side of the gizmo, the Volumes command on the Sound screen lets you set the volume for three types of sound events, as shown in Figure 19-5. Table 19-1 describes the items found in the Volumes window control.

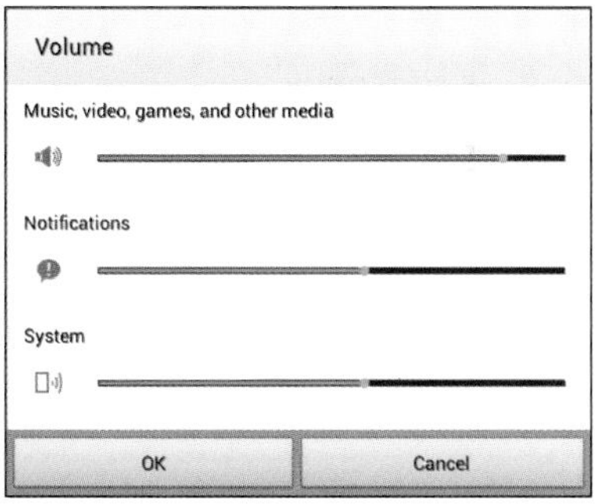

Figure 19-5: Various volume settings.

Table 19-1	Volume Settings
Item	*Volume control*
Alarms	Alarms set by the Clock or Alarm app
Media	Sounds made by most apps, music that plays, videos, games, and so on
Notifications	Notification sounds
System	Sounds used by the tablet or the Android operating system, warnings, feedback, and so on

The System sounds are those generated by the Android operating system, such as when locking or unlocking the screen, connecting to a dock, and so on.

Default Notification: Choose which sound you want to hear for a notification alert. Choose a sound or choose Silent (at the top of the list) for no sound. This item may be titled Ringtone on some tablets.

You can put the Android tablet in Silent mode by pressing the Down Volume button all the way down until the sound is set to 0, or silence.

Changing display settings

The Settings app's Display item contains options and settings for adjusting the touchscreen. Among the more popular items are these:

Sleep Timeout: When does the tablet lock itself? The Sleep option lets you set that value. Choose Sleep or Screen Timeout on the Display screen. Choose an inactivity interval. The tablet dutifully locks itself after you ignore for that time span.

Brightness: Probably the key thing you want to adjust visually on an Android tablet is screen brightness. In the Settings app, touch the Display entry to view the Display screen. Choose the Brightness item to see the Brightness window.

Move the slider to the left to make the screen dim; move the slider to the right to brighten the screen.

If you place a check mark by the Automatic Brightness item, the tablet automatically adjusts its brightness based on the ambient light in the room. That option doesn't please everyone; if that group includes you, remove the check mark by Automatic Brightness and set the brightness manually.

A Brightness setting may also be found in the Quick Settings shade or in the Quick Settings area on the Notifications shade.

Maintenance and Troubleshooting

In This Chapter

▶ Cleaning an Android tablet

▶ Checking on the battery

▶ Saving battery power

▶ Solving annoying problems

▶ Searching for support

▶ Troubleshooting issues

▶ Getting answers

*M*aintenance for your Android tablet is a lot easier than in the old days. Back in the 1970s, tablet computer owners were required to completely disassemble their devices and hand clean every nut and sprocket with solvent and a wire brush. Special cloth was required to sop up all the electrical oil. It was a nightmare, which is why most people never did maintenance back then.

Today things are different. Android tablet maintenance is really rather carefree, involving little more than cleaning the thing every so often. No disassembly is required. Beyond covering maintenance, this chapter offers suggestions for using the battery, gives you some helpful tips, and provides a Q&A section.

The Maintenance Chore

Relax. Maintenance of an Android tablet is simple and quick. Basically, I can summarize it in three words: Keep it clean. Beyond that, another maintenance task worthy of attention is backing up the information stored on your tablet.

Keeping it clean

You probably already keep your Android tablet clean. Perhaps you're one of those people who use their sleeves to wipe the touchscreen. Of course, better than your sleeve is something called a *microfiber cloth*. This item can be found at any computer- or office-supply store.

✔ Never use any liquid to clean the touchscreen — especially ammonia or alcohol. Those substances damage the touchscreen, rendering it unable to detect your input. Further, such harsh chemicals can smudge the display, making it more difficult to see.

✔ Touchscreen-safe screen cleaners are available for those times your sleeve or even a microfiber cloth won't cut it. Ensure that you get a screen cleaner designed for a touchscreen.

✔ If the screen keeps getting dirty, consider adding a screen protector. This specially designed cover prevents the screen from getting scratched or dirty but also lets you use your finger on the touchscreen. Be sure that the screen protector is designed for use with the specific brand and model of your Android tablet.

Backing up your stuff

A *backup* is a safety copy of information. For your Android tablet, the backup copy includes contact information, music, photos, video, and apps you've installed, plus any settings you've made to customize your tablet. Copying that information to another source is one way to keep the information safe in case anything happens to your tablet.

Yes, a backup is a good thing. Lamentably, there's no universal method of backing up the stuff on your Android tablet.

Your Google account information is backed up automatically. That information includes the tablet's address book (see Chapter 5), Gmail inbox, and Calendar app appointments. Because that information automatically syncs with the Internet, a backup is always present.

To confirm that your Google account information is being backed up, heed these steps:

1. **At the Home screen, touch the Apps icon.**

2. **Choose Settings.**

3. **Display your Google account information.**

   On some laptops, choose Google from below the Accounts heading. On other laptops, choose the Accounts and Sync item, and then you'll find your Google account.

4. **Touch the green Sync icon.**

   The Sync icon appears similar to what's shown in the margin.

5. **Ensure that check marks appear by every item in the list.**

   Yeah, there are a lot of items. Each needs a check mark if you want that item backed up.

6. **Touch the Back icon twice to return to the main Settings app screen.**

7. **Choose Backup & Reset.**

   The command may also read as Back Up and Reset, or some such similar variation.

8. **Ensure that a check mark appears by the item Back Up My Data.**

   You should see a blue check mark there. If not, touch the square to add one.

Beyond your Google account, which is automatically backed up, the rest of the information can be manually backed up. You can copy files from the tablet's internal storage to your computer as a form of backup. See Chapter 17 for information on manually copying files and folders between the Android tablet and your computer.

Yes, I agree: Manual backup isn't an example of technology making your life easier.

A backup of the data stored on an Android tablet would include all data, including photos, videos, and music. Specifically, the folders you should copy are DCIM, Download, and Music. Additional folders to copy include folders named after apps you've downloaded, such as Aldiko, Kindle, Kobo, layar, and other folders named after the apps that created them.

Updating the system

Every so often, a new version of the Android tablet's operating system becomes available. It's an *Android* update because Android is the name of the operating system, not because the Android tablet thinks that it's some type of robot.

When an automatic update occurs, you see an alert or a message indicating that a system upgrade is available, similar to what's shown in Figure 20-1.

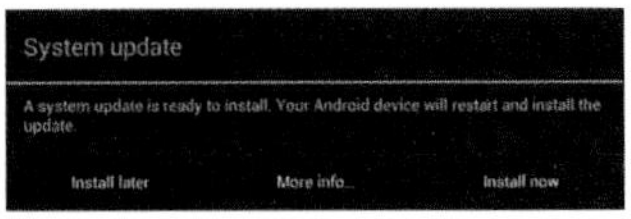

You usually have three options:

System update

A system update is ready to install. Your Android device will restart and install the update.

Install later   More info...   Install now

Figure 20-1: An Android update looms in your tablet's future.

- ✔ Install Now
- ✔ Install Later
- ✔ More Info

My advice is to choose Install Now and get it over with — unless you're doing something urgent, in which case you can put off the update until later by choosing Install Later.

- ✔ If possible, connect the Android tablet to a power source during an update.
- ✔ Some updates may simply present themselves with an Install and Restart button.
- ✔ You can manually check for updates: In the Settings app, choose About Tablet (or About Device) and then choose System Updates. When the system is up-to-date, the screen tells you so. Otherwise, you find directions for updating the Android operating system.
- ✔ Touching the Check Now button isn't magic. If an update is available, the tablet lets you know.
- ✔ Non-Android system updates might also be issued. For example, the tablet's manufacturer may send out an update to the Android tablet's guts. This type of update is often called a *firmware* update. As with Android updates, my advice is to accept all firmware updates.

Battery Care and Feeding

Perhaps the most important item you can monitor and maintain on your Android tablet is its battery. The battery supplies the necessary electrical juice by which the device operates. Without battery power, your tablet is basically an expensive trivet. Keep an eye on the battery.

Monitoring the battery

You can find information about the Android tablet's battery status at the same location as other status icons, either at the top or bottom of the screen.

The icons used to display battery status vary in orientation and color, but generally look similar to the samples shown in Figure 20-2.

Fully charged   Starting to drain   Low; charge soon   Very low; stop using and charge at once!   Charging

Figure 20-2: Battery status icons.

You might also see an icon for a dead battery, but for some reason I can't get my Android tablet to turn on and display that icon.

The next section describes features that consume battery power and how to deal with battery issues. It also shows a more accurate way to gauge how much battery power is left.

Heed those low-battery warnings! The Android tablet alerts you whenever the battery level gets low, at about 15 percent capacity, as shown in Figure 20-3. Connect to a power supply at once!

Another warning appears when the battery level gets below 5 percent, but why wait for that? Take action at the 15 percent warning.

Figure 20-3: A low-battery warning.

✔ When the battery level is too low, the Android tablet shuts itself off.

✔ The best way to deal with low battery power is to connect the tablet to a power source: Either plug it into a wall socket or connect it to a computer by using a USB cable. The tablet begins charging itself immediately; plus, you can use the device while it's charging.

✔ You don't have to fully charge the Android tablet to use it. When you have only 20 minutes to charge and get only a 70 percent battery level, that's great. Well, it's not great, but it's far better than a lower battery level.

✔ Battery percentage values are best-guess estimates. Your Android tablet has a hearty battery that can last for hours. But when the battery meter gets low, the battery drains faster. So, if you get 8 hours of use from the tablet and the battery meter shows 20 percent left, those numbers don't imply that 20 percent equals 2 more hours of use. In practice, the amount of time you have left is much less than that. As a rule, when the battery percentage value gets low, the battery appears to drain faster.

Determining what is sucking up power

An Android tablet is smart enough to know which of its features and apps use the most battery power. You can check it out for yourself:

1. **At the Home screen, touch the Apps icon.**

2. **Choose Settings.**

3. **Choose Battery.**

   You see a screen similar to the one shown in Figure 20-4.

The number and variety of items listed on the Battery screen depend on what you've been doing between charges and how many apps you're using.

Carefully note which applications consume the most battery power. You can curb your use of these programs to conserve juice — though, honestly, your savings are negligible. See the next section for battery-saving advice.

Figure 20-4: Things that drain the battery.

 ✔ You can touch any item listed on the Battery screen to see further details for that item. On the Use Details screen you can review what specifically is drawing power. Buttons are available on some screens that let you disable features that may be drawing too much power.

 ✔ Not everything you've done shows up on the Battery Use screen. (Refer to Figure 20-4.) For example, even after I read a Kindle book for about half an hour, Kindle didn't show up. Also, I've seen the Gallery app show up from time to time, even though I've not used it.

Extending battery life

A surefire way to make a battery last a good long time is to never turn on the device in the first place. That's kind of impractical, so rather than let you use your Android tablet as an expensive paperweight, I offer a smattering of suggestions you can follow to help prolong battery life in your tablet.

Lower the volume: Additionally, consider lowering the volume for the various noises the Android tablet makes, especially notifications. Information on setting volume options is also found in Chapter 19.

Dim the screen: Refer to Figure 20-4, and you can see that the display (labeled Screen) sucks down quite a lot of battery power. Although a dim screen can be more difficult to see, especially outdoors, it definitely saves on battery life.

Turn off Bluetooth: When you're not using Bluetooth, turn it off. See Chapter 16 for information on Bluetooth.

Turn off Wi-Fi: Because I tend to use Wi-Fi in only one spot, I keep the tablet plugged in. Away from a single location, however, Wi-Fi "wanders" and isn't useful for an Internet connection anyway. So why not turn it off? Refer to Chapter 16 for information on Wi-Fi.

Disable GPS: The GPS services are handy for finding yourself and places nearby, but they too use a lot of power. Disable the GPS by choosing the Location Access or Location Services item in the Settings app, and then removing all the check marks. Also see Chapter 10 for information on the location services.

Help and Troubleshooting

Wouldn't it be great if you could have an avuncular Mr. Wizard-type available at a moment's notice? He could just walk in and, with a happy smile on his face and a reassuring hand on your shoulder, let you know what the problem is and how to fix it. Then he'd give you a cookie. Never mind that such a thing would be creepy — getting helpful advice is worth it.

Fixing random and annoying problems

Here are some typical problems you may encounter on your Android tablet and my suggestions for a solution.

General trouble: For just about any problem or minor quirk, consider restarting the tablet by turning it off and then turning it on again. This procedure will most likely fix a majority of the annoying problems you encounter.

Check the cellular data connection: As you move about, the cellular signal can change. In fact, you may observe the status bar icon change from 4G to 3G to even the dreaded 1X or — worse — nothing, depending on the strength and availability of the cellular data service.

My advice for random signal weirdness is to wait. Oftentimes, the signal comes back after a few minutes. If it doesn't, the cellular data network might be down, or you may just be in an area with lousy service. Consider changing your location.

Check the Wi-Fi connection: Ensure that the Wi-Fi network is set up properly and working. This process usually involves pestering the person who configured the Wi-Fi router or, in a coffee shop, bothering the cheerful person with the bad haircut who serves you coffee.

Reset the Wi-Fi connection: Perhaps the issue isn't with the tablet at all but rather with the Wi-Fi network. Some networks have a "lease time" after which your tablet might be disconnected. If so, follow the directions in Chapter 16 for turning off the tablet's Wi-Fi and then turn it on again. That often solves the issue.

Music is playing and you want it to stop: It's awesome that your tablet continues to play music while you do other things. Getting the music to stop quickly, however, requires some skill. You can access the play controls for the Play Music app from a number of locations. They're found on the Lock screen, for example. You can also find them on the Notification shade.

An app has run amok: Sometimes, apps that misbehave let you know. You see a warning on the screen announcing the app's stubborn disposition, such as the warning shown in Figure 20-5. When that happens, touch the Force Close button to shut down the errant app.

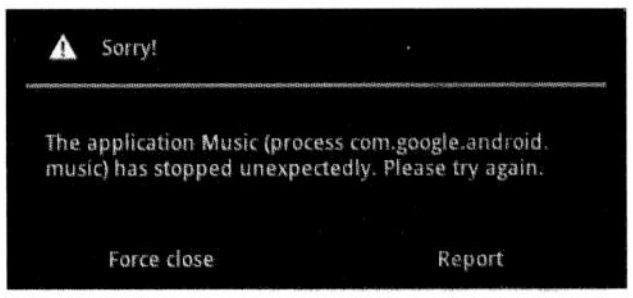

⚠ Sorry!

The application Music (process com.google.android.music) has stopped unexpectedly. Please try again.

Force close   Report

Figure 20-5: Halting an app run amok.

When you don't see a warning or when an app appears to be unduly obstinate, you can shut 'er down the manual way, by following these steps:

1. **Open the Settings app.**

2. **Choose Apps or Applications.**

3. **Choose the Running category from the top of the screen.**

4. **Choose the app that's causing you distress.**

   For example, a program doesn't start or says that it's busy or has some other issue.

5. **Touch the Stop button.**

   The app stops.

After stopping the program, try opening it again to see whether it works. If the program continues to run amok, contact its developer: Open the Play Store app. Search for the app you're having trouble with in the Play Store (not in the My Apps list). When you find the app's information screen, scroll down the See Details list. Choose the Send Email item. Send the developer a message describing the problem.

Reset the Android tablet software: When all else fails, you can do the drastic thing and reset all tablet software, essentially returning it to the state it was in when it first popped out of the box. Obviously, do not perform this step lightly. In fact, consider finding support (see the later section "Getting support") before you start the following process:

1. **Open the Settings app.**
2. **Choose Backup & Reset.**
3. **Choose Factory Data Reset.**
4. **Touch the Reset Tablet button.**

   The button could be titled Reset Device instead of Reset Tablet.

5. **Touch the Erase Everything or Delete All button to confirm.**

   All the information you've set or stored on the Android tablet is purged. That includes apps you've downloaded, music, synchronized accounts, everything.

Again, do not follow these steps unless you're certain that they will fix the problem or you're under orders to do so from someone in tech support.

You can also choose to reset the tablet's software and erase everything should you ever return or sell your Android tablet. Of course, you probably love your tablet so much that the mere thought of selling it makes you blanch.

Getting support

You can use several sources for support for your Android tablet. So no matter how isolated you feel, help is amply available.

For app issues, contact the developer in the Play Store app, which is covered in Chapter 15. For issues with the Play Store, contact Google at

```
support.google.com/googleplay
```

If you have a cellular tablet, and are an active mobile data subscriber, you can get help from the cellular provider. Table 20-1 lists contact information on U.S. cellular providers.

Table 20-1		U.S. Cellular Providers
Provider	*Toll free*	*Website*
AT&T	800-331-0500	www.att.com/esupport
Sprint Nextel	800-211-4727	mysprint.sprint.com
T-Mobile	800-866-2453	www.t-mobile.com/Contact.aspx
Verizon	800-922-0204	http://support.vzw.com/clc

Support might also be available from your tablet's manufacturer, such as Asus, Samsung, or whatever. Information for support can be found in those random papers and pamphlets included in the box your Android tablet came in. Remember how in Chapter 1 I told you not to throw that stuff out? This is why.

When contacting support, it helps to know the device's ID and Android operating system version number:

1. **At the Home screen, touch the Apps icon.**

2. **Choose Settings.**

3. **Choose About Tablet or About Device.**

    The tablet's model number, as well as the Android version, is listed on the About screen.

Jot down the model number and Android version! Do it right here:

Model Number: _____

Android Version: _____

Valuable Android Tablet Q&A

I love Q&A! Not only is it an effective way to express certain problems and solutions, but some of the questions might also cover things I've been wanting to ask.

I can't turn the tablet on (or off)!

Yes, sometimes an Android tablet locks up. It's frustrating, but I've discovered that if you press and hold the Power button for about 8 seconds, the tablet turns either off or on, depending on which state it's in.

I've had a program lock my tablet tight when the 8-second Power switch trick didn't work. In that case, I waited 12 minutes or so, just letting the tablet sit there and do nothing. Then I pressed and held the Power button for about 8 seconds, and it turned itself back on.

The touchscreen doesn't work!

A touchscreen, such as the one on the Android tablet, requires a human finger for proper interaction. The tablet interprets the static potential between the human finger and the device to determine where the touchscreen is being touched.

You cannot use the touchscreen when you're wearing gloves, unless they're specially designed static-carrying gloves that claim to work on touchscreens.

The touchscreen might fail also when the battery power is low or when the Android tablet has been physically damaged.

I've been informed that there is an Android app for cats. That implies that the touchscreen can also interpret a feline paw for proper interaction. Either that, or the cat can hold a human finger in its mouth and manipulate the app that way. Because I don't have the app, I can't tell for certain.

The battery doesn't charge!

Start from the source: Is the wall socket providing power? Is the cord plugged in? The cable may be damaged, so try another cable.

When charging from a USB port on a computer, ensure that the computer is turned on. Most computers don't provide USB power when they're turned off.

The tablet gets so hot that it turns itself off!

Yikes! An overheating gadget can be a nasty problem. Judge how hot the tablet is by seeing whether you can hold it in your hand: When it's too hot to hold, it's *too* hot. If you're using the tablet to cook an egg, it's too hot.

Turn off your Android tablet and let the battery cool.

If the overheating problem continues, have the Android tablet looked at for potential repair. The battery might need to be replaced. As far as I can tell, there's no way to remove and replace the Android tablet battery by yourself.

Do not continue to use any gizmo that's too hot! The heat damages the electronics. It can also start a fire.

My tablet doesn't do landscape mode!

Not every app takes advantage of the tablet's capability to reorient itself when you rotate the device between portrait and landscape modes — or even upside-down mode. For example, many games set their orientations one way and refuse to change, no matter how you hold the tablet. So, just because the app doesn't go into horizontal or vertical mode, that doesn't mean anything is broken.

Confirm that the orientation lock isn't on: Check the Quick Settings shade or the Quick Settings button on the Notification shade. Ensure that the rotation lock item isn't turned on; if so, the screen doesn't reorient itself.

Part V

The Part of Tens

Enjoy an additional *Android Tablets For Dummies* Part of Tens chapter online at Dummies.com: www.dummies.com.

In this part . . .

- Behold ten useful tips and tricks for getting the most from your Android tablet.

- Find out ten important things you shouldn't forget.

- Discover ten useful, free apps that help boost your tablet's capabilities.

Ten Tips, Tricks, and Shortcuts

In This Chapter

▶ Reviewing recent apps

▶ Turning off the 4G signal

▶ Adding a contact widget

▶ Avoiding the sleep timeout

▶ Using settings widgets

▶ Removing the vocal dirty word filter

▶ Setting locations for your schedule

▶ Using the task manager

▶ Finding your wayward Android tablet

▶ Adding more users

A *tip* is a small suggestion, a word of advice often spoken from bruising experience or knowledge passed along from someone with bruising experience. A *trick,* which is something not many know, usually causes amazement or surprise. A *shortcut* is a quick way to get home, even though it crosses the old graveyard and you never quite know whether Old Man Witherspoon is the groundskeeper or a zombie.

I'd like to think that just about everything in this book is a tip, trick, or shortcut for using an Android tablet. Even so, I've distilled a list of items in this chapter that are definitely worthy of note.

Summon a Recent App

I have to kick myself every time I return to the Apps screen to, once again, page through the parade of icons to dig up an app I just opened. Why bother? Because I can summon the list of recently opened apps by touching the Recent Apps icon at the bottom of the Home screen.

Using the Recent Apps icon is the best way you can switch between two running apps. So when you need to switch between, for example, the Email and Calendar apps, just touch the Recent Apps icon and choose the bottom item on the list. It's effectively the same thing as the Alt+Tab key combination in Windows.

Disable Fast Mobile Data

With the über-speed of the 4G LTE network, it's easy to blow by your monthly data plan allowance. If you're cheap (like me), you probably have an allowance of only 2GB (gigabytes) of data per month before another charge pops onto your bill. To help avoid that, you can get a higher-capacity data plan, or you can just choose to forego the 4G LTE experience.

To limit the tablet to use only the 3G (or slower) networks, follow these steps:

1. **At the Home screen, touch the Apps icon.**
2. **Choose Settings.**
3. **Choose More.**
4. **Choose Mobile Networks.**
5. **Choose Network Mode.**
6. **Choose CDMA.**
7. **Choose Automatic.**

To reactivate the 4G LTE network, repeat these steps but choose LTE/CDMA in Step 6.

Changing the network doesn't alter the tablet's mobile data service limit. All it does is ensure that you'll take longer to get to that limit. So in a way, this trick is more about self-torture than saving money. But still, I find if I have to wait for something too long over the cellular connection, I'll just put off that activity until I get a Wi-Fi connection.

TIP

In the same vein, avoid updating your Android apps until you have a Wi-Fi connection. Sure, you can update when you have a cellular connection, but why waste that routine operation on your precious mobile data quota? Wait for Wi-Fi.

Create a Contact Widget

The people you contact most often are deserving of their own icons on your Android tablet's Home screen. You just don't realize how useful such a thing is until you have one.

To create a contact screen shortcut, follow these steps:

1. **At the Home screen, touch the Apps icon.**
2. **Choose the Widgets category from the top of the screen.**
3. **Long-press the Contact widget and position it on the Home screen.**
4. **Choose a contact from the Contacts list.**

   Preferably, choose someone whom you frequently and electronically contact.

An icon representing the contact appears on the screen. If the contact has an associated picture, you see the picture. Otherwise, you see a generic contact icon, but it has a teeny menu indicator in the lower-right corner. If you touch the widget, a menu appears, displaying a list of quick tasks for the contact, similar to what's shown in Figure 21-1.

Choose a quick task for a contact by touching the task's icon, as shown in Figure 21-1. For some contacts with lots of quick tasks, you may have to scroll the quick tasks left or right to see them all.

The number of quick task icons that appears for a contact depends on how much information you have available for the contact, such as e-mail address; cell phone number (for texting); or linked contacts for Facebook, Skype, Twitter, and so on.

Contact screen shortcut

Contact quick tasks

Details for selected quick task

Figure 21-1: Quick tasks for a contact screen shortcut.

✔ To hide the quick contact information, simply touch another part of the Home screen or touch the Back icon.

✔ A contact's Facebook status may appear below the name, which isn't shown in Figure 21-1.

✔ Just touch the contact screen widget to see the quick tasks. When you long-press the widget, the tablet believes that you want to move or delete the icon.

Keep the Tablet Awake

Your Android tablet sports a screen timeout, after which the display goes dark and the tablet automatically locks. You can set that timeout value as described elsewhere in this book, but you're limited to 30 minutes. To make that value infinity — so that the tablet stays awake as long as it's plugged in — obey these steps:

1. **At the Home screen, touch the Apps icon.**

2. **Start the Settings app.**

3. **Choose Developer Options.**

    The Developer Options item is there, though it may be hidden. To unhide it, choose About Device or About Tablet. Scroll to the bottom of that screen and tap the Build Number item seven times. That's the super secret way to unveil the Developer Options item.

4. **Place a blue check mark by the Stay Awake setting.**

As long as you leave the tablet plugged in, the screen won't dim.

✔ Not every tablet features a Stay Awake setting in the Developer Options area.

✔ You'll need to lock the screen when you're away. Otherwise, having the screen on for long periods of time could damage the device.

✔ Some tablets sport a *daydream* feature. When the tablet is left on long enough, the screen changes to a pattern or picture, kind of like a computer's screen saver. Touch the screen to jostle the tablet out of its daydream.

Add Settings Widgets

You can instantly slap down a shortcut to your favorite locations in the Settings app by creating a Settings widget. Here's how it works:

1. **Touch the Apps icon to summon the Apps screen.**

2. **Choose the Widgets category.**

3. **Scroll through the list until you find the Settings Shortcut widget.**

4. **Long-press the Settings Shortcut widget and place it on the Home screen.**

   Detailed directions are offered in Chapter 19.

5. **Choose an item from the list.**

   The item represents a shortcut to a specific spot in the Settings app, something that you probably change often.

Touch the Settings Shortcut widget to quickly access its associated feature. For example, to quickly access the Bluetooth screen, create a Bluetooth shortcut widget.

   ✔ Don't worry about where the shortcut icon is placed. You can move shortcut icons just like anything else on the Home screen. See Chapter 19.

   ✔ If you can't decide which Settings item to place on the Home screen, just put a shortcut to the Settings app itself. I find myself using that app often enough that a shortcut is warranted.

Add Spice to Dictation

I feel that too few people use dictation, despite how handy it can be. Whether or not you use it, you might notice that it occasionally censors some of the words you utter. Perhaps you're the kind of person who won't put up with that kind of s***.

Relax, b******. You can lift the vocal censorship ban by following these steps:

1. **Open the Settings app.**

2. **Choose Language & Input.**

3. **Touch the Settings icon by the item Google Voice Typing.**

4. **Remove the check mark by the option Block Offensive Words.**

And just what are offensive words? I would think that *censorship* would be an offensive word. But no; apparently the words s***, c***, and even innocent little old a****** are deemed offensive by Google Voice. What the h***?

Enter Location Information for Events

When you create an event for the Calendar app, be sure to enter the event location. You can type either an address (if you know it) or the name of the location. The key is to type the text as you would type it in the Maps app when searching for a location. That way, you can touch the event location and the Android tablet displays it on the touchscreen. Finding an appointment couldn't be easier.

 ✔ See Chapter 10 for more information about the Maps app.

 ✔ See Chapter 14 for details about the Calendar app.

Visit the Task Manager

Some Android tablets come with a Task Manager app, which you can use to examine the list of running apps and halt apps run amok. Even if your tablet has such an app, you can use this little trick to view running apps:

1. **Open the Settings app.**

2. **Choose the Apps or Applications or Application Manager item.**

3. **Choose the Running category.**

    You'll see a list of apps currently active on your Android tablet, similar to what's shown in Figure 21-2. Some of the items are apps, such as the Weather Channel app shown in the figure, but others can be services. Some apps may even have double entries, showing that the apps are doing more than one thing at a time.

4. **Choose an app to examine more details.**

    The details break down the app's usage of the tablet's resources into an organized list of exhaustive information few people understand.

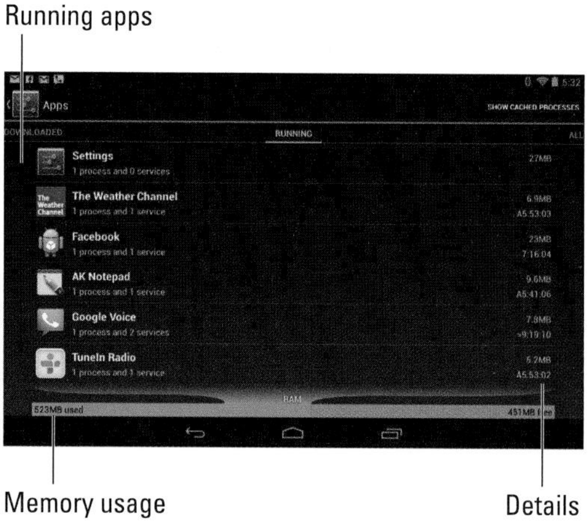

Running apps

Memory usage   Details

Figure 21-2: Apps running on the Android tablet.

Some tablets have specific task manager apps. You'll find them on the Apps screen, but they may also show up in unusual places. I've seen a Task Manger button appear when the recent apps list is displayed. (Touch the Recent Apps icon to see recent apps.) On some Samsung tablets, you'll find a Task Manager mini-app when you touch the up-chevron at the bottom of the screen.

When examining an item, you can touch the Stop button to halt that app or service. Even though that process is necessary to halt apps run amok, I don't recommend that you go about and randomly stop apps and services. The end result could render the tablet unstable, requiring you to power off or reset the tablet to regain control.

Find Your Lost Tablet

Someday you may lose your Android tablet — for a panic-filled few seconds or forever. The hardware solution is to weld a heavy object to the tablet, such as a bowling ball or furnace, yet that kind of defeats the entire mobile/wireless paradigm. The software solution is to use a cell phone locator service.

Even though an Android tablet isn't a cell phone, you can use the same apps that cell phones use to help find a wayward Android tablet. Those apps use the cellular signal as well as the tablet's GPS to help locate a missing gizmo.

Many apps available at the Google Play Store can help locate your Android tablet. I've not tried them all. Here are some suggestions:

- Plan B from Lookout Mobile Security
- Norton Mobile Security
- Security Pro

Most of these services require that you set up a web page account to assist in locating your Android tablet. They also enable services that send updates to the Internet. The updates assist in tracking your Android tablet, in case it becomes lost or is stolen.

Add Another User

Computers have had the capability to allow multiple users for some time — even though I believe few people use that feature. The whole motif of the personal computer is supposed to be one computer, one person, right? Your

Android tablet should be the same, but just like your computer, your tablet can have more than one user account.

Over my objections, some tablets allow you to configure multiple users — several people who can have their own custom Home screen, widgets, and other options on a single tablet.

To add another user, follow these steps:

1. **Open the Settings app and choose Users.**

   If you don't see a Users category, your tablet doesn't have this feature.

2. **Touch the Add User button.**

3. **Read through the information (or not) and touch OK.**

4. **Configure the new user.**

   Touch the Set Up Now button to configure the user or, better, hand the tablet to the other user and let that person configure it. The configuration process is basically the same setup procedure you suffered through when you first turned on the tablet.

All accounts on the tablet are listed at the bottom of the lock screen. To have someone else use the tablet, lock the screen and then have the other user unlock the tablet. Touch the user account circle at the bottom of the screen to use the tablet as that person.

- ✓ I highly recommend that you apply a PIN or password to your account if you're going to have multiple users on a single Android tablet.

- ✓ The tablet's first user (most likely you) is the main user, the one who has primary administrative control.

- ✓ When you're done using the tablet, lock the screen. Other users can then access their own accounts.

- ✓ You can check to see which account you're using by viewing the Quick Actions shade. The current user is shown as an icon in the shade.

- ✓ Remove an account by visiting the Users screen in the Settings app. Touch the Trash icon next to an account to remove it. Touch the Delete button to confirm.

- ✓ I don't like having separate users on my tablet. It makes a simple device complicated. With the tablet's low cost, it just makes more sense to have a second user get his or her own Android tablet. And, of course, his or her own copy of *Android Tablets For Dummies* as well.

Ten Things to Remember

*H*ave you ever tried to tie a string around your finger to remember something? I've not attempted that technique just yet. The main reason is that I keep forgetting to buy string and have no way to remind myself.

For your Android tablet, some things are definitely worth remembering. Out of the long, long list, I've come up with ten good ones.

Use Dictation

Dictation is such a handy feature, don't forget to use it! You can dictate most text instead of typing it. Just touch the Microphone key on the keyboard — or anywhere you see the Microphone icon — and begin speaking. Your utterances are translated to text. If you have a tablet that runs Android Jelly Bean, the translation is instantaneous.

See Chapter 3 for more information on Android tablet dictation.

Change Orientation

Apps such as Chrome, Play Books, and even Email can look much better in a horizontal orientation, while apps such as the web browser, Kindle, and even Email can look much better in a vertical orientation. The key to changing orientation is to rotate the tablet to view the app the way you like best. Rotate!

- ✔ Not every app changes its orientation. Some apps, specifically some games, appear only in one orientation, landscape or portrait.

- ✔ Some apps, such as Play Books, have screen rotation settings that let you lock the orientation to the way you want regardless of what the tablet is doing.

- ✔ The 10-inch Android tablets tend to use landscape orientation as the tablet's standard viewing mode. Smaller tablets, 8- and 7-inch models, present information vertically.

Orientation Lock

The opposite of remembering that the tablet can change orientation (see the preceding section) is forgetting that it has an orientation lock feature. When engaged, the orientation lock prevents the screen from adjusting between landscape and portrait modes: The screen stays fixed in whichever orientation it was in when you set the orientation lock.

You'll find the orientation lock in the Quick Settings shade. Or if your tablet lacks a Quick Settings shade, look for the orientation lock Quick Setting on the Notification shade.

Use the Keyboard Suggestions

Don't forget to take advantage of the suggestions that appear above the onscreen keyboard when you're typing text. In fact, you don't even need to touch a suggestion; to replace your text with the highlighted suggestion, simply touch the onscreen keyboard's Space key. Zap! The word appears.

To ensure that suggestions are enabled, follow these steps:

1. **Start the Settings app.**
2. **Choose Language & Input.**

   What happens next depends on the tablet. Try these steps first:

3. **Touch the Settings icon by the Android Keyboard item.**
4. **Choose Advanced Settings.**
5. **Ensure that there is a check mark by the Next Word Prediction item.**

   This item might also be titled Next-Word Suggestions.

If those last three steps don't work, substitute these steps:

3. **On the Language & Input screen, choose the Default item.**
4. **Choose Configure Input Methods.**
5. **Touch the Settings (gear) icon next to the currently selected keyboard.**
6. **Ensure that a check mark appears by XT9, the predictive text option.**

Also refer to Chapter 4 for additional information on using the keyboard suggestions.

Things That Consume Lots of Battery Juice

Four items on an Android tablet suck down battery power faster than a massive alien fleet is defeated by a plucky antihero who just wants the girl:

- Wi-Fi networking
- Bluetooth
- GPS
- Navigation

Wi-Fi networking, Bluetooth, and GPS require extra power for their wireless radios. The amount isn't much, but it's enough that I would consider shutting them down when battery power gets low.

Navigation is certainly handy, but the battery drains rapidly because the tablet's touchscreen is on the entire time and dictating text to you. If possible, try to plug the tablet into the car's power socket when you're navigating.

See Chapter 20 for more information on managing the tablet's battery.

Use a Docking Stand

When I'm not on the road, I tend to keep my tablet in one spot: in a multimedia stand designed to support my Android tablet brand. The stand is a helpful way to hold the tablet, to keep it propped up and easy to access. Because I use the stand as home base for my tablet, I always know where it is, and because I don't have the cleanest of desktops, I can always find the tablet despite ominous swells in seas of paper.

- ✔ Not every Android tablet has a companion docking stand. Sending the tablet's manufacturer a weepy letter begging them to produce such a stand doesn't seem to help.

- ✔ Given the choice of a multimedia stand or a keyboard dock, I prefer the multimedia stand. While keyboard stands are nice, they occupy too much room for my desktop. The multimedia stand for my tablet also offers USB and HDMI output, which is nice to have.

Make Phone Calls

Yeah, I know: It's not a phone. Even Android tablets that use the cellular data system for Internet access cannot make phone calls. Why let that stop you?

Using apps such as Google Talk and Skype, you can place phone calls and video chat with your friends. Skype even lets you dial into real phones, providing you boost your account with some Skype Credit. See Chapter 9 for details.

Mind Your Schedule

The Calendar app can certainly be handy to remind you of upcoming dates and generally keep you on schedule. A great way to augment the calendar is to employ the Calendar widget on the Home screen.

The Calendar widget lists the current date and then a long list of upcoming appointments. It's a great way to check your schedule, especially when you use your tablet all the time. I recommend sticking the Calendar widget right on the center Home screen panel.

See Chapter 19 for information on adding widgets to the Home screen; Chapter 14 covers the Calendar app.

Snap a Pic of That Contact

Here's something I always forget: Whenever you're near one of your contacts, take the person's picture. Sure, some people are bashful, but most folks are flattered. The idea is to build up the tablet's address book so that all your contacts have photos.

When taking a picture, be sure to show it to the person before you assign it to the contact. Let them decide whether it's good enough. Or, if you just want to be rude, assign a crummy looking picture. Heck, you don't even have to do that: Just assign to a contact a random picture of anything. A plant. A rock. Your cat. But seriously, keep in mind that your tablet can take a contact's picture the next time you meet up with that person.

See Chapter 11 for more information on using the tablet's camera and assigning a picture to a contact.

Use Google Search

Google is known worldwide for its searching capabilities and its popular website. By gum, the word *Google* is synonymous with searching. So please don't forget that your Android tablet, which uses the Google Android operating system, has a powerful Search command. It's even called Google Search in case you forget who provides it to you.

The Search command is not only powerful but also available all over. You can touch the Search icon in any app where you can find it. Use it to search for information, locations, people — you name it. It's handy.

Ten Great Free Apps

More than 500,000 apps are available at the Google Play Store — so many that it would take you more than a relaxing evening to discover them all. Rather than list every single app, I've culled from the lot some apps that I find exceptional — that show the diversity of the Google Play Store but also how well your tablet can run Android apps.

Every app listed in this chapter is free; see Chapter 15 for directions on finding them using the Google Play Store.

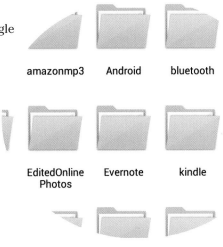

amazonmp3   Android   bluetooth

EditedOnline   Evernote   kindle
Photos

AK Notepad

One program that most Android tablets are missing out of the box is a notepad. A good choice for an app to fill that void is AK Notepad. Use it to type or dictate short messages and memos, which I find handy.

For example, before a recent visit to the hardware store, I made (dictated) a list of items I needed by using AK Notepad. I also keep some important items as notes — things that I often forget or don't care to remember, such as frequent flyer numbers, which cartridges I need for my laser printer, and my dress shirt and suit size (like I ever need that info).

ASTRO File Manager

Consider yourself fortunate when your Android tablet comes with a file manager app — even when you never plan on using the thing. Even if your tablet came with a file manager, consider getting another one. The one I recommend is ASTRO, which does a lot more than get you dirty exploring the bowels of your tablet's storage system.

For example, as a bonus, ASTRO can also be used to access files on your Wi-Fi network. It takes some configuration, which isn't the easiest thing, but after this feature set up, you can use the app to access your computer over your Wi-Fi network.

Dropbox

One solid way to share files between your computer, laptop, and tablet is to use the file-sharing and synchronization utility Dropbox. You need to obtain an account at `www.dropbox.com`. Then install the Dropbox software on your computer to share files there. Finally, get the Dropbox app for your Android tablet to access and view those shared files.

With Dropbox, there is no need to synchronize files between your computer and your tablet. Any files stored in the Dropbox folders are automatically synchronized.

Google Finance

The Google Finance app is an excellent market-tracking tool for folks who are obsessed with the stock market or want to keep an eye on their portfolios. The app offers you an overview of the market and updates to your stocks as well as links to financial news.

To get the most from this app, configure Google Finance on the web, using a computer. You can create a list of stocks to watch, which is then instantly synchronized with your Android tablet. You can visit Google Finance on the web at `www.google.com/finance`.

Avoiding Android viruses

How can you tell which apps are legitimate and which might be viruses or evil apps that do odd things to your tablet? Well, you can't. In fact, most people can't, because most evil apps don't advertise themselves as such.

The key to knowing whether an app is evil is to look at what it does, as described in Chapter 15. If a simple grocery-list app uses the tablet's e-mail service and the app doesn't need to send e-mail messages, it's suspect.

In the history of the Android operating system, only a handful of malicious apps have been distributed, and most of them were found in Asia. Google routinely removes these apps from the

Google Play Store, and a feature of the Android operating system even lets Google remove apps from your tablet, so you're pretty safe.

Generally speaking, avoid "hacker" apps, porn, and apps that use social engineering to make you do things that you wouldn't otherwise do, such as text an overseas number to see racy pictures of politicians or celebrities.

Also, I highly recommend that you abstain from obtaining apps from anything but the official Google Play Store. The Amazon Market is okay, but some other unofficial markets are basically distribution points for illegal or infected software. Avoid them.

As with other Google services, Google Finance is provided to you for free, as part of your Google account.

Google Sky Map

Ever look up into the night sky and say, "What the heck is that?" Unless it's a bird, an airplane, a satellite, or a UFO, the Google Sky Map can help you find what it is. You may discover that a particularly bright star in the sky is, in fact, the planet Jupiter.

The Google Sky Map app is elegant. It basically turns your Android tablet into a window you can look through to identify things in the night sky. Just start the app and hold up the tablet to the sky. Pan the tablet to identify planets, stars, and constellations.

Google Sky Map promotes using a tablet without touching it. For this reason, the screen goes blank after a spell, which is merely the tablet's power-saving mode. If you plan extensive stargazing with the Google Sky Map, consider resetting the screen timeout. Refer to Chapter 19 for information on this topic.

Movies

The Movies app is your gateway to Hollywood. Well, more like your tablet's gateway. The app lists films that are currently running and are opening, and it has links to your local theaters with showtimes and other information. The Movies app is also tied into the popular Rotten Tomatoes website for reviews and feedback. If you enjoy going to the movies, you'll find the Movies app a valuable addition to your Android tablet's app library.

SportsTap

I admit to not being a sports nut, so it's difficult for me to identify with the craving to have the latest scores, news, and schedules. The sports nuts in my life, however, tell me that the very best app for that purpose is a handy thing named SportsTap.

Rather than blather on about something I'm not into, just take my advice and obtain SportsTap. I believe you'll be thrilled.

TuneIn Radio

I know I mentioned this app back in Chapter 13, but I really do recommend it. One of the favorite ways that my Android tablet entertains me is as a little radio I keep by my workstation. I use the TuneIn Radio app to find a favorite Internet radio station, and then I sit back and work.

While TuneIn Radio is playing, you can do other things with your tablet, such as check Facebook or answer an e-mail. You can return to the TuneIn Radio app by choosing the triangle notification icon. Or just keep it going and enjoy the tunes.

Voice Recorder

All Android tablets can record your voice or other sounds, but few tablets come with a sound recording app. That's why I recommend the Voice Recorder. It's a good, basic app for performing this task.

Voice Recorder features an elegant and simple interface: Touch the big Record icon to start recording. Make a note for yourself or record a friend doing his Daffy Duck impression.

Previous recordings are stored in a list on the Voice Recorder's main screen. Each recording is shown with its title, the date and time of the recording, and the recording duration.

Zedge

The Zedge program is a helpful resource for finding wallpapers and ringtones — millions of them. It's a sharing app, so you can access wallpapers and ringtones created by other Android users as well as share your own. If you're looking for a specific sound or something special for Home screen wallpaper, Zedge is the best place to start your search.

Index

Apple & Mac

iPad For Dummies,
5th Edition
978-1-118-49823-1

iPhone 5 For Dummies,
6th Edition
978-1-118-35201-4

MacBook For Dummies,
4th Edition
978-1-118-20920-2

OS X Mountain Lion
For Dummies
978-1-118-39418-2

Blogging & Social Media

Facebook For Dummies,
4th Edition
978-1-118-09562-1

Mom Blogging
For Dummies
978-1-118-03843-7

Pinterest For Dummies
978-1-118-32800-2

WordPress For Dummies,
5th Edition
978-1-118-38318-6

Business

Commodities For Dummies,
2nd Edition
978-1-118-01687-9

Investing For Dummies,
6th Edition
978-0-470-90545-6

Personal Finance
For Dummies,
7th Edition
978-1-118-11785-9

QuickBooks 2013
For Dummies
978-1-118-35641-8

Small Business Marketing Kit
For Dummies,
3rd Edition
978-1-118-31183-7

Careers

Job Interviews
For Dummies,
4th Edition
978-1-118-11290-8

Job Searching with
Social Media
For Dummies
978-0-470-93072-4

Personal Branding
For Dummies
978-1-118-11792-7

Resumes For Dummies,
6th Edition
978-0-470-87361-8

Success as a Mediator
For Dummies
978-1-118-07862-4

Diet & Nutrition

Belly Fat Diet For Dummies
978-1-118-34585-6

Eating Clean For Dummies
978-1-118-00013-7

Nutrition For Dummies,
5th Edition
978-0-470-93231-5

Digital Photography

Digital Photography
For Dummies,
7th Edition
978-1-118-09203-3

Digital SLR Cameras &
Photography For Dummies,
4th Edition
978-1-118-14489-3

Photoshop Elements 11
For Dummies
978-1-118-40821-6

Gardening

Herb Gardening
For Dummies,
2nd Edition
978-0-470-61778-6

Vegetable Gardening
For Dummies,
2nd Edition
978-0-470-49870-5

Health

Anti-Inflammation Diet
For Dummies
978-1-118-02381-5

Diabetes For Dummies,
3rd Edition
978-0-470-27086-8

Living Paleo For Dummies
978-1-118-29405-5

Hobbies

Beekeeping
For Dummies
978-0-470-43065-1

eBay For Dummies,
7th Edition
978-1-118-09806-6

Raising Chickens
For Dummies
978-0-470-46544-8

Wine For Dummies,
5th Edition
978-1-118-28872-6

Writing Young Adult Fiction
For Dummies
978-0-470-94954-2

Language &
Foreign Language

500 Spanish Verbs
For Dummies
978-1-118-02382-2

English Grammar
For Dummies,
2nd Edition
978-0-470-54664-2

French All-in One
For Dummies
978-1-118-22815-9

German Essentials
For Dummies
978-1-118-18422-6

Italian For Dummies,
2nd Edition
978-1-118-00465-4

e Available in print and e-book formats.

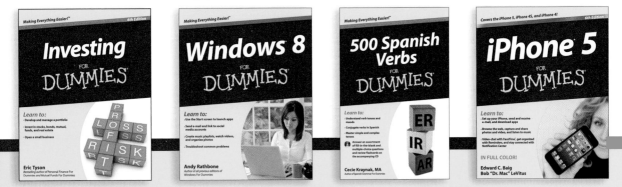

Math & Science

Algebra I For Dummies,
2nd Edition
978-0-470-55964-2

Anatomy and Physiology
For Dummies,
2nd Edition
978-0-470-92326-9

Astronomy For Dummies,
3rd Edition
978-1-118-37697-3

Biology For Dummies,
2nd Edition
978-0-470-59875-7

Chemistry For Dummies,
2nd Edition
978-1-1180-0730-3

Pre-Algebra Essentials
For Dummies
978-0-470-61838-7

Microsoft Office

Excel 2013 For Dummies
978-1-118-51012-4

Office 2013 All-in-One
For Dummies
978-1-118-51636-2

PowerPoint 2013
For Dummies
978-1-118-50253-2

Word 2013 For Dummies
978-1-118-49123-2

Music

Blues Harmonica
For Dummies
978-1-118-25269-7

Guitar For Dummies,
3rd Edition
978-1-118-11554-1

iPod & iTunes
For Dummies,
10th Edition
978-1-118-50864-0

Programming

Android Application
Development For
Dummies, 2nd Edition
978-1-118-38710-8

iOS 6 Application
Development For Dummies
978-1-118-50880-0

Java For Dummies,
5th Edition
978-0-470-37173-2

Religion & Inspiration

The Bible For Dummies
978-0-7645-5296-0

Buddhism For Dummies,
2nd Edition
978-1-118-02379-2

Catholicism For Dummies,
2nd Edition
978-1-118-07778-8

Self-Help & Relationships

Bipolar Disorder
For Dummies,
2nd Edition
978-1-118-33882-7

Meditation For Dummies,
3rd Edition
978-1-118-29144-3

Seniors

Computers For Seniors
For Dummies,
3rd Edition
978-1-118-11553-4

iPad For Seniors
For Dummies,
5th Edition
978-1-118-49708-1

Social Security
For Dummies
978-1-118-20573-0

Smartphones & Tablets

Android Phones
For Dummies
978-1-118-16952-0

Kindle Fire HD
For Dummies
978-1-118-42223-6

NOOK HD For Dummies,
Portable Edition
978-1-118-39498-4

Surface For Dummies
978-1-118-49634-3

Test Prep

ACT For Dummies,
5th Edition
978-1-118-01259-8

ASVAB For Dummies,
3rd Edition
978-0-470-63760-9

GRE For Dummies,
7th Edition
978-0-470-88921-3

Officer Candidate Tests,
For Dummies
978-0-470-59876-4

Physician's Assistant Exam
For Dummies
978-1-118-11556-5

Series 7 Exam
For Dummies
978-0-470-09932-2

Windows 8

Windows 8 For Dummies
978-1-118-13461-0

Windows 8 For Dummies,
Book + DVD Bundle
978-1-118-27167-4

Windows 8 All-in-One
For Dummies
978-1-118-11920-4

Available in print and e-book formats.

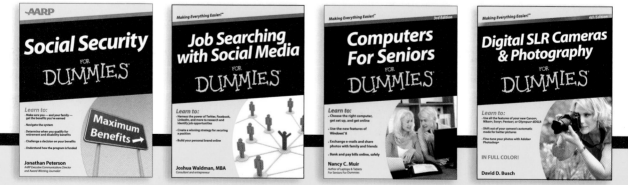

Take Dummies with you everywhere you go!

Whether you're excited about e-books, want more from the web, must have your mobile apps, or swept up in social media, Dummies makes everything easier .

Dummies products make life easier!

- DIY
- Consumer Electronics
- Crafts
- Software
- Cookware
- Hobbies
- Videos
- Music
- Games
- and More!

For more information, go to **Dummies.com**® and search the store by category.

FOR
DUMMIES
A Wiley Brand